James Drummond

Via, Veritas, Vita

Lectures on Christianity in its Most Simple and Intelligible Form

James Drummond

Via, Veritas, Vita
Lectures on Christianity in its Most Simple and Intelligible Form

ISBN/EAN: 9783337164867

Printed in Europe, USA, Canada, Australia, Japan

Cover: Foto ©Lupo / pixelio.de

More available books at **www.hansebooks.com**

THE HIBBERT LECTURES.

Now that the present series of Hibbert Lectures have been brought to a close, it may be of advantage to place on record a short account of their origin and purpose, and of the manner in which the plan has been carried out.

The Trust Fund was established on the most liberal and comprehensive basis. It was to be applied in the manner deemed "most conducive to the spread of Christianity in its most simple and intelligible form, and to the unfettered exercise of private judgment in matters of religion," and no dogmatic or denominational test was imposed upon its administration. Such a fund seemed to offer an admirable opportunity for the establishment of a lectureship in which religious questions should be treated, by members of various churches, with reverent impartiality, and with no object in view but the investigation of truth, and the scholarly exposition of the best results of thought and study. Owing chiefly to the exertions of Dr. Martineau and the Rev. J. E. Carpenter, a letter was addressed to the Trustees by several scholars, some of them men of the highest eminence, requesting them to found a lectureship which should be free from "traditional restraints," and should exhibit "clearly from time to time some of the most important results of recent study in the great fields of Philosophy, of Biblical Criticism and Comparative Religion."

This proposal was warmly welcomed by the Trustees, as affording an unexampled opportunity for illustrating the great principle of unfettered scholarship in matters of religion, and as enabling them to extend the benefits of the Trust to a wider public than had hitherto been possible. Accordingly, a scheme of lectures was carefully prepared, which was to be followed as far as circumstances would permit, but was necessarily subject to variation owing to the necessity of obtaining the services of competent lecturers. The scheme, however, was more coherent, and was carried out with more regard to a definite purpose than was immediately apparent to the public. It appeared to the Trustees that the sympathetic study of every form of religion would be a valuable preparation for understanding its highest and purest expression in Christianity, which would not occupy its true position till it was brought into friendly comparison with other forms of faith. Moreover, this larger survey, it was thought, would prepare the way for a philosophy of religion, without which it would be impossible to place Christianity on its true intellectual ground. Especially an exposition of the older Hebrew religion, as the root out of which Christianity sprang, would aid the interpretation of its own richer and more spiritual development. It was further desirable that some of the great movements of Christianity, both near the time of its inception and at the epoch of the Reformation, should be exhibited from the point of view of the critical historian, so as to throw light on the genius of the religion in its most creative periods; and that the influence of the Græco-Roman world on Christian thought and practice should be carefully traced, so that the original essence of the religion might be separated from the accretions which it slowly gathered around it as it struggled for the mastery of the world.

According to this scheme, which it was not possible to carry out with completeness or in systematic order, the lectures which were actually delivered fall into certain groups. First, a series of valuable contributions to the study of Comparative Religion, has been supplied by the lectures of Professor Max Müller on the Religions of India, of Mr. P. Le Page Renouf on the Religion of Ancient Egypt, of Professor T. W. Rhys Davids on Indian Buddhism, of Professor Albert Réville on the Ancient Religion of Mexico and Peru, of Professor J. Rhys on Celtic Heathendom, of Professor Sayce on the Religion of Ancient Assyria and Babylonia, and of Mr. Montefiore on the Religion of the Ancient Hebrews. More philosophical in their conception and execution were the lectures of Professor Kuenen on National Religions and Universal Religions, and of Count Goblet d'Alviella on the Origin and Growth of the Idea of God; while those of Professor C. B. Upton on the Bases of Religious Belief were purely philosophical, and dealt with the most urgent questions of the present day. Connected with the history of Christianity were the lectures of M. Ernest Renan on the Influence of the Institutions, Thought and Culture of Rome on Christianity, and the Development of the Catholic Church; of the Rev. Charles Beard on the Reformation in its Relation to Modern Thought and Knowledge; of Professor Pfleiderer on the Influence of the Apostle Paul on the Development of Christianity; and of the Rev. Dr. Hatch on the Influence of Greek Ideas and Usages upon the Christian Church. The course was suitably closed by Dr. Drummond's lectures on Christianity in its most simple and intelligible form, which sought to deduce from the New Testament, under the illumination of the various previous studies, the fundamental and essential teachings of the Gospel, and to exhibit those permanent spiritual roots from which the various forms of theology and practice have sprung in accordance with the growing or declining culture and the predominant sentiment of successive ages.

Thus the lectures, considered as a whole, constitute, if not a complete, nevertheless a regularly organised structure, all tending to the realisation of a free and spiritual religion, under the still living inspiration which breathed in him whom Christians recognise as the Way, the Truth, and the Life, and which he bequeathed as a permanent possession to mankind. Where all have been so conscientiously executed, none need be selected for special approval. The Trustees may justly feel that they have bestowed upon the public an important collection of volumes, and have illustrated the possibility of discussing religious themes with the same single-minded love of truth and the same freedom from doctrinal obligation as are brought to the study of science and of history; and they have a well-grounded confidence that their pioneer effort has not been without its influence in preparing men for a larger and more discerning treatment of the things of faith. In providing for a lectureship of Ecclesiastical History at Oxford, which shall give special attention to those churches that have kept themselves free from the fetters of dogma, they believe that they are continuing the same work under another name, and serving the cause of that pure and undefiled religion to which the Trust is dedicated.

Dr. WILLIAMS'S LIBRARY,
December, 1894.

THE HIBBERT LECTURES,
1894.

THE HIBBERT LECTURES, 1894.

VIA, VERITAS, VITA:

Lectures

ON

"CHRISTIANITY IN ITS MOST SIMPLE AND INTELLIGIBLE FORM."

DELIVERED IN OXFORD AND LONDON

IN APRIL AND MAY, 1894.

BY

JAMES DRUMMOND,

M.A. (OXON.), LL.D., HON. LITT. D. (DUBLIN);
PRINCIPAL OF MANCHESTER COLLEGE, OXFORD.

SECOND EDITION.

WILLIAMS AND NORGATE,
14, HENRIETTA STREET, COVENT GARDEN, LONDON;
20, SOUTH FREDERICK STREET, EDINBURGH;
AND 7, BROAD STREET, OXFORD.

1895.

PREFACE.

Of the inadequacy of the Lectures contained in this volume no one can be more fully aware than the author. Numerous questions which are under discussion at the present day have been passed over in silence, or alluded to only to be dismissed for want of space. All criticism of the primitive documents of Christianity has necessarily been omitted, and the exegesis of particular passages has not been accompanied by the full and careful examination on which my own opinions have been based. I understood that the object of the Lectures was to give a general description of the spiritual teaching of Christianity, avoiding as far as possible the purely doctrinal controversies which have so often called off men's attention from more fundamental matters. For this attempt I had at least one qualification, that in my early days I was not placed under the bias of any catechism or denominational formula, but was left to form my ideas from repeated and independent reading of the New Testament. That I have succeeded in fathoming its deepest thoughts I do not for a moment pretend; and I know full well that my exposition must bear the marks of personal limitation, and, it may be, of misapprehension. But man can live only by what he understands and appropriates; and though my views are incomplete, and my statement of them can be little more than a summary of selected thoughts, I trust that these Lectures may at least call attention to some important, and too often neglected, aspects of Christianity.

The limitations of space have likewise forbidden me to refer frequently or at any length to the writings of other students. Numerous writers have no doubt been helpful and suggestive; but, for the substance of this volume, I am not conscious of any special indebtedness which I am bound to acknowledge. Wendt's *Die Lehre Jesu* I read with profound interest; but my Lectures were already sketched out before I did so, and I do not think any portion of them is due to the influence of that valuable treatise.

With this short explanation I send forth my work, hoping that it may do something to foster the growth of pure and undefiled religion, and help to recall men from erections of wood, hay and stubble, to the one foundation, which is so highly extolled in words, so despised and rejected in practice. To all of every name and Church who love the Lord Jesus Christ in sincerity I humbly dedicate these Lectures.

JAMES DRUMMOND.

OXFORD,
September, 1894.

TABLE OF CONTENTS.

LECTURE I.

ESSENTIAL CHARACTER OF CHRISTIANITY. THE CHRISTIAN
CHURCH ... ... 3—38

Purpose and method of the Course, pp. 3-6.
The source of information, 6. Essential character of Christianity, 7-13. Not limited to the teaching of Jesus, but embraces the total specific effect of his life and teaching, 13-15.
The Christian Church. Its origin, 15-22: In what sense Jesus was its Founder, 15-18; its early growth, 18-19; "the communion of the Holy Spirit," 19-20; missionary activity, 20-22. Its formative idea, 22-25. Conditions of membership, 26-27. Character of its government, 27-29. Obligations of its ritual, 29-33. Its living tradition, 33-35. Its teaching function, 35-38.

LECTURE II.

THE BIBLE.—I. THE EARLIEST CHRISTIAN VIEW ... 41—78

The Church existed before the Bible was complete, 41-42. Nevertheless, the Old Testament formed a Christian Canon from the first, 42-44. Infallibility of the Bible generally assumed, 44-45. Change of view in modern times, 45-47. Christ's use of the Old Testament, 47-71 : his view must be gathered from occasional utterances, 48. He accepted, in some sense, the authority of the Scriptures, 48-50. In appeals to prophecy he never dwells on minute details, 51-54. He places the moral above the ritual law, 55-57. His arguments based upon Scripture are opposed to the notion of a binding authority, 57-62. Words of Scripture treated as a commandment of God, 62-64. Evidence afforded by the Sermon on the Mount, 64-69. Conclusion, 69-71.

St. Paul's view, 71-77 : He looked upon the Old Testament as "holy Scriptures," 72-73 ; yet thought the old Covenant superseded by the new, 73-74. These two positions reconciled by his doctrine of the letter and the spirit, 74-75. This distinction applied to interpretation, 75-76. His difference from Philo, 76-77. Agreement with the view of Christ, 77.

LECTURE III.

THE BIBLE.—II. THE MODERN VIEW ... ... 81—120

The ancient view and its modern adherents, 81-83. The change of view which is in progress, 84. Causes of the change, 85-95 : (i) Science, 85-87; (ii) Literary and historical criticism, 87-92 ; (iii) Moral and spiritual criticism, 92-95. Result, the Bible no longer a decisive authority, 95. Nevertheless, its religious value is attested by Christian experience, 96-101 : (i) It holds up a mirror to the conscience, 98; (ii) It brings home spiritual truths to the mind, 98-99; (iii) It deepens devout feeling, 99-100 ; (iv) It gives comfort in sorrow, 100-101. Analogies in

CONTENTS. xi

other literature do not rob it of its unique position, 101-102.

Reconciliation of the critical and religious views, 102-120:—
The Christian philosophy of the subject, 102-110: "The deep things of God" revealed in consciousness, 102-104; the highest form of life known to Christians as "the Spirit of Christ" (the "Christian consciousness"), 104-105; truths involved in the Christian consciousness, 105-108; distinction in the kinds of truth, and limits of inspiration, 108-110.

Mode in which the Bible reveals truth, 110-117: The New Testament discloses the Spirit of Christ, 110-112; presents doctrines ready formed, 112-115; criterion by which to distinguish these, 115; the position of the Old Testament, 115-117.

Reason for the unique position of the Bible in Christendom, 117-119. Sources of its authority, 119-120.

LECTURE IV.

THE KINGDOM OF GOD ... ... 123—166

The Kingdom of God a fundamental thought in Christ's teaching, 123-125. Principles of interpretation, 125-128. The use of the phrase among the Jews, 128-131.

The view of Jesus, 131-166:—"The Kingdom of God is within you," 131-134. It is a present kingdom, 134-146. It comprises an indeterminate community, 146-155. Conditions of admission to it, 155-161. The kingdom not only present, but future, 161-162. The "coming of the Son of Man," 163-164. The slow and silent advent of the kingdom, 164-166.

LECTURE V.

THE DOCTRINE OF GOD ... ... 169—206

Need of return to original spiritual experiences, 169-170.
The fundamental idea that of Fatherhood, 170. Comparison with Philo, 171-172; and with the Old Testament, 172-176. Essential character of the Christian ideal, 176-180.
The way in which God is known, 180-189: through religious experience, 180-183; through the person of Christ, 183-187; through the divinity of human goodness, 187-188; from the action of God in nature, 188.
General character of Christ's teaching about God, 189-190.
His leading ideas, 190-201: the unity of God, 190-192. His sovereignty, 192-193. His omnipresence, and omniscience, 193-195. The Hearer of prayer, 195-197. Forgiving, 197-198. Leaves man responsible, 198-201.
Developments, 201-206: practical, 201-202; intellectual, 203-206.

LECTURE VI.

ETHICS.—I. ... ... 209—243

Christianity profoundly ethical, 209-210. Its view of the supreme good, 210-212. Goodness, not in outward actions, but in the inward life, 212-215. Deductions from this principle, 215-225 :—freedom from the law, 215-216; sin inward as well as outward, 216-218; need of conversion, 218-221; practical duty insisted upon, 221-223; self-denial required, 223-225.
Particular virtues, 225-243 :—
Want of system in Christ's teaching, 225-227. Summary of the Law, 227-228.

CONTENTS. xiii

PAGE

Love to God, 229-243 : Allegiance must be undivided, 229-230. The power of faith, 230-233. Faithfulness, 233-234. Vigilance, 234-235. Sincerity, 235-236. Humility, 236-239. Prayer, 239-243.

LECTURE VII.

ETHICS.—II. ... ... 247—280

Particular virtues (continued) 247-269 :—
Love to man, 247-258 : Love the supreme term, 247-248. Ground on which Love to man rests, 248-249. Unlimited in its range, 249-251. Inflicts no injury, 251-252. Requires us to give, 252-254 ; and to help to heal the moral evils of the world, 254-256. The special relations of life to be regulated by love, 257. Christ's view of marriage, 257-258.
Duties towards the lower animals, 258-261.
Duties towards self, 261-269: Openness to truth, 261-262. Purity, 262-265. Swearing, 265-266. The possession of riches, 266-269.
The future life, and its law of retribution, 269-278.
Unity of moral conception in the New Testament, 278-280.

LECTURE VIII.

THE MOTIVE POWER OF CHRISTIANITY ... ... 283—318

Statement of the question ; Christianity a religion of redemption, 283-284.
Power of ideas, 285-292: Christ as a Teacher, 285. Remarks on the phrase, "a mere man," 285-286. Saving efficacy of truth recognized in the New Testament, 286-288. Effect of Christian teaching on Jew and Gentile, 288-289. A Christianity without Christ might still have great power

PAGE

for good, 289-291. Nevertheless, the view which limits Christianity to the enunciation of truth is inadequate, 291-292.

Power of Christ's personality, 292-317: Doctrine of his person, 292-312: The spiritual fact in the experience of the first disciples, 293; interpreted through the philosophy and vocabulary of the time, 294. The doctrine of the Logos, 294-312: Meaning of the term, 294-297. Heraclitus; and the Stoics, 297-300. The Jews of Alexandria (Philo), 300-304. The Scriptures as "the Word of God," 304-306. The Johannine view, 307-312. Its relation to Hebrew and Greek thought, 307-308. "The Word made flesh" a fact of experience, 308-309. The Divine Thought in nature, 309-310; in man, 310-311; in the prophets, 311; "made flesh," 312. Bearing of this doctrine on the method of revelation of God and man, 312-315. The charter of spiritual freedom, 315-317.

Power of the Church of Christ, as a community of brethren, who perpetuate the life of Divine Sonship among men, 317-318.

INDEX OF SUBJECTS 321

INDEX OF PASSAGES OF SCRIPTURE REFERRED TO 325

CORRIGENDA.

P. 164, l. 6, *for* angel's *read* angels'.
P. 195, heading, *for* BEARER *read* HEARER.
P. 231, l. 14, *for* as its noblest *read* so its noblest.

LECTURE I.
ESSENTIAL CHARACTER OF CHRISTIANITY.
THE CHRISTIAN CHURCH.

LECTURE I.

ESSENTIAL CHARACTER OF CHRISTIANITY. THE CHRISTIAN CHURCH.

THE task to which I have been invited by the courtesy of the Hibbert Trustees is one of no ordinary difficulty, and one which I would not have ventured spontaneously to undertake. It is to treat, within the limit of a short Course of Lectures, a large and complex subject, which bristles with controversy at every point, and to discuss with the impartiality of a critical historian a religion which not only pulsates all around us, and affects the mind with the varying feelings of agreement or dissent, but, as the chief power in my own life, commands a veneration which those who stand outside might regard as a blind survival from an antiquated past.

In order to escape from the former difficulty I must

eschew all controversy, and confine myself to an exposition, necessarily from my own point of view, of some of the leading thoughts of Christianity; and indeed the title which has been assigned to these Lectures, "Christianity in its most Simple and Intelligible Form," suggests the avoidance of the separating lines which divide the several sects, and the selection of those dominating features which might be supposed to present themselves to the eye of a distant spectator. The matters about which we wrangle are not necessarily the most important, but rather help to divert the attention from what is really vital and essential. It was shown by the lamented Dr. Hatch, in his learned and valuable course of Hibbert Lectures, that the metaphysical systems with which Christianity has become associated were not part of the original Gospel, but resulted from the exercise of the human intellect upon the problems which Christianity presented; and whatever may be the utility or the truth of these systems, it will be our duty to endeavour to get behind them, and ascertain the root-ideas of which they are the more or less imperfect expression. These ideas are the common heritage of Christendom, too often overlaid and forgotten amid piles of controversial disquisition, sometimes denied and blasphemed by the rage of contending parties; and it is the special work of our time to recover the fundamental spiritual facts which can alone justify any system of doctrine, to see and feel them in the simple beauty of their original presentment, and then, if need be, to retranslate them into forms of thought, not through the medium of Rabbinical lore or Greek philosophy, but in accordance with modern knowledge, and with the altered mental view which that knowledge has generated.

The procedure thus indicated will to a large extent relieve us of the second difficulty. By avoiding controversy it will be possible to speak without the feelings of a partizan, and to look with a more judicial eye upon the various subjects which may come before us. But in trying to shun the controversial temper, we must not forget that the treatment of the subjects must be open to question, and kindly and suggestive criticism will be always welcome. The limitations of individual thought must make any exposition sadly defective; and I am deeply and even painfully conscious that I can only sketch a few of the thoughts which Christianity has spoken to a single mind, and that goodly pearls of truth may have escaped the observation of too dim an eye. But in regard to an inherited veneration we need have no alarm. No system of life and thought can be understood by one who stands unsympathetically outside it; and this, as we shall see, is peculiarly true of Christianity. Love is the great interpreter; and if to the shrewd critic it sometimes appears to press beyond the outward facts, it is only that it pierces to the divine ideal, and sees the imperishable truth behind the transient form.

In entering on our subject, the first question which presents itself relates to the source of our information. Are we to confine ourselves to the teaching of Jesus, and believe that Christianity is to be found there complete and unalterable? Or are we to include the Apostolic age, and maintain that Christ's immediate disciples were authorized exponents of his doctrine, but that the living word of God died with the last of the Apostles? Or are we to cast our survey down the ages, and suppose that the original inspiration is still unexhausted, and brings new messages of truth and light to those who have ears to hear? Our answer to these questions must depend on our conception of the essential character of Christianity, whether it is primarily a doctrine, or a law, or a mode of interior and spiritual life.

There are certain great sayings in the New Testament which may help to determine this problem:— "Not every one that saith unto me, Lord, Lord, shall enter into the kingdom of heaven; but he that doeth the will of my Father which is in heaven."[1] "Whosoever shall do the will of my Father which is in heaven, he is my brother, and sister, and mother."[2] "By this shall all men know that ye are my disciples, if ye have love one to another."[3] "The law of the Spirit of life in Christ Jesus made me free from the law of sin and death; .... if any man hath not the Spirit of Christ, he is none of his, ... as many as are led by the Spirit of God, these are sons of God."[4] "Now abideth faith, hope, love, these three; and the greatest of these is love."[5] "We all, with unveiled face reflecting as a mirror the glory of the Lord, are transformed into the same image from glory to glory, even as from the Lord the Spirit."[6] "Pure religion

[1] Matt. vii. 21. [2] Matt. xii. 50.
[3] John xiii. 35. [4] Rom. viii. 2, 9, 14.
[5] 1 Cor. xiii. 13. [6] 2 Cor. iii. 18

and undefiled before our God and Father is this, to visit the fatherless and widows in their affliction, and to keep himself unspotted from the world."[1] "Ye may become partakers of the Divine nature."[2] "Hereby know we that we abide in him, and he in us, because he hath given us of his Spirit. .... He that abideth in love, abideth in God, and God abideth in him."[3] These are only samples of sayings with similar import, and have been taken, not from a single book, but from several writers of markedly different temperament and intellectual tendency. Their common underlying sentiment is expressed with varying degrees of fulness and force; but they all point to something different from a law of duty or of ritual, which it would be possible mechanically to obey, and from a doctrine to which it would be possible to give a lifeless assent. They imply an inward experience of life with God of a peculiar and vivid kind; the consciousness of a spirit breathed over the disordered passions and desires, and reducing them to the peace and harmony of love. Whatever may be its source, whatever its channel of communication, whatever the implicit thought on which it rests, whatever the duties or the worship

[1] James i. 27.   [2] 2 Peter i. 4.   [3] 1 John iv. 13, 16.

which it requires, I regard the presence of this mighty and transforming Spirit as the fundamental and permanent fact in Christianity.

The doctrine and ritual of Christendom have undergone momentous changes, development or corruption, according to the point of view of the observer, and at this day present themselves in irreconcilable variety; and nevertheless we recognize in Christianity a certain self-identity running through the altered ages, and extending over the most discordant sects. The belief of the first generation that Jesus would speedily return as the triumphant Messiah to establish upon earth a kingdom of the saints, though it nerved the efforts of the missionary, gave point and force to the preacher's exhortation, and consoled the martyr amid the pangs of death, faded away under the teachings of history; and yet the Gospel lost none of its earnestness and power. Justin Martyr assures us that those who were in all respects orthodox Christians knew that there would be a resurrection of the flesh, and a thousand years in a restored and adorned Jerusalem;[1] but knowledge passes away, and this immature conception yielded to larger and more spiritual views.

[1] Dial. 80.

Nevertheless Christianity remained, and only increased in strength by adapting itself to changing intellectual conditions, and infusing itself into every variety of temperament. It refuses to be bound by the ignorance of man; and when we have tied it up with the most ingenious knots of ceremony and dogma, it often slips away, leaving us in that arrogant self-righteousness which was and is its most deadly foe, and robing the heretic in the sweet simplicity and gracious lowliness of Christ. Where, then, are we to find that element which binds together Catholic and Protestant, Quaker and Ritualist, Calvinist and Arminian, Unitarian and Trinitarian, in the unity of a common name, and marks them as belonging to the same religious genus? We can find it only in the quality of the inward life. We may describe this as the life of Christ within the heart, as a life of saintly fellowship with God, as the life of sonship, as the incorporation of the Divine life in humanity. This is what its greatest teachers have recognized as its essence. Whatever else might admit of dispute, it was an undeniable fact of experience that it had entered as a new power into their lives; and whatever importance they may have attached to sacrament or dogma, the end in view was always the inward holiness and love which belong to the children of God.[1] Christianity, then, is, as St. Paul declared, a religion of the spirit, not of the letter; and, though Christendom is still so blind to its own real glory, this is its grand and distinctive mark. "Spirit" and "life" are among the great words of the New Testament; and these do not suggest a dead deposit which, like a sacred mummy, must be wrapped in swathing bands, and guarded from attack, but vivid forces which find ever new expression in activity and thought, and reach their highest development by freely mingling in the progressive movement of mankind.

If this view be correct, it is clear that we cannot regard Christianity simply as a truth or a system of truths, which, as Theodore Parker said, would be just as true if Herod or Catiline had taught them, and which, like the truths of astronomy or biology, when once discovered become the property of the race, resting exclusively on their own evidence, and leaving to the discoverer, some religious Newton or Darwin, only an historical or antiquarian interest. He who

---

[1] See a very striking description of his own change quoted from Cyprian, Ep. i. ad Donatum in *Neander's Memorials of Christian Life*, p. 15 : Bohn.

discovers a truth of science hands it over as an impersonal gift to mankind, and the value of the truth has no connection with the life of him who first propounded it. He might sink into as complete oblivion as the great astronomers of Chaldea; but the science would remain with unimpaired vitality and value. But a special type of religious life cannot be so easily detached from him in whom it was first enshrined. It cannot be taught like a lesson in mathematics or chemistry, but must enter as a refining power into the mind, transmuting its dross into fine gold, and cleansing that inward eye by which spiritual truth is discerned. It spreads, not by the calculable process of the intellect, but, as it were, by a holy contagion of exalted feeling; and hence he who introduces it into the world becomes at once its inspirer and its norm, giving life through the communion of faith and love, and restoring that life to pristine purity when it has strayed into extravagance and error. If conscious sonship be the essence of Christianity, then he to whom that sonship was such an absorbing reality that he made it a reality to the world, must stand in an undying relation to that spiritual movement of which he is not only the ancient source, but is still the source in multitudes of hearts; and those who are within that movement cannot come to him with the cold curiosity of historians, but with the veneration and love of disciples. Nevertheless, as disciples they desire not so much to receive, on his authority, some truth of the intellect, as to be imbued, through his influence, with the same spirit.

These remarks will enable us to answer the question with which we started. Christianity, as a living spirit in the world, does not begin and end with the oral teaching of Jesus himself, but must embrace the total specific effect of his life and teaching upon the human soul. We may expect, indeed, to find the fundamental principles of his religion enunciated in his recorded discourses, and we may apply these principles as a test to various ecclesiastical developments; but we have no right to expect a completed system of thought or a final judgment upon the various questions to which, in the course of time, his own teaching necessarily gave rise. His own teaching was couched in the language of the day, and addressed to the wants of the day; and succeeding ages had their own problems, which had to be solved, not by the express words of the Master, but by his spirit working through the imperfect intelligence and knowledge of the several periods. An excellent example is furnished by the earliest controversy which arose within the Church. Were the Gentiles to be admitted without imposing on them the observance of the Jewish Law? Here was a question which was vital to the future of Christianity, and yet it was impossible to appeal to the decision of Jesus, for the question had not arisen in his time. St. Paul decided it by his clear perception of the spirit of Christ, in which the solution was virtually involved. His arguments, when stripped of their temporary form and colour, amount to this: that the spirit of Christ, the spirit of sonship, exempted men from subserviency to the Law, not by the lowering of duty or the abolition of moral distinctions, but by lifting them into the righteousness of God, where the eternal requirements of moral obligation were fulfilled with a spontaneous freedom and completeness that were not possible at any lower stage. To be in Christ was *ipso facto* to be independent of the Law, and therefore to impose it on the Gentiles was practically to deny the faith. Here, then, was a momentous theological decision, which went clearly beyond the express teaching of Jesus. All will now admit that it was a grand and wise decision, and that Paul, in stepping boldly forth into the freedom of the spirit, interpreted correctly the true genius of Christianity, rather than those who shut themselves up in the oldness of the letter, and maintained that a dead Christ, whom they had known after the flesh, had nothing more to teach the world. So to others likewise the Spirit may have spoken words of truth, and some of the profound sayings of the Fourth Gospel, even if they were not actually spoken by the mortal lips of Jesus, may have been breathed in the interpreting soul of a genuine seer, and be a true expression of his doctrine. And when the aged seer closed his dying eyes, the Spirit did not die, but continued, and still continues to bear witness; and never has it been more active than in our own day, when it is engaged in the solution, not of speculative, but of practical problems.

We are now prepared to deduce the idea of the Christian Church. In the view which we have taken, it is a question of comparatively small importance whether Jesus himself founded and constituted a Church or not; for a distinct society, with suitable organization, grew necessarily out of the movement which he

10   I. THE CHRISTIAN CHURCH.

initiated. It is certainly remarkable that in three of the Gospels the word Church does not occur, and in the remaining one it is used only on two occasions,[1] of which one alone has any bearing upon the subject. The celebrated declaration, "On this rock will I build my Church, and the gates of hell shall not prevail against it," is omitted in the parallel accounts, and is therefore exposed to the suspicion of a later date; for

---

[1] Matt. xvi. 18, xviii. 17. Mr. W. H. Lowe shows that ἐκκλησία in the latter passage refers neither to the Christian Church nor to the Jewish Synagogue, but simply to a body of *ten* persons, which in Hebrew is called עֵדָה, a congregation, ten being the number required by Rabbinic law for various more solemn religious acts. (*The Fragment of Talmud Babli*, 1879, p. 65, note Cc.) The added words, "What things soever ye shall bind on earth shall be bound in heaven: and what things soever ye shall loose on earth shall be loosed in heaven," have been understood as conveying to the Church the prerogative of forgiveness and condemnation. Yet the words are addressed, not to the Church, but to the disciples, who were desired to report to the Church the impenitence of an offending brother. If we interpret the words by the context, the meaning seems to be that if the disciples acted in the just and forgiving spirit which was inculcated, their binding and loosing would correspond with the verdict of heaven. To suppose that the statement was intended to confer even on the Apostles an arbitrary and unconditional power of forgiving or not at their discretion, would be quite contrary to the whole tenor of the chapter. I am arguing on the supposition that the words have been correctly attributed to Christ; but some critics might show reason for doubt.

we can hardly suppose that two of the Evangelists would deliberately omit a saying which constituted the very basis of ecclesiastical authority.[1] At all events, it would be impossible in any scientific treatment to regard this statement as an adequate foundation for the enormous superstructure of ecclesiastical assumption which has been built upon it. We must infer from these facts that the notion of a Church entered very little or not at all into Christ's teaching, and that in speaking of him as the Founder of the Church we express rather the unpremeditated consequence than the explicit purpose of his life and doctrine. He speaks, indeed, frequently of " the kingdom of heaven," or " the kingdom of God; " but he nowhere identifies this with a Church, or ascribes to it any definite organization. From among his disciples he selected an inner group, to enjoy a closer intimacy with himself, and to extend, through the medium of their word,

[1] Professor A. B. Bruce accepts the saying as genuine on the ground that "it is far too remarkable to have proceeded from any one but Jesus." He thinks the third Evangelist may have omitted it owing to "a consciousness that the words were being used already for party purposes," and that Mark may have omitted it owing to the "modesty" of Peter, under whose influence he wrote. (*The Kingdom of God; or, Christ's Teaching according to the Synoptical Gospels*, pp. 260 sqq.)

the area of his preaching; and this may show that he contemplated a large movement of reform on lines peculiar to himself. But there is no evidence that he made his Apostles the nucleus of a society, which was to be constituted under fixed rules, and placed under the direction of a hierarchy. It seems to have been his immediate purpose to scatter his great spiritual principles broadcast on the world, and allow them to germinate freely where and how they would.[1]

Nevertheless, a distinct society of "Brethren" appears to have grown up almost immediately after the departure of Jesus from the world; and within twenty or thirty years we find "Assemblies" (commonly translated "Churches") of these "Brethren" or "Saints" scattered over the Roman empire, and the idea of the collective Church, united as a single organism, already formulated by St. Paul. We cannot enter into the question of the mode in which these Churches were constituted. The researches of Dr. Hatch and others have made it probable that the organization was based upon existing lines, and was slowly elaborated to meet the growing necessities of the movement; and there is really no evidence that

[1] See, especially, the parable of the Sower.

the Church is a "divinely constituted society," in the sense that it owes all the details of its government to the express appointment of men acting under a divine sanction. Indeed, this kind of legal and inflexible constitution is inconsistent with the spirituality and freedom of primitive Christianity, when the general body of believers were "an elect race, a royal priesthood," "to offer up spiritual sacrifices;"[1] and it was only through the intrusion of lower elements of thought, and the needs of a world-wide empire, which had ceased to be a kingdom of saints, that a vast organized authority gradually asserted itself, and claimed to represent on earth the prerogative of God. But in another and higher sense the Church was of divine origin. As human society has arisen out of the nature which God has implanted in the heart of man, so the Christian society arose out of that new spirit which separated all who received it from the superstition and immorality around them. It may be sufficient to notice two elements in the Christian consciousness which led to the formation of a Church.

"The communion of the Holy Spirit" is one of the great ideas of Christendom. These words came ori-

[1] 1 Peter ii. 9, 5.

ginally from the glowing heart of Paul, when he saw the Corinthian disciples wrangling about superficial questions, and forgetting the deep and inward life with God, without which Christianity was nothing but a name. The words have lived on, and passed into the devotions of the Church; and if they have too often degenerated into a heartless formula, which Christians honour with their lips and disown in practice, still they bear witness to an ideal which has been never wholly lost. Nothing unites men so powerfully as common religious sympathies and aspirations, and those who share in any degree the communion of the Spirit are drawn together as brother to brother; for before the majesty of this hidden life of God in the soul all lower estrangements dwindle into insignificance. Out of this life the Church arose, as a community of brethren and children of God; and the members met together to express their sense of brotherhood, to offer common worship, and to give and receive the strength and encouragement which spring from the consciousness of common aims and hopes.

Further, Christianity has always been a missionary religion. Christ himself was a "teacher;" and to teach and reform the world, to go about doing good, to bring spiritual riches down into the abodes of poverty, to carry the torch of divine life and light into the darkest haunts of sin,—this has always been part of the duty of Christendom, and was a marked feature of the original movement. If the anticipation of a speedy judgment coming upon the world gave greater energy to the labours of the missionary, these labours were generated and sustained by the new philanthropy, which overleapt the barriers of wealth and class, of nation and sect, and saw in the most squalid of earth's sufferers a child of God whom the spirit of Christ could redeem. According to the splendid vision of the Apocalyptic seer, the kingdoms of the world would become the kingdom of the Lord and of his Christ, and the tabernacle of God would be with men, and he would wipe away every tear from their eyes.[1] But before this could come to pass, the missionary had to travel, footsore, from land to land; the Apostle had to become familiar with peril, and nakedness, and hunger; the martyr had to illumine the night with his flaming body, or to yield his blood under the claws of lions for the amusement of a brutal

[1] Rev. xi. 15, xxi. 3, 4.

mob. The dream has not been fulfilled; but all over the Roman empire arose an army of men and women who were ready to die at any moment for this new enterprize of love; and though they were scorned by the wealth and culture of their day, and it is still the fashion in some quarters to deride their superstition and folly, I for my part cannot but venerate these steadfast champions of righteousness, and would humbly lay a wreath of honour upon the tombs of that noble army of martyrs. The vast and dangerous task on which these men were engaged could not be accomplished by individual effort. Association, method, organization, were essential to their purpose; and thus the beneficence of Christianity was another element which led by a natural process to the formation of a Church.

We must conclude, then, that even if Jesus did not constitute the Church by any express command, still its formation is a genuine and inevitable outcome of the Christian principle; and in this sense we may speak of Christ as the Founder of the Church.

We must now ask, What is the formative idea by which this association of brethren was governed, and by its appropriation of which it is to be judged?

St. Paul compares it to a temple in which the Spirit of God dwells.[1] What was true of the individual was true in a fuller sense of the assembly. All had been baptized severally into the same spirit, and therefore all collectively formed one body, animated by one spirit. But a body is an organism controlled by one pervading life, and yet having a variety of functions which are allotted to different members. So the Church is an organism which finds the complete expression of its life only in its corporate unity, and manifests an endless variety of gift, and aim, and operation, through the individuals composing it.[2] With this lofty idea, it was natural that the new society should be called "the Church of God;"[3] for it was the living sanctuary

---

[1] 1 Cor. iii. 16, said in immediate reference to the Corinthian believers.

[2] See this idea worked out in 1 Cor. xii., where we may remark in passing that instead of "bishops, priests and deacons," as we might expect in accordance with ecclesiastical theory, we have "apostles, prophets and teachers."

[3] See 1 Cor. i. 2, x. 32, xi. 22, xv. 9; 2 Cor. i. 1; Gal. i. 13; 1 Tim. iii. 5, 15. In 1 Cor. xi. 16, 1 Thess. ii. 14, and 2 Thess. i. 4, the expression is used in the plural. See also the opening of Clem. ad Cor., of the Epistle of Polycarp, and of the Epistle on the Martyrdom of Polycarp. In some of the Ignatian Epistles the expression is used with the addition of the name of Christ (Ad

where God revealed his Spirit, if not with greater depth and power, yet with greater richness and manifold fulness, than was possible to the solitary soul. Christ was the head of the body, the full receptacle of the divine life of love, from whom it was distributed to the several parts;[1] and we are therefore justified in saying that the Christian Church, according to its idea, is a society for the extension and perpetuation of the spirit of life in Christ. As a man without his spirit is none of his, so a Church without his spirit is none of his; and no assumption of Apostolical succession, or of any other outward and material links, can alter the divine facts, and make lowliness, purity and love, anything but Christlike—hatred, worldliness and arrogance, anything but diabolical. In all the sects of Christendom there is some attempt to express this divine idea of the Church, and so far as they express it they are parts of the Church of Christ; in all, I suppose, there is some admixture of selfish and degrading

Philadelph. and *Ad Smyrn.* The simpler expression is used in the plural, *Ad Trall.* xii.).

[1] Eph. iv. 15, 16, i. 22, 23; Col. i. 18, 19. Even if, as some critics suppose, these words are not Paul's, they are at all events not inconsistent with his thought, and they express one of the purest and noblest ideas of primitive Christianity.

elements, for the Spirit of God takes little heed of the lines of human organization. Hence a distinction has been drawn between the visible and the invisible Church. The visible Church consists at present of a number of organizations, which include unworthy as well as worthy members, and, in their devotion to what is non-essential, regard one another with more or less of suspicion and hostility. The invisible Church consists of the men, wherever found, who make the spirit of Christ the sovereign guide of their lives, and exhibit, at least in some faint and trembling gleams, the love of the Father in the world. These men belong to one another, and form one sacred band, though their communion may not be known and realized till the dreams of earth are passed. Here they are kept apart by the subtilties of theologians, the pretensions of ecclesiastics, the false or limited aims of sectarian leaders; but even now they can see the barriers crumbling beneath the power of the Spirit, and surely the day must come when they shall step across the ruins, and, recognizing on one another's foreheads the new name, will find themselves side by side, a great army of brothers marching into the kingdom of God.

If we proceed to inquire into the constitution of

the Church, we enter on a subject which has filled volumes of controversy, and cannot possibly be discussed within our prescribed limits. I can only indicate in the briefest way the principles which seem to me to lie at the root of the question.

The conditions of membership ought to correspond with the essential character of the religion; and therefore a sincere desire to live under the guidance of the Spirit of God ought to be a sufficient qualification. And so it practically was in the earliest times. Christ himself preached the necessity of repentance, of returning to the purity and simplicity of childhood, of taking up the cross daily and following him. As we have already seen, those who did the will of God were his spiritual kindred; and we have not only no evidence that he insisted on the adoption of an elaborate theological creed or a particular form of ritual, but such insistence is utterly remote from the whole tone and method of his teaching. Even when the Church was more fully constituted, the initial declaration of faith was of the simplest kind, and almost a startling variety of belief was to be found among the disciples; and it was only by slow degrees that the opinions of majorities received the force of irreversible laws, and Paul's principle that "knowledge passes away," and permanence is to be found only in the Spirit, was contemptuously trodden under foot. From that time Christianity, though never without faithful witnesses, became less and less a religion of the Spirit, more and more a religion of the letter and the form, till things were done in the name of the Gospel which might have sent a tremor of shame through the denizens of hell.[1] But the Spirit is slowly breaking its fetters, and Christ is rising from the tomb in which his professed followers have buried him. The intellect is re-asserting its rights, and finding that Christianity is not a spirit of bondage to fear, but a spirit of sonship which gives a free and exalted life to the noblest powers of the mind.

In regard to the government of the Church, I can only express my own conviction that the idea of a sacred order, clerical or sacerdotal, is quite alien to the original principles of Christianity.[2] The general

[1] It is sufficient to mention the Inquisition, the Massacre of St. Bartholomew, and the doings of the Spaniards in the Netherlands.

[2] I may refer especially to Lightfoot's admirable essay on "The Christian Ministry," in his *Epistle to the Philippians*. It may be worth while calling attention to the familiar, but disregarded, fact, that neither Jesus himself, nor, so far as we know, any of his

body of believers were "kings and priests to God,"[1] enjoying, like the ideal Stoic, a royal freedom and prerogative, and, like the ideal servant of the sanctuary, an immediate communion with the Father. According to the record, Christ expressly forbade his disciples to have any titles of distinction, on the ground that they were all brothers;[2] and Paul declared that all were one man in Christ, for all were sons of God.[3] Still every society requires officers for the direction and administration of its affairs, and at a comparatively early period the Church was organized agreeably to the system which has prevailed in its largest sections ever since. Such an organization, though I believe it arose out of practical necessities, and took form from existing usages, is perfectly legitimate, and runs counter to the primitive Gospel only when it lays claim to a special divine authority, and invests its officers with clerical or sacerdotal functions. This violation of the earlier idea stole in very naturally from older and less spiritual systems, but has con-

Apostles, sprung from the sacerdotal line. Peter and John are expressly called ἰδιῶται, "laymen" (Acts iv. 13).

[1] Rev. i. 6; see also v. 10 and xx. 6.
[2] Matt. xxiii. 8 sqq.   [3] Gal. iii. 26 sqq.

tributed not a little to the obscuring, if not the destruction, of some of the grandest principles of Christ's teaching. Its pretensions are refuted, not only by history and interpretation, but by experience; for men of the noblest Christian character are found outside as well as inside the episcopal portions of Christendom. Organization, then, is a matter of convenience, not of prescription; and the Spirit, whose expression and organ it is, may freely adapt it to the wants of different times and places.

A similar remark applies to the observance of ritual. Not only is no particular form of worship enjoined in the earliest documents of Christianity, but principles are laid down which militate against the imposition of any rigid ceremonial. The controlling principle of the movement is expressed in the words, "Neither in this mountain, nor in Jerusalem, shall ye worship the Father..... God is Spirit: and they that worship him must worship in spirit and truth."[1] Christians were not to "observe days, and months, and seasons, and years,"[2] and were not to allow any man to judge them "in meat, or in drink, or in respect of a feast-day, or a new moon, or a Sabbath-day."[3] Christ's

[1] John iv. 21, 24.   [2] Gal. iv. 10.   [3] Col. ii. 16.

own directions might almost seem to forbid the public services of religion: "When ye pray, ye shall not be as the hypocrites: for they love to stand and pray in the synagogues and in the corners of the streets, that they may be seen of men. . . . . But thou, when thou prayest, enter into thine inner chamber, and having shut thy door, pray to thy Father which is in secret. . . . . When thou fastest, anoint thy head and wash thy face; that thou be not seen of men to fast, but of thy Father which is in secret."[1] Yet as he himself appears to have attended the services of the synagogue, we may fairly take these words, not as a prohibition of all public worship, but as a protest against ostentation and insincerity, and a warning that we must reserve for the eye of God alone those acts of devotion and self-discipline in which we are not uniting with our fellow-men. Here, too, the instincts and requirements of human nature must have free play under the guidance of the Spirit. From the first, Christians have been drawn together in the communion of worship; and thus time and place were necessarily pre-arranged, days and buildings were set apart, and some decorous order of service became requisite. No

[1] Matt. vi. 5, 6, 17, 18.

order is illegitimate that expresses and fosters the Christian life, and extends to every time and place the consecration which signalizes the Sabbath and the Church; none is legitimate which substitutes the form for the spirit, or creates a sense of merit in scrupulous attention to a ceremonial.

A few words must be said here about the observances which are known as sacraments. Whatever may be thought about other rites, there can be no doubt that Baptism and the Lord's Supper have been observed by the vast majority of Christians from the earliest times; and it may therefore be contended, with some show of reason, that they were enjoined by Christ himself as an essential part of his religion. This long and wide-spread continuity of usage makes these rites peculiarly impressive symbols of the unity of Christendom; and for my part I accept and deeply value them as venerable witnesses of a large and undying fellowship, and as helps, consecrated by the piety of ages, in our own dedication to that life which for so many centuries has been struggling against the evil in the world. But it is impossible to prove that Christ formally constituted them a part of his religion for all time;[1] and there is nothing whatever to justify the ascription to him of teaching which attaches value to the material elements, or attributes a sacramental efficacy to the mere performance of a rite. This, indeed, is quite contrary to the whole tenor of his teaching, which invariably lays the stress on that which is within, not on that which is without. He offended the Pharisees by saying that "there is nothing from without the man that going into him can defile him .... because it goeth not into his heart;"[2] and it is only analogous reasoning to say that nothing from

---

[1] The injunction, "This do in remembrance of me," is not found in Matthew or Mark. In Luke the words are at least of doubtful authenticity. In Westcott and Hort's edition the conclusion is reached that there is "no moral doubt that the words in question were absent from the original text of Lc." The Fourth Gospel makes no allusion to the institution, and therefore its evidence is purely negative. The fact, however, remains, that this important precept, if Westcott and Hort are right, rests ultimately on the sole testimony of Paul. But even if the words were used, they were spoken simply to the disciples then present, and there is nothing to suggest their application to the followers of Christ for all time. I may refer the reader to an essay by Professor Percy Gardner on *The Origin of the Lord's Supper* (Macmillan and Co., 1893), though I am unable to accept its more important conclusions.

[2] Mark vii. 15, 19; Matt. xv. 10 sqq.

without can sanctify a man, because it enters not his heart. Here, too, men must exercise the freedom of Christian judgment, and be fully persuaded in their own minds.

There are one or two other questions on which we must touch before we conclude. From all that has been said it follows that the Church, so far as it answers to its idea, is the ever-living witness and organ of the life of sonship, and that Christians, therefore, are not bound by a legal or dogmatic revelation incorporated once for all in ancient documents. The life which was brought into the world by Christ has remained as a permanent force, ever striving for a fuller and larger realization, and applying present insight to the solution of new problems of thought and practice. It is indeed kept pure and true to its ideal by constant reference to its original source; but that source fails of its intended object if the languid waters are allowed to sink into a stagnant marsh, and the living streams no longer flow over the wilderness, clothing it with freshness and verdure. There is, therefore, room in the Church for a true theological development. It is the business of theology to express in terms of thought the implicit contents of the spirit.

Here, then, are two elements of growth. The contents of the spirit gradually unfold themselves in consciousness under the experience and discipline of life; and from time to time men of higher spiritual power than their fellows arise, and, owing to exceptional gifts, bring new phases of the spirit to light, or clearly reveal what before was only dimly discerned. And, again, thought has its own law of development, and often requires centuries to work out its logical results; and as every system of thought must correspond with the known facts of the universe, it is checked and controlled, and liable even to be completely reversed, by the advance of knowledge. Thus theology grew as men became more clearly conscious of the problems which their Christian experience suggested, and it necessarily took form from the knowledge and philosophy of the time. Unfortunately, the definitions of theologians, when ratified by the votes of a general council, were regarded as the infallible utterances of Divine wisdom, and an anathema was pronounced on all who questioned their validity. This, as it appears to me, was a complete departure from Christian principle; and it has plunged the Church into trouble and confusion, and perhaps more than anything else has imperilled the very existence of the religion. If Christians all spoke with the free voice of untrammelled thought, their assertion of Christian truth would be a thousand-fold more impressive than it is; and if thought could freely adapt itself to the vast changes in our knowledge, the oracles of the Spirit would not be silent amid the decaying walls of mediæval dogma.

This leads me, finally, to say a few words about the teaching function of the Church. In accordance with the view that the Church is not a dead mechanism, but a living organism, it is not simply to copy the earliest examples, and limit its instruction by the elementary wants of the first converts. Experience has widened; knowledge has increased; doubts and difficulties peculiar to the time are continually pressing upon the mind. In order to meet this condition of things, a body of men is required who are fitted both by natural gifts and by careful training for a position of high responsibility and of no ordinary difficulty. They ought to combine, at least in some humble fashion, the functions of the prophet and the scholar. They ought themselves to be penetrated with that spirit of sonship, the meaning and contents of which they have to unfold, so that they may speak with authority of what they have seen and known, and bring forth ancient truth with the originality of new experience. They ought to be equipped with the learning belonging to their own department of inquiry, and to be possessed of sufficient general culture to understand the position of theology in the circle of the sciences, and to appreciate the enormous growth in human knowledge, and the profound changes which have taken place, not only in men's formal belief, but even to a greater extent in the whole attitude of thought towards spiritual things. They would thus be saved from the feeble and querulous denials of new knowledge which only make religion ridiculous, and be able to offer at least some little contribution towards that re-statement of religious truth which the intelligence of the age requires.

On such a body of men two obligations ought to be imposed. As teachers of religion, they ought to have no end in view but the ascertaining and enunciation of truth; as teachers of ethics, they ought to view every question of practice from the side of the purest morality. They fall from the duties of their high office when they become the lifeless depositories of an ancient creed, and judge every political and social movement by its bearing on the interests of their own sect. It is not theirs to hand down unbroken the fossils of what was once a living faith, but to guide the evolving life of their own time towards the realization of that formative ideal which through the ages has been the divinest power of our growing humanity. They must have known in themselves the vivid play of intellect and soul, and have seen, at least in gleams of sympathetic light, the spirit of sonship illumining their own consciousness. For them Christianity must be living, and not dead, and possess all the variety and adaptability of life. They would then speak with the genuine authority of men competent to deal with their subject, and Christianity, expressing itself through a freer and nobler organ than ever before, would enter on a new career of beneficent activity. I do not indeed envy the man who can find no authority in Christendom as it has existed hitherto, and is not impressed by its long and wonderful history. With all its errors, and weaknesses, and sins, it has borne a noble testimony to an unseen kingdom of truth and righteousness; and if it has sometimes appeared to sink into the kingdoms of the world, yet, through its lowly saints and its daring preachers and martyrs, it has proved that the life of God in the soul of man is a profound reality. It is these who speak to our hearts and rebuke our doubts. They come to us, a great throng, from every kindred and tongue and sect; and if they do not bear a commission from a hierarchy, they have the seal of God upon their souls, and their names are in the book of Life. The Holy Spirit will not be bound by our human rules, but, paying no heed to our corporations and successions, "bloweth where it listeth," and now leaves the priest alone in his empty pride, and again kindles prophetic fire in some wanderer from the beaten ways. When this fact is frankly recognized, and it is seen that Christians give an unconstrained assent to the reality of things spiritual and eternal, that they are not the prejudiced upholders of an effete system, but the thankful guardians of a heavenly life, which with perennial youth adapts itself to ever new surroundings, the Church of God which is in Christ will have a word of greater and more convincing power, and, laying aside its bitter controversies, and its vain and unspiritual pretensions, unite its scattered forces, and march to new victories over ignorance, superstition and sin.

LECTURE II.
THE BIBLE.—I.

LECTURE II.

THE BIBLE.—I.

In the last Lecture we had frequent occasion to quote portions of the New Testament; and while we treated Christianity as in its essence a spirit of life, with its own laws of growth and adaptability, and with its living word for each successive age, still we referred to the New Testament as containing the most authentic account of its large and governing ideas. The question is thus opened into the nature of the Christian Scriptures, and the place which they occupy in the religious life of Christendom. That sacred Scriptures have played a prominent part in the direction of Christian thought and practice from the first, is simply an historical fact. It is not true that the Church existed before the Bible, except in this sense, that it existed before the Bible was complete. Churches were established in various countries before the books of the New Testament were written, and had become conscious of their corporate unity before these books were collected into an accepted Canon. This is undoubtedly a weighty fact, and confirms the view already taken, that Christianity is not bound by its earliest expression, but seeks new forms of utterance as circumstances require. It is significant that Christ himself wrote nothing; though, if it had been his purpose to promulgate a new law or to establish a dogmatic system, it would have been his natural course to write it down with all plainness, and demand the obedience or belief of his disciples. But instead of this, he enunciated large principles of life and thought, which were capable of various embodiment, and which he taught with greater clearness and power through the quality and force of his character than through his words. The personal impression of his own Sonship to God, an impression handed down by the living tradition of souls quickened by the same Spirit, is the most precious inheritance which he has bequeathed to mankind. But while all this is true, it is also true that the Old Testament is more ancient than the Christian Church, and formed an accepted canon of Holy Scripture before Christ and his Apostles began to disturb the traditional orthodoxy of the Jews.[1] So far as our scanty records enable us to judge, it seems probable that the first Christian missionaries went forth with these venerable writings in their hands. Not only did they appeal to their authority before Jews and proselytes, but St. Paul, in addressing Gentile Churches, assumes that the disciples are familiar with their contents.[2] Heathen philosophers were converted to Christianity by reading the Old Testament, especially the Prophets;[3] and in the earliest account which we possess of the regular Sunday services, we are told that the memoirs of the Apostles or the writings of the Prophets were read.[4] It is a reasonable inference that before the books of the New Testament were written, and at a time when the

---

[1] The fact that doubts existed about the precise limits of the Canon does not affect the truth of this general statement.

[2] See Gal., 1 and 2 Cor., and I would add Rom., *passim*.

[3] See Justin Martyr, *Dial.* 7 sq.; Tatian, *Orat. ad Græc.* 29; Theophilus of Ant. *Ad Aut.* I. 14; Clem. Al. *Cohort ad Gent.* i. pp. 3 and 8 (Potter); and for the inspiration of the Prophets, and the evidence they afford of the truth of Christianity, see Athenagoras, *Supplic.* 9.

[4] Justin Martyr, *Ap.* I. 67.

Jewish element in the Church was influential, the Old Testament was the Christian Bible, and that it stood in a relation to Christian life and thought, if not identical with, at least similar to, that which at a later time was fulfilled by the two Testaments in combination.[1] I think, therefore, that we are justified in affirming that not only were sacred Scriptures produced by the Church as a result of its own activity, and as a more exact expression of its own peculiar life, but that from the first a Bible was accepted as one of the foundations of the faith, as an authority in controversy, and as a source from which the religious spirit might derive nourishment and strength.

It is hardly necessary to say that throughout the history of the Church a position has been assigned to the Bible which places it quite apart from all other religious literature. It has been customary to attribute to it a unique kind of inspiration, and to recognize it as the supreme source, or one of two co-ordinate sources, of saving truth and moral discipline. The limits of this inspiration have not been precisely defined by ecclesiastical authority; but practically the infalli-

---

[1] I may refer here to 1 Tim. iv. 13, where the connection suggests public reading of the Scriptures.

bility of Scripture has been generally maintained by Christians, and it has been commonly assumed till very recent times that attacks on the credibility of any portion of it could proceed only from infidelity. In the Roman Catholic Church the Council of Trent declared that God was the author of the Old and New Testaments;[1] and this certainly seems to imply their miraculous origin and absolute perfection, as similar language would not have been used about any other collection of books. The sixth Article of the Church of England is much less explicit, because its object is to assert "the sufficiency," and not the authority, of Scripture; but in the acknowledgment of the books as "Canonical," and as the final court of appeal in all questions of faith, the view of their inspiration prevalent at the time is virtually adopted. The ordinary Protestant view is clearly set forth in the Westminster "Confession of Faith." God is there pronounced to be "the author" of the Bible, "the Word of God written," and its "infallible truth and Divine authority," are accepted.[2]

At the present day an increasing number of men

[1] Sessio Quarta, Decretum de Canonicis Scripturis.
[2] Chap. i.

are becoming convinced that this doctrine is contrary to fact, and cannot be maintained; and among these men are not only opponents of Christianity in all its forms, but also believers who feel that Christianity is the breath of their life, and that in the rejection of this ancient doctrine they are only getting nearer to the heart of the religion. Among important groups of theologians the question is, not how they shall defend this dogma as the last stronghold of the Gospel against the swarming hordes of atheism and immorality, but how they shall rid Christianity of what has become an obscuration and an encumbrance, and still retain all the spiritual value of the ancient creed. To them, as to their predecessors, the Bible has been a book of life, enriching their thought, purifying their hearts, strengthening their better purposes; and it holds a place in their religious affections, and in the Services of the Church, which no other literature can claim. It is one of the questions of our time whether this state of mind can be justified, and whether it will be possible finally to harmonize the encroaching demands of honest criticism with the inherited veneration of a devout heart. Can we have a new doctrine of the Bible, and still leave Christianity among the living forces of the world? Before surveying this question in its modern aspects, it may be well to turn to the New Testament, and see whether we can gain any light from the teaching and practice of Christ, or from the writings of the great Apostle of the Gentiles.

As we have already observed, a body of sacred Scripture was in existence before the birth of Christ; and the most rigid theory of its inspiration had become fully established. As the son of Sirach says, all the utterances of wisdom "are the book of the covenant of God most high, the Law which Moses commanded, an inheritance to the synagogues of Jacob."[1] From the decision of the Law and the Prophets there was no further appeal; and even those who, with the help of allegory, extracted their own philosophy out of the Bible, assumed its inspiration down to the minutest details. Jesus grew up in the midst of this belief; and so far as mere critical opinions are concerned, we have no evidence that he ever examined them, or felt any difficulty in accepting the popular view. It was not his office to be a critic or a philosopher. His judgments were based on religion; and where current

[1] Ecclus. xxiv. 23.

opinion did not wound his religious sensibility, he was content to let it pass. We need not be surprised, therefore, that there is no distinct statement of what he thought on the question of Biblical inspiration, and that we have to gather his view from occasional utterances, and from the use which he is said to have made of the Old Testament.

That he accepted in some sense the authority of the Scriptures is apparent from his appeal to prophecy, and from some of his arguments with his adversaries. He seems to have placed himself clearly within the line of Hebrew development, and to have regarded his mission as the fulfilment of an ancient providential plan. David had foreseen the times of the Messiah;[1] and "Moses and the Prophets" were competent to teach men the way of life.[2] To use his own comparison, Jesus brought forth out of his treasure things old as well as new.[3] Nevertheless, he was conscious that his principles were new, and would require new forms of expression; for an old garment could not be safely patched with a piece of undressed cloth, and new wine

---

[1] Mark xii. 36; Matt. xxii. 43; Luke xx. 42.
[2] Luke xvi. 29.
[3] Matt. xiii. 52.

would burst old skins.[1] Accordingly, his teaching as a whole is not an exposition of Scripture; nor does he commend Scripture as the one Divine authority by which he himself and his disciples were alike bound. If we were content to follow only the records in the Gospels, I do not suppose that any one would imagine that Christ intended a sacred book, either new or old, to be the permanent basis of his religion. A greater than Solomon, a greater than Moses and the Prophets, was close to every son of man who had ears to hear; and those who knew what spirit they were of could reverently distinguish the Divine voice in the past from the human passion and error with which it was so often mingled. One passage, indeed, may seem to militate against this view. We are told that he "spake to the multitudes and to his disciples, saying, The Scribes and the Pharisees sit on Moses' seat: all things therefore whatsoever they bid you, these do and observe."[2] This, however, has not been received by any school of Christians as a commandment for all time, and it is one to which Jesus himself did not conform. It was intended to bring out vividly the

[1] Mark ii. 21 sq.; Matt. ix. 16 sq.; Luke v. 36 sqq.
[2] Matt. xxiii. 1—3.

contrast in worth between profession and practice, and we must regard it as addressed only to the people then present, and understand it in a large sense:—Do you, the people of Palestine, obey the authorized interpreters of your ancient Law, but do not imitate their conduct. If we interpret it more strictly, it becomes quite inconsistent with the very speech of which it forms the beginning,[1] and with the warning to beware of the leaven of the Pharisees and Sadducees, which, according to Matthew, the disciples understood of the *teaching* of these sects.[2] We must turn, then, to other passages as indications of Christ's real position.

[1] Especially verses 16 sqq. I am content to accept the saying as authentic, though it is found only in Matt., as I think these strong expressions must always be interpreted with some laxity, and with due regard to the context. As the words are the introduction to a tremendous indictment of the whole Pharisaic spirit and teaching, I cannot suppose that they are meant for a covert fling at St. Paul. An illustration of Christ's application of the rule is found in his direction to the leper to go and show himself to the priest, and offer for his purification what Moses commanded (Mark i. 44; Matt. viii. 4; Luke v. 14). He would not stir men up to revolt against innocent customs, or sanction their breaking the law without spiritual understanding. See the very suggestive interpolation in *Codex Bezæ*, after Luke vi. 4: "On the same day, having observed a certain man working on the sabbath, he said to him, Man, if thou knowest what thou doest, thou art blessed; but if thou knowest not, thou art accursed, and a transgressor of the law."

[2] Mark viii. 14 sqq.; Matt. xvi. 5 sqq.; Luke xii. 1.

It is remarkable that in his appeals to prophecy he never dwells on minute details, such as would indicate a miraculous foreknowledge on the part of the writers, but refers to general expressions of spiritual insight which found in himself a marked fulfilment. Thus, when he announced to the people of Nazareth that the words of Isaiah were fulfilled, "the Spirit of the Lord is upon me, because he anointed me to preach good tidings to the poor," he adopted words which admirably described the purpose of his mission, but are applicable to all who labour in the same spirit. In alluding to his own rejection, he cited the words, " The stone which the builders rejected became the head of the corner: this was from the Lord, and it is marvellous in our eyes."[1] This was a statement strictly applicable, but by no means limited in its application. Again, when the children in the temple were shouting, " Hosanna to the Son of David!" and the chief priests and scribes expressed their indignation, he replied, "Yea: did ye never read, Out of the mouth of babes and sucklings thou hast perfected praise?"[2] This quotation was extremely apt; but there is no evi-

[1] Mark xii. 10 sq.; Matt. xxi. 42; Luke xx. 17 sq.
[2] Matt. xxi. 15 sq.

dence either that it was a prediction, or that Jesus regarded it as such.

There is a similar vagueness in relation to his sufferings. He finds support in the prophetic announcement of the providential law that the righteous must suffer for the benefit of the world, and perceives that he, more than any man, must exemplify that law:—"The Son of Man goeth, even as it is written of him;"[1] "It is written, I will smite the shepherd, and the sheep shall be scattered abroad;"[2] "I was daily with you in the temple teaching, and ye took me not: but this is done that the Scriptures might be fulfilled;"[3] "All things that are written by the Prophets shall be accomplished unto the Son of Man;"[4] "This which is written must be fulfilled in me, And he was reckoned with transgressors;"[5]

---

[1] Mark xiv. 21; Matt. xxvi. 24. Luke changes "as it is written" into "as it hath been determined," xxii. 22.

[2] Mark xiv. 27; Matt. xxvi. 31.

[3] Mark xiv. 49; Matt. xxvi. 55 sq. For the last words Luke substitutes, "This is your hour, and the power of darkness," xxii. 53.

[4] Luke xviii. 31.

[5] Luke xxii. 37.

"How, then, should the Scriptures be fulfilled, that thus it must be?"[1]

It is obvious that the well-known argument from prophecy could not be built on such quotations as these. They are of that general kind which a devout man naturally applies to his own case; and while they lend no sanction to the idea that the Prophets had a miraculous foreknowledge of particular events, they show that Jesus found in the Scriptures a support for the religious life, and valued the Prophets as the preachers of divine truth.

One other passage remains, which shows how ready he was to interpret the Prophets in the spirit, and not in the letter. "His disciples asked him, saying, Why then say the Scribes that Elijah must first

---

[1] Matt. xxvi. 54. A similar remark will apply to Luke xxi. 22, if that be a genuine saying. For the meaning attached in Hebrew literature to the expression "fulfil," I may refer to a note by Mr. W. H. Lowe, *The Fragment of Talmud Babli*, p. 69, in which he says that one of its uses is to denote doing "something which fits in exactly with (or practically illustrates) the words of Scripture.... In this latter usage .... the Scripture may even have been written long *after* the event, which is said 'to establish it,' e.g. 'Aboth de Rabbi Nathan, i. 5. It is said that Adam sinned in the seventh hour from his creation *to establish what is written* (Ps. xlix. 13), 'Man cannot live over a single night in honour.'"

come? And he answered and said, Elijah indeed cometh, and shall restore all things: but I say unto you, that Elijah is come already, and they knew him not, but did unto him whatsoever they listed. Even so shall the Son of Man also suffer of them. Then understood the disciples that he spake unto them of John the Baptist."[1] The opinion of the Scribes was founded on the prediction of Malachi,[2] and Jesus accordingly accepts it as true in a certain sense. But how completely he rationalizes it, bringing it within the domain of current events, and holding out no hope of a real return of the great prophet who had gone up to heaven in the chariot of fire. The literalists knew that John the Baptist was not Elijah, and, blind to the spirit of prophecy in him, rejected the only Elijah they were to have; Jesus, unfettered by the hard rules of an outward authority, recognized the spiritual identity of the two preachers of righteousness, and drew from the ancient words a lesson which was contained in their substance rather than their form.

We must now turn to some passages of a different

[1] Matt. xvii. 11 sqq.; Mark ix. 11 sqq. See also Matt. xi. 14.
[2] iv. 5.

kind. In his denunciation of the Scribes and Pharisees, he says: "Woe unto you, Scribes and Pharisees, hypocrites! For ye tithe mint and anise and cummin, and have left undone the weightier matters of the Law, judgment, and mercy, and faith: but these ye ought to have done, and not to have left the other undone. Ye blind guides, which strain out the gnat and swallow the camel."[1] The commandment to pay tithe is contained in Leviticus;[2] and therefore those who were under the obligations of the Levitical Law did well to observe it. But how vehement is Christ's indignation that such observance should be placed above, or on a level with, the moral law! What blind guides he sees in men who can go wrong on such a point! It is clear that he places the conscience above the written law, and requires it to discriminate, to pick and choose, and, instead of binding itself to the letter of commandments supposed to be all alike divine, to follow the healthy judgments of an uncorrupted moral nature. He thus blamed the Pharisees for not doing what in modern times men have been blamed by his supposed representatives for doing.

A similar train of thought is found in his answer

[1] Matt. xxiii. 23 sq.   [2] xxvii. 30.

to the lawyer who asked, "Which is the great commandment in the Law?" He replied by repeating the commandments to love God, and to love one's neighbour, and added: "On these two commandments hangeth the whole Law, and the Prophets."[1] Mark tells us further that the Scribe assented, and declared that such love was "much more than all whole burnt-offerings and sacrifices;" and Jesus was so pleased that he rejoined, "Thou art not far from the kingdom of God."[2] Here we have the same selection, the same distinction between the moral and the ritual, and the same approval of the former as constituting the sum and substance of the ancient Scriptures. Again, when one asked him what he should do to inherit eternal life, Jesus told him to keep the commandments: "Do not kill; do not commit adultery; do not steal; do not bear false witness; do not defraud; honour thy father and mother;" and, Matthew adds, "thou shalt love thy neighbour as thyself;" and when the questioner

---

[1] Matt. xxii. 35 sqq.

[2] Mark. xii. 28 sqq. See also the similar incident in Luke x. 25 sqq., and the saying in Matt. vii. 12: "All things, therefore, whatsoever ye would that men should do unto you, even so do ye also unto them: for this is the Law and the Prophets."

wished for something further, he was desired to sell his goods and give to the poor, and come and follow Christ.[1] Here there is the same insistence on the moral virtues; and when these are not thought sufficient, they are only put to a severer test. There is not a word about studying the Scriptures, or attending public worship, or believing certain statements, or offering sacrifices, or submission to the priest. The whole ceremonial law is quietly set aside, and Jesus picks out commandments which are not only engraven on stone, but on the universal conscience of civilized mankind. Perhaps we shall best appreciate the significance of this fact if we reflect on the scorn with which most of the professed disciples of Christ would treat such an answer at the present day.

We must next attend to some passages in which he bases an argument upon the Scriptures. On several occasions he deliberately broke the Pharisaic rules in regard to the observance of the Sabbath, and thereby gave great offence to the Sabbatarians, who knew that he was not from God because he kept not the Sabbath.[2] It was necessary, therefore, to defend himself; and on

[1] Mark x. 17 sqq.; Matt. xix. 16 sqq.; Luke xviii. 18 sqq.
[2] John ix. 16.

one occasion when his disciples broke the Sabbath by plucking ears of corn, and so brought down on their Master the rebuke of the Pharisees, he appealed to the example of David, who had eaten the shewbread, and thus under the stress of hunger had violated the Law. From this he drew a universal principle, only applying it to the case of the Sabbath: "The Sabbath was made for man, not man for the Sabbath: so that the Son of Man is Lord even of the Sabbath."[1] I follow Mark's account because the other Gospels omit a most important clause, and thereby break the thread of the argument, and lose the universal principle. The connection of thought seems to be this,—the example of David proves that ritual observances must give way to human necessities, and therefore even the Sabbath is intended only for the furtherance of human welfare, and the mode in which it should be kept is amenable to human judgment. The appeal to an historical incident does not tell us much about Christ's view of the authority of Scripture; but he gives it a startling application when he extracts from it a spiritual principle which is directly opposed to the notion of an external authority, before which the individual judg-

[1] Mark ii. 23 sqq.; Matt. xii. 1 sqq.; Luke vi. 1 sqq.

ment must bow in servile obedience. Matthew adds a most interesting argument: "If ye had known what this meaneth, I desire mercy and not sacrifice,[1] ye would not have condemned the guiltless."[2] The utterance of the Prophet is here treated as authoritative; but it is precisely the kind of utterance that is ratified by the enlightened spirit of man, and veils its profound and far-reaching meaning from those who are blinded by their subservience to the letter. We must further remark that Jesus makes no allusion to the commandment respecting the Sabbath, although it was one of the ten. In referring to the commandments, he invariably ignores it; and when he has to defend himself, he does not complain that the Pharisees have gone wrong in their interpretation, and assert that he himself is keeping strictly within the scriptural lines. While citing the Scripture as containing words which appeal to what is noblest in man, he never for a moment lays stress upon them as an over-ruling authority. It also deserves notice in this connection that he defends his violation of the Sabbath

[1] Hosea vi. 6.

[2] The same passage is quoted in Matt. ix. 13. Was it a favourite text with Jesus?

by calling in the aid of reason. "Is it lawful," he asked, "on the Sabbath-day to do good or to do harm? to save a life, or to kill?" "What man shall there be of you, that shall have one sheep, and if this fall into a pit on the Sabbath-day, will he not lay hold on it and lift it out? How much then is a man of more value than a sheep! Wherefore it is lawful to do good on the Sabbath-day." And for once we hear of his anger as he looked round about upon the blind ritualists of his time.[1] In the Fourth Gospel there is a yet higher flight: "My Father worketh even until now, and I work."[2] The ancient story of rest on the seventh day is calmly set aside; the Divine activity in the perpetual processes of nature is recognized; and this natural revelation is placed above the written command, and turned into a rule for human action. Of course the orthodox Jews could see in this nothing but flat blasphemy and personal arrogance.

In relation to another question, that of divorce, Jesus went so far as to say that Moses, for the hardness of the people's heart, had written a commandment

---

[1] Mark iii. 1 sqq.; Matt. xii. 9 sqq.; Luke vi. 6 sqq. Compare also Luke xiv. 1 sqq., and xii. 10 sqq.

[2] v. 17.

which fell below the original Divine purpose: in other words, the Law of Moses did not come up to the requirements of ideal morality, and a more august law was written in the very constitution of our nature. He gave his own view in one of those grand and pregnant sentences in which his teaching abounds: "What God has joined together, let not man put asunder."[1]

Two other references to Scripture throw but little light upon his views. "Is it not written," he asked in the temple, "my house shall be called a house of prayer for all the nations? But ye have made it a den of robbers."[2] In his reply to the question of the Sadducees, he said that they erred from not knowing the Scriptures and the power of God, and he referred to what they might have "read in the book of Moses, in the place concerning the bush, how God spake unto him, saying, I am the God of Abraham, and the God of Isaac, and the God of Jacob;" and then he added his own impressive comment: "He is not the God of the dead, but of the living."[3] These

---

[1] Mark x. 2 sqq.; Matt. xix. 3 sqq.

[2] Mark xi. 17; Matt. xxi. 13; Luke xix. 46.

[3] Mark xii. 26 sq.; Matt. xxii. 31 sq.; Luke xx. 37. The differences in the mode of reference are worth noticing, Luke ascribing

passages, however, exhibit the same disposition that we have already noticed, to appeal to Scripture in support of great spiritual principles which might be discovered within the soul itself, and to which the soul alone could furnish the interpretation.

Another saying calls for careful consideration, because in it the Scripture seems to be accepted as "the word of God," in contrast with "the tradition of men." The Pharisees were shocked because the disciples of Jesus did not conform to a traditional rule about the washing of hands. Jesus, who never shows the least mercy to this kind of formal and external religion, immediately charges them with hypocrisy, and quotes against them the prophecy of Isaiah: "This people honoureth me with their lips, but their heart is far from me. But in vain do they worship me, teaching as their doctrines the precepts of men." These words were singularly applicable to the case; but though Jesus treated them as a prophecy, we need not suppose that he looked upon them as intended by the Prophet to have this particular limitation. The words were true in Isaiah's time, and were a prophecy

the words exclusively to Moses, Matthew to God, and Mark, with greater fulness, taking a position between the two.

against hypocrites of all time. But what follows is of more importance: "Full well do ye reject the commandment of God, that ye may keep your tradition. For Moses said (or as Matthew has it, God said), Honour thy father and thy mother; and, He that speaketh evil of father or mother, let him die the death;" but the Pharisees had made this void by their tradition.[1] Now here some words of Scripture are treated as a commandment of God; but we have once more to remark that the commandment selected is one which the unperverted conscience emphatically confirms, while a false religion set up the fancied obligations of a supernatural authority above the divine claims of natural duty and affection. Perhaps we may be allowed to conjecture that Jesus intended to limit "the commandment of God" to the words taken from the Ten Commandments, and that he added the terrible penalty only to show the extreme importance which Moses attached to the duty in question; for we cannot believe, consistently with the general tenor of his teaching, that he would himself have sanctioned this vindictive punishment. But be this as it may, the rebuke uttered against the Pharisees is followed

[1] Mark vii. 1 sqq.; Matt. xv. 1 sqq.

by a declaration of principle, to which we have already alluded, whereby not only the teaching of the Pharisees, but the teaching of parts of the Old Testament itself, is directly contravened: "There is nothing from without the man that going into him can defile him; but the things which proceed out of the man are those that defile the man." To this principle we must give the utmost latitude; for otherwise it would not cover the question at issue, which related, not to the nature of the food, but to the washing of the hands. It therefore repudiates not only the distinction of kinds of food as religiously clean or unclean,[1] but all reliance upon formal and external acts, and throws men back exclusively on the condition of the thoughts and affections which their conduct reveals. If we take this passage, then, as a whole, it confirms the indications which we have previously noticed, that Christ did not accept the Old Testament as a uniform utterance of divinely authenticated oracles, but discriminated as the word of God that alone which commended itself to the pure heart and conscience.

We are now prepared for the startling evidence afforded by the Sermon on the Mount.[2] Jesus there

---

[1] See Levit. xi.   [2] Matt. v. 21 sqq.

deals, not with ritual, but with moral precepts, where we should expect to find his confidence in the Bible most strongly asserted. But no; he deals with one commandment after another, not as "the word of God," but as that which "was said to them of old time." Some of these he treats as insufficient, and gives them a large extension. "Thou shalt not kill," is transformed into an injunction against the anger or contempt which may be the root of murderous passion. "Thou shalt not forswear thyself, but shalt perform unto the Lord thine oaths," becomes a prohibition against swearing at all, and an approval of the simple speech of plain veracity. "Thou shalt not commit adultery," is enlarged into a principle of inward purity. But the law of divorce, laid down in Deuteronomy,[1] is condemned as immoral. The law of retaliation, "An eye for an eye, and a tooth for a tooth," is condemned with equal emphasis. "Thou shalt love thy neighbour and hate thine enemy,"[2] is transfigured into a universal love which embraces enemies and persecutors. It seems clear that, to use the cant phrase of modern

[1] xxiv. 1 sqq.
[2] This expresses the sense rather than the exact words of the Law.

disciples of the Pharisees, Jesus did not "believe in the Bible," but used it with a freedom and discrimination which soon raised against him a swarm of implacable enemies, who, in the charitable judgment of Paul, had "a zeal for God, but not according to knowledge."[1]

How, then, it will be asked, are we to understand the words in which the permanence of the Law is asserted?—"Think not that I came to destroy the Law or the Prophets: I came not to destroy, but to fulfil. For verily I say unto you, till heaven and earth pass away, one jot or one tittle shall in no wise pass away from the Law till all things be accomplished."[2] Some writers have supposed that these words are so plainly directed against the teaching of St. Paul that they cannot be authentic, but owe their origin to the conflicts of the Apostolic age. This seems to me a needless criticism, partly because the words, if interpreted by their context, yield a sense which is agreeable to the rest of Christ's teaching, partly because their substance is given by Luke also,[3] and partly because St. Paul himself writes as though he were acquainted with them, and understood them

[1] Rom. x. 2.   [2] Matt. v. 17 sq.   [3] xvi. 17.

in a sense favourable to his own views. According to him, the very object of freedom from the Law through the sending of Christ was "that the ordinance of the Law might be fulfilled in us;" "He that loveth his neighbour hath fulfilled the Law;" "The whole Law is fulfilled in one word, even in this, 'Thou shalt love thy neighbour as thyself.'"[1] If Paul could use such language at the very time when he was proving that the Law had served its purpose, and that it contained "weak and beggarly elements" to which only the unspiritual could return, surely Christ might guard himself against suspicions of antinomianism by saying that he had no thought of relaxing the high obligations which were laid upon men by the ancient reli-

[1] It is well to notice the Greek words. Οὐκ ἦλθον καταλῦσαι ἀλλὰ πληρῶσαι. ... ἐὰν μὴ περισσεύσῃ ὑμῶν ἡ δικαιοσύνη πλεῖον τῶν γραμματέων καὶ Φαρισαίων κ. τ. λ. (Matt. v. 17, 20). Ἵνα τὸ δικαίωμα τοῦ νόμου πληρωθῇ ἐν ἡμῖν τοῖς μὴ κατὰ σάρκα περιπατοῦσιν ἀλλὰ κατὰ πνεῦμα (thus reaching the higher righteousness by reversing the Pharisaic method; Rom. viii. 4). Ὁ γὰρ ἀγαπῶν τὸν ἕτερον νόμον πεπλήρωκεν. ... πλήρωμα οὖν νόμου ἡ ἀγάπη (Rom. xiii. 8, 10). Again, Ὃς ἐὰν οὖν λύσῃ μίαν τῶν ἐντολῶν τούτων τῶν ἐλαχίστων (Matt. v. 19), compared with εἴ τις ἑτέρα ἐντολή, ἐν τῷ λόγῳ τούτῳ ἀνακεφαλαιοῦται (Rom. xiii. 9), and ὁ γὰρ πᾶς νόμος ἐν ἑνὶ λόγῳ πεπλήρωται, ἐν τῷ Ἀγαπήσεις τὸν πλησίον σου ὡς σεαυτόν (Gal. v. 14). Compare also, Νόμον οὖν καταργοῦμεν διὰ τῆς πίστεως; Μὴ γένοιτο· ἀλλὰ νόμον ἱστάνομεν (Rom. iii. 31).

gion; nay, that he intended to carry them to a finer perfection and a greater strictness. It is clear that in the passages quoted from Paul he means by the Law the moral law, that which might be accepted by the conscience as the eternal law of God; and Christ may have used it in the same sense. I do not mean that an explicit distinction was drawn between the moral and the ceremonial. The Law was regarded as a whole; but it was perceived by the more enlightened minds that, as a whole, it had a moral and spiritual significance, and that its ritual requirements were only symbolic veils of spiritual ideas. As soon, therefore, as the spiritual ideas were realized in life, the foreshadowing symbol fell away of itself, being lost in its fulfilment. It was possible, accordingly, for Paul to say that "the *whole* Law" was fulfilled in the commandment to love one's neighbour, because this was the culminating idea which gave life and meaning to the whole. In the same way, Jesus refers to every portion of the Law, while at the same time his mind instinctively seizes on the ethical portion as the true expression of its idea, and as alone imparting to it any permanent value. All the examples which follow are from the moral law, and they illustrate what Jesus meant by "fulfilling." He did not mean adhering to the letter of the commandment, but penetrating to the spirit of goodness which the commandment sought to embody, and giving to that a nobler and more complete expression. He sums up his meaning in one brief and memorable sentence: "All things, therefore, whatsoever ye would that men should do unto you, even so do ye also unto them: for this is the Law and the Prophets."[1] It was in this large sense, then, that he came not to destroy, but to fulfil. In the kingdom of heaven there was no lowering of the divine requirements. There was to be no explaining away of the commandment to honour one's father and mother, no quibbling distinctions as to the binding nature of oaths, no defining of the term neighbour so as to suit one's narrow and selfish passions; but the divine idea of the old religion was to be carried out in the minutest particulars, till its grandest dream passed into waking reality, and men became the sons of their Father in heaven through participation in his spirit of love.[2]

If, now, we put these various lines of evidence together, we obtain a pretty distinct conception of

[1] Matt. vii. 12.   [2] Matt. v. 44 sq.

Christ's view of the Old Testament. It is clear, in the first place, that he did not, out of repugnance to some portions of its teaching, place himself in revolutionary antagonism to it, as Marcion did at a later time. He set himself in the same line as Moses and the Prophets, and received the Old Testament as the records of their teaching. Many a sublime passage must have found an echo in his heart, and the words of psalmist and seer have often flashed a revealing light into the workings of his own mind. The God whose voice he heard in his own soul was the God who had spoken to them, and he was summoned to carry on and complete their work by leading Israel, and through Israel mankind, to the fulfilment of that Divine idea which for so many ages had been slowly unfolding itself through the imperfect conditions of Hebrew history. But the very notion of fulfilment, of completion, of enlargement, implies the previous existence of the incomplete and limited, and a mingling of the transient and erroneous with the true and permanent; and we have seen that this was clearly recognized by Jesus. The presence and operation of God were no guarantee of infallibility, for they were seen through the dimness of human vision, and the divine message was expressed through the halting forms of human speech. Discrimination was necessary. In the passionate righteousness of Elijah the righteousness had to be separated from the passion. In the Law of Moses, what was allowed in order to prevent worse evils had to be distinguished from the creative thought of God. The ultimate authority, therefore, must be within; and he who would draw forth the grandest lessons of the Old Testament must go to it with "spiritual discernment," and bring its various thoughts into the presence of God, to be tested by the fire of his Spirit. It was thus that Jesus dealt with the Scriptures; and it was through this reverent freedom that he drew down on himself the wrath of the blind guides who knew that God had spoken to Moses, but who had neither eyes nor ears for his living word among themselves.

We have been obliged to infer Christ's view of the Old Testament from the use which he actually makes of it, as, owing to the occasional and unsystematic character of his teaching, he did not find it necessary to reduce his thoughts on the subject to a precise form. To a certain extent, the same remark is true of Paul; but he was compelled by the exigencies of controversy to frame a theory of the relation which the Old Testament bore to the new teaching, and to present this theory to his own thought in a shape sufficiently definite for argumentative purposes. Revolutionary, and even blasphemous, as his views appeared to his fellow-countrymen, he retained his veneration for the ancient Scriptures, and looked upon the manifestation of the spirit of sonship in Christ as the full revelation of the idea which had guided the providential history of the Jewish race. The intentions of God were not carried out by spasmodic and irrational methods. One determining thought had been guiding the education of mankind; and it was only when the fulness of the time came, and men were ready to pass out of the immaturity and subjection of childhood, that the Son of God appeared in order to lead the world into its spiritual manhood.[1] This being so, the Gospel furnished a new key to the Old Testament; for it was now possible to detect the underlying idea beneath the temporary forms and imperfect hints by which it sought to manifest itself amid the lower conditions of spiritual culture, while the grander passages flashed forth with a new brilliancy as they seemed to

---

[1] See especially Rom. vii. and viii., and Gal. iii. and iv.

issue from the very spirit which Christ had brought into the world. But without this inward illumination it was impossible to understand the old words aright. A veil lay upon the heart, and the more diligently the letter was studied, and the more vehemently it was defended, the more impenetrable the veil became.[1]

Paul, therefore, accepted in a certain sense the authority of the Old Testament. He constantly appealed to it in argument. He regarded incidents recorded in it as "our examples ... written for our admonition."[2] He looked upon Jesus as the Messiah, sprung from the seed of David, and foretold by the Prophets in "Holy Scriptures."[3] He thought of the Jews as the chosen olive, into which the Gentiles were only grafted.[4] He believed in the promise made to Abraham, and saw in the Gospel the final realization of that faith which had marked the founder of the Hebrew race.[5] Yet, on the other hand, his great and characteristic contention was that the old covenant had been superseded by a new, and that the very portion of the Old Testament which in Judaism had been considered fundamental had sunk

[1] See especially Rom. x., 1 Cor. ii., 2 Cor. iii.
[2] 1 Cor. x. 6, 11.   [3] Rom. i. 1 sqq.
[4] Rom. xi. 16 sqq.   [5] Rom. iv.; Gal. iii.

away, and become a useless or mischievous relic of an outgrown past. He dismisses some of its injunctions as "weak and beggarly elements," and treats with withering scorn those who placed any reliance on its ceremonial requirements.[1] It appears, therefore, that he accepted the Old Testament just so far as it approved itself to the new Christian spirit, and whatever ran counter to that spirit he rejected without hesitation. As we have seen, he followed his Master in interpreting the essence of the Law, which he found in the commandment to love one's neighbour; and for the one thing which is of avail under the Gospel he selected, not obedience to or belief in the Scriptures, "but faith working through love," a "new creation" in the heart, an inward detachment from the world, and self-surrender to God in the spirit of Christ.[2]

How, then, were these two positions reconciled in the mind of Paul? By his doctrine of the letter and the spirit. He had died to the Law, so that he served "in newness of the spirit, and not in oldness of the letter."[3] His ministry was "not of the letter, but of

[1] Gal. iii. 1 sqq., v. 6 sqq.
[2] See especially Gal. v. 6, vi. 14 sqq.; Rom. vi. 1 sqq.
[3] Rom. vii. 6.

the spirit: for the letter killeth, but the spirit giveth life;" and for the Law written on tables of stone he would substitute a more glorious and permanent ministration, written on the heart "with the Spirit of the living God."[1] The distinction of the letter and the spirit reminds us of the system of allegorical interpretation which had been already brought to such perfection by Philo, and which was subsequently adopted by Christian commentators. Was this what Paul meant? I think not; for he seems to refer, not to two kinds of interpretation, but to the contrast between a written word and the word of the spirit within the heart. "Faith working through love" is not a mode of interpreting, but of living; and Paul believed that Christians were emancipated from all dependence on an authoritative Scripture, and were committed to the free leading of the Spirit of God. The Scriptures seen in the light of that Spirit might be of the highest value; treated as an authority by which the Spirit was to be quenched, they could produce nothing but spiritual death.

This last remark suggests the possibility of carrying over the distinction between the letter and the spirit

[1] 2 Cor. iii.

into the interpretation of the Bible, and I think that Paul did so, although this was not his immediate intention when he used the words. In this aspect of the subject we find the key to his meaning at the end of the second chapter of Romans: "He is not a Jew which is one outwardly, neither is that circumcision which is outward in the flesh: but he is a Jew which is one inwardly; and circumcision is that of the heart, in the spirit, not in the letter." This certainly reminds one of allegorical interpretation; but it is allegory in its most sober and simple form. It is not an importation of philosophical ideas into a plain narrative, which at first sight seems to have nothing to do with such recondite thoughts, but an attempt to pass behind the superficial meaning of things into their permanent spiritual essence. The purest example of this is found in the teaching of Christ, as when he extends the prohibition against killing to the angry passions. But Paul goes beyond this, and admits the use of allegory,[1] though we must say that he uses it with great caution and moderation when we compare his practice with that of Philo. He was not driven to it by his theory. Philo had to bring the infallible word,

[1] 1 Cor. ix. 9 sq., x. 1 sqq.; Gal. iv. 21 sqq.

however unworthy it appeared, into harmony with the highest wisdom; Paul saw in the Old Testament much that was temporary and imperfect, a preparatory discipline which was destined to pass away, and so, under the guidance of the Spirit, he could enter into its deeper portions, and see that Spirit striving to weave a heavenly pattern out of human infirmity and sin, while he could allow the childish notions of a barbarous age, or the ceremonial requirements of a rude people, to drop off, not as wholly undivine, but as temporary incidents in the education of the world.

We conclude, then, that Paul followed the example of Christ, at once in his respect for the ancient Scriptures, as embodying words of God, and in his free dealing with them, as falling short of the absolute standard of right and truth. We may assume that in matters of history, which are tested by intellectual criticism, Christ and his Apostle accepted the opinion of their day; in matters of faith and practice, which are tested by spiritual criticism, they freely and trustfully followed the leading of the Spirit within them, which bore its own witness that it was from God.[1]

---

[1] A correspondent has called my attention to the familiar text, 2 Tim. iii. 16 : "Every scripture inspired of God is also profitable

for teaching," &c. This is said in immediate connection with "the sacred writings," and there can be no doubt that the Old Testament is referred to, and treated as inspired. We must remark, however, that the genuineness of this Epistle has been widely doubted in modern times, so that we cannot appeal to it without hesitation as representing Paul's opinion. But the verse contains in fact nothing inconsistent with the exposition given above. That Paul believed that the Old Testament was θεόπνευστος I see no reason to doubt: the question is whether he regarded inspiration as carrying with it a universal and literal infallibility, and on this point the text is absolutely silent. A similar remark will apply to the words of another writer, the author of the second Epistle ascribed to Peter: "No prophecy ever came by the will of man: but men spake from God, being moved by the Holy Spirit" (i. 21). We must learn to recognize the presence and operation of God in that which is imperfect; and much needless scepticism would be prevented if we habitually distinguished the "inspired" and the "infallible."

LECTURE III.
THE BIBLE.—II.

LECTURE III.

THE BIBLE.—II.

IN the last Lecture I started the question whether we can have a new doctrine of the Bible, and still retain Christianity among the living forces of the world. As a preparation for answering that question, I endeavoured to ascertain what position was taken by Christ himself, and by the great Apostle of the Gentiles, in relation to the ancient Scriptures. That position, we saw reason to believe, was widely different from .that which has been generally occupied by the Christian Church. The infallibility of the Bible, as being from beginning to end a wholly exceptional and miraculous book, has been virtually a fundamental dogma of Christendom, and has failed to secure the same precise and rigid definition as other dogmas simply because it was so universally accepted. Even where the Church has been recognized as a co-ordinate authority, the Bible has been regarded as in every respect the Word of God; and any error attaching to its use lay, not in its own imperfect ideas or language, but in faulty interpretation. This doctrine is still maintained as vital and necessary by all who stand upon the old lines; and they look with consternation on the encroaching tide of criticism, which is slowly crumbling away the ancient landmarks in almost every section of the Church, and in the nobler and more spiritual thought of our time they can detect nothing but an irreverent rationalism. It is not very long[1] since a document was issued by a number of the clergy of the Church of England to put a ban upon the labours of scholars who in all humility and devoutness are seeking after truth, and showing how it is possible to preserve the Divine treasure when the earthen vessel which contained it is worn or broken. These gentlemen do not speak as careful and competent students, but as "messengers, watchmen, and stewards of the Lord, who have received the Holy Ghost to be faithful dispensers of the Word of God;" and after a declaration of their belief in "all the

[1] Unfortunately, I have not a note of the exact date.

Canonical Scriptures" as "inspired by the Holy Ghost," they proceed to say:

"We believe these Scriptures because they have the authority of Divine revelation; and wholly independent of our own or of any human approval of the probability or possibility of their subject-matter; and independently of our own or of any human and finite comprehension thereof.

"And we believe that any judgment, either for or against them, formed on the ground of such approval or comprehension, or of the want thereof, is inapplicable to the matter of Divine revelation.

"And we believe the Holy Scriptures to have this Divine authority, on the testimony of the universal Church, the spouse and body of Christ, the witness and keeper of Holy Writ. So that no opinion of the fact or form of Divine revelation, grounded on literary criticism of the Scriptures themselves, can be admitted to interfere with the traditionary testimony of the Church when that has been once ascertained and verified by appeal to antiquity."

To an outsider this attempt to stop the progress of human thought by an assertion of authority can only prove how thickly the Judaic veil still lies upon the heart of many nominal Christians, and illustrate the power which an inherited and ignorant prejudice can exercise upon the minds of good men. But the pity of it is that this teaching is fast destroying the reverence for the Bible in the hearts of the English people. There are numbers who, in revolt against this dogma, can now see in the Bible nothing but a bundle of "lies" (this word is often used), and find a keen pleasure in every cheap and flippant sneer against a collection of books of whose spiritual meaning and value they are utterly ignorant; and thus the narrow dogmatism of religion produces the narrower and meaner dogmatism of no-religion.[1]

Thanks, however, to the despised critics, and to the general advance of knowledge, the night is passing away, and the dawn is shedding its orient beams upon the world. For an ever-increasing number the dogma which has so long obscured and dishonoured the Bible has passed away; and yet their reverence for it has

[1] Mr. Gore's well-known essay in *Lux Mundi* is an earnest attempt, from the point of view of the High Church, to meet this danger by making large concessions in regard to the Old Testament; but I doubt whether he fully appreciates the profundity of the change, and whether some of his opponents do not see more clearly the logical consequences of his position.

remained with them, I will not say unimpaired, but augmented and deepened. Let us briefly review the grounds of these two really coincident, but at first sight antithetical, positions.

The great change, which is still in progress, in the doctrine of Biblical inspiration has been brought about by a variety of causes. These must be briefly indicated, without any attempt to discuss their validity or to estimate the value of apologetic arguments,—an attempt which would carry us far beyond our prescribed limits.

First, then, it is a simple fact that the advance of science has shattered what was believed to be the scientific teaching of the Bible until scientific men pronounced that teaching to be erroneous. When the results of the investigation of nature could no longer be denied, the difficulty was met, in the conservative interest, by giving a new interpretation to the Bible. Supposing this interpretation to be correct, instead of being, as I believe it is, a wresting of Holy Scripture in favour of a baseless dogma, still what a strange authority that is for the guidance of men which is certain to be misinterpreted until science steps in, and tells us plainly what the supposed authority had expressed in words which seemed designed for the very purpose of leading men into error. For instance, no plain and unbiassed man could read the first chapter of Genesis, and think that the author meant by the days, with their evening and their morning, anything but the days with which we are familiar in ordinary speech; and to say that the days mean millions of years, in order to force the narrative into agreement with geology, is very like blasphemy against the Spirit of Truth, who must have foreseen that such a mode of speech would establish for thousands of years a false scientific dogma of the first magnitude. By this process, too, that noble chapter is brought down from the heights of true inspiration, which by its dignity and grandeur has given it a unique place among ancient cosmogonies, and placed on the level of a sagacious magic, like the ambiguous oracles of Delphi. We must refer also to the Biblical astronomy, which did not prevent the long dominance of the Ptolemaic system, or place the Church, with its infallible interpretations, on the side of Copernicus and Galileo. And, again, the date of man's appearance upon the earth, and the story of the Fall, are not borne out by the study of fossil remains and historical monuments. We must add an influence which, though not often reduced to precise argument, has undoubtedly wrought a profound change in current modes of thought, the conception of the continuity and inviolability of natural law. This conception was not unknown to the ancients, or among them to the Hebrews; but the two sciences which have so enormously enlarged our perspective through time and space, have given to the laws of nature a vastness of range which dwarfs all our previous conceptions, and reduces human history to a momentary apparition amid the worlds and ages; and it becomes increasingly difficult to fit into the probabilities of our tiny globe an idea of miracle which was suitable enough to a world that occupied the spacious and dignified centre of the universe. Under the influence of such considerations, the infallibility of the Bible is, for multitudes of men, irrecoverably gone; and those who endeavour to re-establish it, instead of trying to find a place for spiritual truth amid the new facts of knowledge, are but beating the air, and injuring the cause of religion by setting it in opposition to the progress of culture.

Coincidently with the advance of science, historical

and literary criticism has had a conspicuous share in undermining the ancient dogma. Criticism is necessarily a slow and tentative process, and starts many an hypothesis which will not bear a fuller examination; and it cannot be denied that it sometimes puts on grand airs of impartiality, when it is really under the leading of a strong prejudice, which arises through the reactionary enjoyment of a novel freedom. This has sometimes afforded to the opponents of criticism an opportunity for idle scorn, while they point to the contradictory results which range their divided armies against the solid unity of tradition. They do not perceive that truth must always be reached by the severe testing of conflicting hypotheses, or that a negative conclusion may be established with certainty long before any positive statements can be secured, if indeed they can be proved at all. It is conceivable, for instance, that it might be absolutely demonstrated that a certain book was not written by Moses, and that then every variety of hypothesis might be started as to its authorship or date. These hypotheses would be incompatible with one another, and they might even every one of them be demonstrably false; but this would in no way affect the soundness of the original negative proposition. It would only prove that any positive determination was difficult, and perhaps impossible. Now it is a simple fact that a number of critics distinguished by learning, candour and caution—belonging, moreover, to various denominations, and therefore presumably under the influence of different training and bias—have been led by their investigations to reject with confidence the traditional origin of several Biblical books, especially in the Old Testament. These gentlemen do not claim any miraculous authority; and the consequence is, that they are exercising that real authority which ordinary men ascribe to competent students, and their conclusions are being widely accepted by men who have not sufficient learning to test them by methods of their own. The inevitable effect of this uncertainty about the authorship of books is to shake the belief in their infallibility. It is easy to say that their inspiration is not determined by their date or authorship; and in the higher and more spiritual sense of inspiration this is true. Some great unknown soul may have been moved by the Spirit of God to speak words of life to his fellow-men, and the soul which is kindled by his utterances recognizes the inspiration. But a mechanical infallibility depends on a different sort of proof; and when a book, however exalted may be its religious utterances, is no longer attributed to a well-known prophet who bore a miraculous commission, but to some unknown author or authors, plain men will not believe it to be exempt from human imperfection, or pin their faith to every statement which may happen to occur upon its pages. It would be far better, in my humble judgment, for critics to recognize frankly and fully that the results of their criticism, if true, must radically alter the old doctrine of Biblical inspiration. Religion will be the gainer, though creeds which were founded on imperfect knowledge may have to go.

In addition to the changed view of the authorship of books, a careful investigation of the laws of historical evidence has thrown an air of improbability over many narratives, and details which were easily believed by our forefathers have slowly become incredible to a better-trained and better-informed intelligence. Moreover, the difficulties which have been always felt in harmonizing parallel narratives, such as the two accounts of Christ's birth, press upon the mind with increasing weight when they are found to favour a conclusion to which we are led by so many independent lines of inquiry. It is sometimes said that all such objections are very stale, and have been refuted over and over again. They exhibit, however, a strange vitality, if they rest upon nothing but perversity and error. They have, in fact, never been satisfactorily set aside; and yet we may believe that the Church gave the correct solution of the problem which was submitted to it in ancient times. It was assumed that the divine and the infallible were one; and the alternative presented to the Christian mind was the acceptance of every part of the Bible as alike the Word of God, or yielding to the attacks of unbelievers and renouncing the faith. But this alternative no longer exists. We have learnt that the Spirit of God works through imperfect instruments, and that the highest spiritual exaltation, though it may afford visions and revelations of the Lord, and enable a man to utter truths which he has seen and known, is no guarantee against intellectual error or defective knowledge of fact; and hence it is possible now for a man to remain a Christian, and yield himself to the religious power of his faith, and yet acknowledge that the Word has been made *flesh*, and the human has never been absorbed in the divine.[1]

Another order of criticism—that which is moral and spiritual—has also been applied to the Bible. As we have seen, we have the authority of Christ himself for saying that the morality of the Old Testament is not

[1] The foregoing remarks are only confirmed by Mr. Sayce's interesting work on *The "Higher Criticism" and the Verdict of the Monuments.* Having been invited to curse the higher criticism, he has blessed it—[I observe that this allusion to Balak has been used by Mr. T. Tyler in his review in the *Academy;* but as my words were written before I saw that review, I allow them to stand]—by accepting its large conclusions and method. No man can read that book attentively, and retain the old view of the Bible. There is a "flat contradiction" in the account of the Exodus (p. 257). A statement in Joshua is "inconsistent" with a statement in Judges (p. 309 sq.). "The chronology of the Second Book of Kings is more than forty years in excess" (p. 319). There are "unimportant errors of detail" in the Biblical narrative, "as in all other historical documents" (p. 395). "The Biblical chronology must be rejected" in the Book of Kings (p. 406 sq.). "The Biblical writer has made a mistake" in calling Seve "king of Egypt" (p. 418). "The story of Esther is an example of Jewish Haggadah" (p. 475). The Book of Daniel is not historical (p. 531 sqq.).— These are examples of statements scattered through the book, and it is surely a very significant event that such a work has been published by the "Society for promoting Christian Knowledge." No more damaging blow has been dealt in recent times at the old view of the Bible.

the same as that of the New. To the instances adduced in the last Lecture, let us only add, by way of example, the words, "Happy shall be he that taketh and dasheth thy little ones against the rock,"[1] or the fearful curses of the 109th Psalm, and try to imagine them issuing from the mouth of Christ; and do we not feel an incongruity which proves the presence of a spirit far different from his?[2] Again, there is a religious development in the Bible, from

[1] Ps. cxxxvii. 9.

[2] Professor Sanday says, in reference to the Psalter: "It must be admitted that sometimes we are conscious, not only of human limitations, but of the violence of human passion."—*Inspiration*, the Bampton Lectures for 1893, p. 197. His whole work shows what a profound change is taking place in the views of the most cautious inquirers, who are anxious to conserve all that is of permanent religious value in the older forms of thought. See, for instance, the statement: "There are no doubt well-marked grades of inspiration in the Canon; and there are some books which have their place quite upon the outskirts of it, and one or two in which inspiration is hardly perceptible at all" (p. 208). What a contrast does this present to the manifesto quoted near the beginning of the Lecture!

Mr. Gore quotes from the Fathers some interesting passages in which the moral imperfection of the Old Testament is clearly recognized, and explained through the necessity of adapting moral education to the age and capacity of the persons to be educated. (*Lux Mundi*, essay on the Holy Spirit and Inspiration, p. 329 sqq., 1st ed.)

the simplicity and anthropomorphism of patriarchal faith to the soaring flight and pure spirituality of the Pauline Epistles; and it is one of the inestimable services of modern criticism that it has filled the ancient Scriptures once again with human interest, and shown us how the revelation of God has grown from more to more, while the primeval thought of communion between God and man has slowly unfolded its contents, and adapted itself to successive conditions of the world. Further, the study of comparative religion has given us a fuller knowledge of the religious history of mankind, and has co-ordinated with extra-biblical events much that used to seem quite exceptional. We are at last beginning to believe the old Christian saying that God has never left himself without a witness, and that in every nation he that feareth him and worketh righteousness is accepted of him. It is not that Christianity is sinking down into the common mire of a profane humanity, but that everywhere the heavenly idea has been present, however the falsity and meanness of earth may have failed to comprehend it, and has striven to lead men on towards the divine humanity of Christ. Those who consider these things, and see them in their natural bearing, may indeed place the Bible at the head of religious literature, and give it a unique position in history, and in their own grateful reverence; but they can no longer place it in a class entirely apart, and endow it with a miraculous infallibility.

Such, then, are the reasons which, in so many minds, have shattered the old doctrine of the Bible. To those who are not familiar with the process it naturally appears destructive and alarming, and we cannot be surprised that there is much uneasy questioning and much ineffectual protest. The ground on which men thought they stood has vanished beneath their feet, and the value of the Bible as a mere external authority is gone; for we can no longer assume that a statement is true simply because it is between the covers of the venerable book. Let us not shrink from seeing clearly this inevitable conclusion. The instinct is correct which says, that if a single error be admitted, the whole edifice must crumble into ruins; for if there be an error here, there may be an error there, and the basis of belief must be shifted from the Bible to some other ground of judgment.[1]

---

[1] If I may venture to say so, I think this result is hardly recognized with sufficient clearness in Professor Sanday's admirable

III. THE BIBLE.—II.

Nevertheless, the supreme religious value of the Bible is attested by Christian experience; and it appears to me a rash and unreasonable demand that, because we have ceased to believe in its infallibility,

Bampton Lectures; and perhaps for this reason the final statement of results is not quite so helpful as it would otherwise be. A man who has held the ancient doctrine, and believed that in every line of the Bible he had the words of infallible wisdom, feels himself alone in space when this doctrine crumbles beneath his feet; and for him the "dilemma 'all or nothing,'" which Professor Sanday so justly deprecates (p. 428), is for a time inevitable. It seems to me that we can meet this state of mind only by the frankest and fullest recognition of the reality of the dilemma in regard to the particular phase of thought under consideration, the reliance on an external authority which rests on an infallible basis. For this phase of thought we have to provide a substitute; and though within the realm of spiritual experience and religious reverence towards the Bible there is an unquestionable resemblance between the two views, yet on the intellectual side, when reduced to doctrinal form, they are wholly incompatible. The changed opinion about the Bible is nothing less than a revolution in Christian theology; but it will surely bring, as its final result, a deeper appreciation of the spirit of our religion. The lamented Mr. Aubrey Moore puts the case very clearly when he says: "The religious idea of God must claim and justify itself to the highest known morality, and no amount of authority, ecclesiastical or civil, will make men worship an immoral God. And already that truth has thrown back its light upon questions of Old Testament morality. We no longer say, 'It is in the Bible, approved or allowed by God, and therefore it must be right.' It was this view which, in every age, has given its protection to religious wars and intolerance and persecution." ("The Christian Doctrine of God," in *Lux Mundi*, p. 82.)

we should therefore plunge it down into the common mass of literature, break up the Canon, and read indiscriminately in our public worship whatever happens to strike the private fancy as edifying. To put the question upon no higher ground, the Bible has an historical claim which cannot be altered by any change of doctrine. It contains the records of the origin of Christianity, and the first outpouring of the Christian spirit in literature. It is the fountain from which the stream of Christian inspiration has been fed through all the centuries. It has in consequence a time-honoured wealth of association, and a universality of reverence, which cannot possibly be communicated to any freshly imported literature; and consequently, for those who wish to live in the deepest life of man, and not in the isolation of individual peculiarity, it speaks with an accumulated power which places it alone in the love and gratitude of their hearts. Let us glance at some of the effects which it has wrought in innumerable minds, remembering that these effects are not due to any particular dogma, but are rather the foundation which, through the strength of wonder and thankfulness, has supported a theory that was incapable of rational proof.

First, then, it has held up a mirror to the conscience, reminding man that he stands in presence of the Holy One to whom he must give account, and exhibiting side by side the perfection of righteousness and the soiled and misshapen image of himself. "Be not deceived; God is not mocked; for whatsoever a man soweth, that shall he also reap."[1] "Though I speak with the tongues of men and of angels, and have not love, I have become sounding brass or a tinkling cymbal."[2] "He that loveth not his brother abides in death."[3] Examples might of course be multiplied indefinitely. In the Law, and the Prophets, and the Psalms, as well as in the New Testament, are words that pierce to the central seats of life, and, touching the conscience to the quick, waken there the sleeping echoes, a voice of God within responsive to his word without.

Again, the Bible has brought home to our minds numerous spiritual suggestions or truths at which the heart bounds as though it had discovered some long-sought treasure, or in which the anxious thought rests as giving satisfaction to its difficulties and doubts. "God is Spirit, and they that worship him must wor-

[1] Gal. vi. 7.   [2] 1 Cor. xiii. 1.   [3] 1 John iii. 14.

ship him in spirit and truth."[1] "God is love, and he that abideth in love abideth in God, and God in him."[2] "Blessed are the pure in heart, for they shall see God."[3] These are a few sample grains of gold out of the storehouse, which "skilful money-changers" recognize as genuine; they want no outward guarantee, for they have the witness in themselves.

Once more, the Bible has strengthened and deepened our devout feeling, and caused the many strings of reverent and holy love within the heart to vibrate as to the touch of a heavenly musician. "As the hart panteth after the water-brooks, so panteth my soul after thee, O God."[4] "The Lord is my light and my salvation; whom shall I fear?"[5] "Not my will, but thine, be done."[6] "Father, into thy hands I commend my spirit."[7] "My grace is sufficient for thee; for my power is made perfect in weakness."[8] But passage after passage rushes on the memory, and time would fail were I to attempt even to illustrate the abundance of devotional utterance in the Scriptures, which gives articulate expression to our own unshaped

---

[1] John iv. 24. [2] 1 John iv. 16. [3] Matt. v. 8.
[4] Ps. xlii. 1. [5] Ps. xxvii. 1. [6] Luke xxii. 42.
[7] Ps. xxxi. 5; Luke xxiii. 46. [8] 2 Cor. xii. 9.

yearnings, and falls upon the ear like some half-remembered melody, reminding us of our heavenly home, as of a native land where once we aspired and prayed.

And, lastly, what comfort the Bible has poured upon stricken hearts, bringing trust and hope to assuage the bitterness of grief! "Remember, O Lord, thy tender mercies, and thy loving kindnesses; for they have been ever of old."[1] "Like as a father pitieth his children, so the Lord pitieth them that fear him."[2] "O Lord of hosts, blessed is the man that trusteth in thee."[3] "Comfort ye, comfort ye my people, saith your God."[4] "All things work together for good to those that love God."[5] "Peace I leave with you, my peace I give unto you; not as the world giveth give I unto you. Let not your heart be troubled, neither let it be afraid."[6] How many generations of weepers have treasured such words as these, and pondered them in their hearts! How many baffled combatants for truth and righteousness have gained from them new strength to stand in the evil hour! How many have passed tranquilly through the pain and stress of

[1] Ps. xxv. 6. [2] Ps. ciii. 13. [3] Ps. lxxxiv. 12.
[4] Isaiah xl. 1. [5] Rom. viii. 28. [6] John xiv. 27.

life, because the peace of ancient prophets and martyrs has entered their souls, and breathed upon their passions a holy calm!

Such are a few illustrations of the experience which compels Christians to attach such high value to the Bible. It may be said that such experiences are no isolated phenomena, but have their analogies in connection with all religious literature; and I am far from denying that this is the case, or even that to certain individuals some modern writing speaks with greater power and authority than anything in the Bible. But it remains to be seen whether such writings will wear, whether they will last through the centuries, and spread over many lands, and be cherished among rich and poor, learned and unlearned, as a source of life and healing. There are a few works, such as the Confessions of Augustine, the Imitatio, and the Pilgrim's Progress, which have stood the test of permanence and wide diffusion; but all these bear witness to the Bible, and are only fruitful branches of that vine, the roots of which go down into Hebrew prophecy, and the teaching of Christ and his Apostles. We cannot reverse the facts of history, and glorify the works of Emerson or Carlyle with the blood of martyrs, the faithfulness of confessors, the victorious purity of unnumbered saints, and the hallelujahs of ten thousand churches. And strange as it may appear to those who are under the influence of reaction, it is simply the fact that on the Christian soul, in its anguish of sorrow or of sin, words of the Bible drop as with the power of God; and it listens entranced, as though the heavens were opened, and the Father's voice spoke to the very trial of the moment. How is this?

In order to answer this question, to reconcile the two positions, the critical and the religious, and to see how the Bible, without being infallible, is nevertheless a source of truth of primary value, we must consider what may be called the Christian philosophy of the subject.

Paul, whom we do not class among philosophers, because his penetrating and suggestive thoughts are the immediate utterance of the spirit within him, rather than the result of prolonged investigation and reasoning, has given in a few words the solution of our difficulty. "What man," he asks, "knoweth the things of man but the spirit of man which is in him? So also the things of God knoweth none but the Spirit of God. Now we received not the spirit of the world, but the spirit which is from God, that we may know the things that were graciously given to us by God."[1] The hidden workings of the human mind can be revealed to us only in our own consciousness. Take away our imagination, and for us the oracles of poetry must be for ever silent. Destroy our sense of humour, and the laughter of our neighbours will cease to exhilarate us. Banish from us anger and pity, avarice and generosity, and the contrariety of men's actions towards one another, now inflicting injury, and now assuaging pain, will be a puzzle without a key. And in the same way, how can we know transcendent holiness, justice and love, if these things have never visited our consciousness? Speak of them to a man who has never risen out of his selfishness and impurity, and he will not understand you. Place him in the society of angels, and he will find himself a foreigner, listening to a strange tongue. But let them come to us, as come they do, we know not how—let them enter the domain of consciousness—and they stand revealed as of heavenly lineage, expressions of that eternal life which alone, even upon earth, abides amid the schemes

[1] 1 Cor. ii. 11 sq.

and struggles of successive generations, through the rise and fall of empires, and the pride and decay of philosophies and religions,—the spirit, not of the world, but of God. When once this life takes possession of us; when we find ourselves loving where once we hated; when we honour all men, instead of cherishing contempt towards our supposed inferiors; when our hearts melt with pity towards the degraded and repulsive outcast; when the war of passion yields to an unaccustomed peace, and the clamorous demands of self no longer trouble us; when in every quiet moment the soul flies to God as to its home, and prayer is the most spontaneous language that breaks from the lips,—then we ask for no proofs; the witness is in ourselves, and the spirit which has been given us tells us of the Giver. And if we cannot always live at this height, if sometimes clouds must gather around us, still the revelation once made remains with us, and it is impossible to doubt that the life which we then beheld is the divinest thing that ever rose in our consciousness.

This highest form of interior life is, for Christians, the spirit of Christ, or "the spirit of life in Christ Jesus." It does not concern us at present how much or how little of this spirit has been manifested elsewhere. God reveals himself in many ways, and sends some portion of light to every man born into the world. He has been leading on our race through all the ages by the attraction of spiritual ideals, and his formative thought has been slowly shaping a spiritual cosmos out of the chaos of our void and formless capabilities. But for Christians it is in Christ that these ideal relations of the soul with God, which philosophers and devotees have so often felt after with imperfect touch, have received their true expression; and it is in fellowship of the spirit with him that they have become aware of that life of sonship which is thenceforward the goal of all their hope and striving. This inward and experiential knowledge of the spirit of life in Christ is sometimes described in theology as the Christian consciousness.

Now this life contains certain implicit truths as its logical justification. To draw out these truths, and state them in precise form, requires an intellectual process, and is the work of the theologian. Some, through the very confidence of their faith, may be content with a vague and crude system of doctrine; and a few, in whom the ethical nature is predominant.

may be so absorbed and satisfied with the ideal of goodness itself that they never question it, or pass behind it to its ontological ground. Others may go to the opposite extreme, and lose the simple purity of inward experience in the number and complexity of their dogmas, and their combative assertion that these dogmas alone can render possible the experience which they would interpret. Between these two extremes will be various forms of opinion, differences inevitably arising both from the imperfect measures by which the spirit is given, and from the varying power and knowledge of the intellect which is brought to the task of interpretation. Let me try to indicate, by way of example, a few of the truths and questions which are suggested by the Christian consciousness.

There are some truths which it immediately implies. For instance, it involves a sense of filial relationship to God; and this is formulated in the doctrines of the Fatherhood of God and the sonship of man—doctrines which will come under our consideration in a future Lecture. Again, it contains a feeling of trust, an escape from self and its cares into some higher disposal. Now trust cannot rest on anything lower than personality, and it accordingly implies in God the presence of wisdom, love and will, or at least attributes of which these things in us are the highest known expression.

Again, it raises many questions in regard to its own nature and origin. These questions receive different answers according to the degree of spiritual and intellectual illumination; but their test, in the present connection, is their power of satisfying the highest and most permanent Christian experience. Thus, we may ask, wherein did Christ's wonderful influence consist? Was he man, or was he some heavenly being in the semblance of man? Or was he truly man, but one in whom dwelt the fulness of the Divine nature, so far as it comes into spiritual relations with humanity? Out of these questions grows a doctrine of the Person of Christ (or a Christology), which must not only be agreeable to historical facts, but must explain and justify the inner witness of the soul. Whereas we were blind, now we see: why, and how? We must further ask, in regard to the spirit which wrought in the disciples, and of which we are conscious in ourselves, what is it, and whence comes it? We must, in our minds, distinguish Holiness from Reason or Thought; yet both are alike divine, for they belong to our very notion of God, and we cannot think of God as having ever been without them, or as creating them. Is the distinction which is so clear to our thought a reality in Him, or do all distinctions vanish in the incomprehensible Unity of Being? Here we look into a land of mystery which might well seem too high for our feeble vision; but the daring speculations of theology have sought to pierce the secrets of eternity, and have framed a precise doctrine of the Holy Spirit.

These may serve as examples of the kind of truth that is attested by the Christian consciousness. And here a very important distinction comes into view. It is apparent that to ourselves, as well as to Paul, it is "the deep things of God," and these only that are revealed by the Spirit. In other words, the Christian consciousness stands in relation to moral and spiritual truth, but has nothing to say in regard to merely scientific or historical questions. It may be true that the pure in heart shall see God; and yet no degree of purity of heart can determine the date and authorship of a book, or the occurrence of a particular event. These must be investigated by intellectual methods; and, being dependent on learning and carefully trained judgment, opinion respecting them, however competent, must stand in some near connection with the knowledge and thought of the time. It might often happen that the Prophet would be the least qualified to pronounce an opinion upon such subjects; for the whole of his mental tendency would lie in another direction, and he would have little taste for the minute investigations of the scholar and critic. In all these extraneous matters he would naturally accept the established opinion, and no amount of error in regard to them would affect the reality of his message, or the degree of his inspiration. Let us only try to imagine Isaiah devoting several years to investigating the authorship of the Pentateuch, or even Paul, with his Rabbinical training, producing a ponderous tome on the authenticity of the Book of Daniel, and we shall be at once struck with a sense of incongruity, and perceive how wide apart are the provinces of the inspired teacher and the laborious investigator. It is not surprising, therefore, that some have sought to rescue the infallibility of the Bible by limiting its range, and representing it as an unerring standard in everything relating to faith and morals, while scientific and historical statements reflect the opinions of the time. The distinction is true and valuable, and may teach us the folly of denying the reality of inspiration wherever we can detect a blunder. The rule, however, cannot save the doctrine of infallibility; for we have seen that there is a progress in the moral and religious conceptions of the Bible, and that the older teaching is sometimes superseded and even contradicted by the newer. The reason is clear. The message of the prophet may be of limited range, even in the domain of religion. The Spirit is given in very different measures to different men, and the power of intellectual interpretation and expression varies indefinitely. Hence we may see everywhere the working of the Divine Thought, and feel the power of truths found in immediate communion with God, and yet not be surprised that in its childhood the world thought as a child, and that tongues and prophecies and knowledge continually pass away, while faith and hope and love abide, and unfold into richer beauty and more commanding power as the generations pass.

We must next inquire how, in accordance with the view here presented, the Bible reveals truth.

In the first place, the New Testament discloses the spirit of Christ, which is the foundation and norm of the Christian consciousness. This spirit is disclosed, not only through the records of his acts and teaching in the Gospels, but also through the teaching of his disciples and the character of the early Church. As we proceed, we shall come upon traces of the same commanding spirit, of the same general type of life and doctrine, pervading the earliest documents. I say this in full view of the differences and developments which critics have, in recent times, been fond of pointing out in the several writers of the New Testament. These writers were undoubtedly men of diverse temperament and spiritual gift; but all alike express their unbounded reverence for Christ himself, and in their varying moods and tendencies we see only different phases of the same spirit.[1] The pictures are indeed manifold; yet they blend into one harmonious impression, which, without this manifoldness, would be deficient in fulness and perfection. The spirit of life in Christ Jesus thus revealed, and received into ourselves, becomes within us the spiritual judge of moral and

[1] It is impossible to work out this view in the present Lectures; but the reader will at least find some hints and illustrations on the following pages.

religious truth, discerning what is compatible, and what incompatible, with itself.

Secondly, the New Testament goes beyond this, and presents, ready formed, numerous doctrines which are either the expression or the interpretation of the Christian spirit. Its nearest and most essential truths were inevitably the first to disclose themselves in thought, and to become the subjects of conversation and of teaching; while more remote and speculative ideas did not emerge till the original fervour cooled, and intellectual gained the precedence over spiritual interest. As examples of immediate expressions of the spirit of Christ, we may take such sayings as these:— "Blessed are the merciful;" "Every one who is angry with his brother shall be liable to the judgment;" "Not every one that saith unto me, Lord, Lord, shall enter into the kingdom of heaven, but he that doeth the will of my Father who is in heaven;" "There is one God and Father of all;" "God is love;" "He that hateth his brother walketh in darkness." Such statements as these were vivid truths in the days when Christianity was young; and however they have been obscured or forgotten in later times, they still shine with a pure radiance, and bear witness to their own truth in every Christian heart. Doctrines which give an interpretation of the inward life do not possess the same unerring authentication as the primary truths. Some, however, lay so close to the religious experience that they came with all the force of a primary conviction, such as these:—"Except a man be born from above, he cannot see the kingdom of God;" "I am the vine; ye are the branches,"— statements which gain in the clearness and fulness of their meaning through their figurative setting. Others were revealed distinctly to some, but not to all; for instance, that the Gentiles were fellow-heirs with the Jews, and partakers of the promise,—a truth which was as clear as daylight to Paul, but required argument and discussion to bring it home to those who could not see so far into the meaning of the new life. Others, again, were more purely inferential, and therefore mixed up to a greater extent with current modes of belief, such as the doctrine that Jesus was the Christ, who fulfilled the promises to Israel,—a doctrine which commends itself when spiritually interpreted, and serves to embody the truth that Christianity did not break, but consummated, the religious development of Judaism; but it required explanation, and could only be established by a comparison between the old and the new, and by scriptural and historical evidence.

But we find also in the New Testament another class of doctrines, which are not the expression or interpretation of the Christian consciousness, but the result of local and temporary conditions of belief. For instance, the belief just alluded to, that Jesus was the Messiah, naturally carried with it an acceptance of those elements in the old belief which were not contradicted by Christian experience. The fact of the crucifixion made an impassable gulf between the old and the new views, and must have altered to the very core the conception of the Messiah's work; but the expectations of his earthly glory could not immediately disappear, and hence arose the doctrine that Jesus was to return in person, and establish his kingdom in the world, and this before the first generation of disciples had passed away. It is obvious that a belief of this kind could not grow out of the new life with God; indeed, now that we know it to have been erroneous, I think we can see that it is inconsistent with the finer elements of Christian thought, though this was not so obviously the case as to be immediately perceived by those whose minds had been early imbued with the Messianic notions of the time.

We are thus furnished with a criterion by which we can "try the spirits whether they be of God," a criterion which, though in us, is not of us, and is therefore not wholly subjective. Of course this criterion does not transfer to ourselves the infallibility which we have denied to the Bible; for we suffer both from the limitation of the spirit and the imperfection of our intelligence. Still it is for each man the ground of settled faith, and a principle by which, if he will trust it, he can distinguish doctrines, and separate the permanent from the transient—the spiritual verities which shine by their own light, from the shadows which are cast by the fleeting forms of partial thought and knowledge.

From the New Testament we must turn for a moment to the Old. The Christian Church was sounder in its interpretation of spiritual facts than Marcion, when it insisted on accepting the ancient Scriptures, and recognized one God as operative through all the ages. Nevertheless, the great heretic had something to say for himself; and a theory of inspiration which places Esther on a level with Isaiah, and represents Ecclesiastes as written by the same spirit as the noblest of the Psalms, and exalts a page of imprecations to the rank of the Sermon on the Mount, would make it very difficult to defend the ecclesiastical position. Marcion perceived a true distinction; but taking as his key the fashionable Gnosticism, he gave it a wrong interpretation. In accordance with the line of argument here advanced, we may say that the Old Testament discloses the gradual unfolding of that spirit of life which found its full expression in Christ, and exhibits it working through imperfect human instruments, and even at times allying itself with passion and cruelty. Consequently it presents a larger admixture of the earthly and temporary than the New Testament, and a much greater variety in the spiritual impressiveness of different books. But if it contains much that belongs to an elementary stage of civilization, it abounds in passages which at once bring home to us truths that receive the sanction of the inward witness; and for some phases of religious feeling we find a richer expression in the Old Testament than in the New. Moreover, during the growth of the spiritual life in ourselves, the imperfect manifestations in the Old Testament often seem nearer to us.[1] Our childhood wandered in imagination with the heroes of the olden time, who seemed so close to God; and in maturer years many who cannot soar to the heights of Paul and John, find their aspirations, their sorrows, and their trusts, made vocal in the Psalms. And so we can accept and be grateful for what comes home to us, and turn it into spiritual food, while we have no difficulty in rejecting that which does not commend itself to our riper Christian experience or our augmented knowledge.

Sufficient, perhaps, has now been said to explain why the Bible, though not cut off by a miraculous infallibility from other religious literature, must nevertheless continue to occupy a place by itself in the love and veneration of Christians. Creeds and confessions of faith, books of "Common Prayer," and collections

[1] An interesting example is furnished by the remarks of Mr. Lock upon the value of Esther, quoted in Sanday, *Bampton Lectures*, p. 222 sq. I well remember my own early delight in the Book of Joshua, which, if it appealed to the combativeness of the boy, and contains much that is alien to the spirit of Christ, nevertheless taught lessons of courage and fidelity, in reliance upon the Power above us. If not with the sword of steel, yet with the sword of the spirit, we must all learn to fight, and do valiantly for truth and righteousness.

of hymns, may satisfy wants more or less widely felt; but they are all limited in use, and the Bible alone can be the universal book of Christendom. But this recognition of its solitary place in no way precludes the use in private, or on suitable public occasions, of the rich literature in prose or verse, which from age to age has expressed the living spirit of Christian devotion. I would that that literature were better known, and that we nourished and enlarged our inward life by words of truth or aspiration from every section of the Church. These, too, contain a word of God, and often speak with moving power to our souls; and flowing as they did direct from the spirit in some hour of high communion, they have something of the same pregnant simplicity of diction and depth of spiritual insight as we find in the Bible. Yet dear as they may become to us under the pressure of our individual needs, how often they are but aids to the study of the Bible, and, through the illumination which they shed upon some Biblical saying, enable us to see more clearly into the heart of Psalmist or Prophet or Apostle. How often, too, is their influence transient, exciting a vivid interest during some crisis of our lives, and then, through their want of universality, retreating into a quiet memory of what they once accomplished for us. But to the Bible we turn with undiminished interest as life goes on, and, as we read it with more discriminating intelligence and larger sympathy, find in it continually fresh treasures of life and thought.

Finally, we must ask, is any authority left to it? Say what we will, the mass of men crave the support of some authority; all but the very strongest souls seek the support of something that lies outside of their own feeble, partial and isolated lives. Does the Bible afford this? We have seen that the artificial authority of an infallible standard is gone. But "the letter killeth," and we can only rejoice that the tables of stone are broken which forbade the free movement of intellect and conscience. "The spirit giveth life," and the law of that life is written "on fleshy tables of the heart." There is a natural authority which helps our weakness instead of cramping our strength. The highest authority is found when truths come straight to the soul, and receive that inward response without which religious truth is dead and useless. But this is deepened and confirmed by our veneration for Prophets and Apostles to whom the word of God came with unequalled power, and who gave up their lives to the delivery of their message, and above all by our faith and love towards the great Teacher in whom that word became flesh. And there is a yet further authority, the witness which in all ages, in spite of corruptions of government and perversities of thought, the Church has borne to the great spiritual verities by which alone the soul of man can live; and the passages in the Bible which appeal to our hearts come to us laden with the reverence and faith of many generations, fragrant with the incense of innumerable prayers, and sealed with the blood of saints and martyrs, who found in them their strength, their joy, and their hope.

LECTURE IV.
THE KINGDOM OF GOD.

LECTURE IV.

THE KINGDOM OF GOD.

To give even the most elementary account of Christianity, and make no allusion to the "Kingdom of God," would be to overlook an idea which was fundamental in Christ's teaching. The memory of this great idea is kept alive in Christendom by the Lord's Prayer, which has passed into universal use; but the three Creeds which are supposed to embody the essential features of the Christian religion, take no notice of it.[1] The teaching of the Master appears to be the

[1] The only apparent exception is the statement in the Constantinopolitan form of the Nicene Creed, that Christ's "kingdom shall have no end," which I cannot regard as in any way equivalent. This clause might seem to be directed against Paul's statement that there will be "the end, when he shall deliver up the kingdom to God, even the Father, . . . that God may be all in all" (1 Cor. xv. 24 sqq.). The belief in the Church is the ecclesiastical substitute for Christ's doctrine.

last thing that occurs to the minds of many Christians; and if they can only pronounce some formula descriptive of his nature and person, they think it superfluous to dwell with loving reverence on the principles which he taught. But when from the strife of tongues we turn to the quiet study of the Gospels, we cannot but be struck with the constant recurrence of the phrase, "the Kingdom of God" or "the Kingdom of Heaven," and with the supreme place which the idea conveyed by it occupied in the mind of Jesus. It forms the subject of a number of parables. It is invariably assumed that the attainment of the kingdom of God is the highest end of human activity. It is said to have formed the substance of his preaching, not only at the beginning, when he took up the message of the Baptist, "Repent, for the kingdom of heaven is at hand," but also in the later period of his ministry.[1] It is therefore incumbent upon us to inquire what he meant by this phrase; for while we have admitted that there is a legitimate growth in Christian theology, we have also contended that this must be checked and

---

[1] See Matt. iv. 17, Mark i. 15; Matt. iv. 23, ix. 35; Luke viii. 1. The disciples were to preach in the same strain, Matt. x. 7; Luke x. 9, 11.

DIFFICULTY OF THE SUBJECT. 125

tested by reverting to its source ; and though Christ, in his popular teaching, may have used some ideas and images which no longer appeal to us, we cannot afford to overlook a conception which evidently coloured his entire view of life and its duties.

The inquiry on which we are thus entering is not without its difficulties, for the Gospels do not give an absolutely consistent picture ; and it will be necessary for us to disengage, if we can, the original and dominant idea from various imaginative accessories, which may be due partly to Christ's own poetic adoption of popular figures in setting forth his own deeper thought, partly perhaps to his sharing in some anticipations which were not contrary to the spirit of his life, though not destined to be fulfilled by history, and partly to misunderstanding on the part of his hearers, occasioned by their full participation in the national hopes, and the eagerness with which they endeavoured to recollect any words of his that could justify their confident belief in his second coming as a glorious Judge and King. It is only a reasonable rule of interpretation, in seeking to understand any original thinker, to separate the independent and governing thought from what may be owing to the accidents of time and place. Such a thought is (to use Christ s comparison) like a seed dropped into the ground, which grows by the silent operation of nature, appropriating what is suitable, rejecting what is hurtful to itself; but this process requires time, and centuries may pass away before it is complete. No man, even though his thought is going to revolutionize the world, can disengage himself wholly from the associations of the age in which he lives; indeed, it is one of the conditions of his success that he should start from these associations, and to a large extent adopt their language. But the men of a later age who would enter into his soul must understand him in the spirit, and not in the letter, and extract the fine aroma of his thought from the transient errors which once served as its vehicle, but which, if retained beyond their time, become superstitions, mischievous survivals from a lower state of intelligence or knowledge. Under the guidance of this rule we must assign quite a subordinate place to those long eschatological passages, which read like a Christian version of some Jewish apocalypse, and gather Christ's essential thought from sayings which bear a clearer mark of originality, and are opposed to the passion and prejudice of the hour.

It might be contended at the outset that if Jesus adopted a current phrase, he must have used it in the current sense, for otherwise his language would have been quite misleading. This, however, is true only within certain limits. Words which are expressive of great spiritual ideas or spiritual facts have, so to speak, a fluid meaning, settling down into the moulds of individual minds according to their several capacities. There must of course be some underlying sense which is held in common, and the employment of the same term by a number of people shows that they refer to the same thing, however various may be their conceptions of it. Thus, when we speak of God, there is an undefined meaning which makes our language intelligible, though one may rise to the highest spirituality of thought, another be sunk in the grossest anthropomorphism. The phrase "the Kingdom of God" is no less flexible. It denotes some sort of Divine rule among men, but of what sort the expression itself does not determine. Every man will form his own picture, according to his power of spiritual imagination; and one to whom the reign of God was the highest reality in human life might justly speak of it, although it presented to his inward eye a sublimer form and richer colours than were granted to ordinary apprehension. He would thus appeal to what was ideally best in each man's consciousness, seeking to clear it from the crust of prejudice, and to reveal it in its divine and imperishable beauty.

These remarks receive confirmation from what little we know of the state of opinion in the time of Jesus. There is no evidence that the Kingdom of God was so clearly defined, and so intimately associated with the Messianic expectation, that it was impossible to attach to it a higher and a lower significance. It denoted simply the sovereignty of God. This sovereignty was perpetually exercised even upon earth. God was himself the King of the Jewish race, and his kingdom extended for ever over the Gentiles in judgment.[1] Yet this kingdom was capable of a more glorious revelation, and the time was anticipated when it would be visibly established, and the whole creation would be brought under its rule.[2] An expectation of this sort was naturally associated with the belief in the advent of a Messiah; but the two expressions, the Kingdom of God and the Kingdom of Messiah, are not

[1] *Psalms of Sol.* xvii. 1, 4, 51.
[2] *Sib. Or.* iii. 47 sq.; *Assump. of Moses*, x. 26.

identical. The former is the larger term. It was the chief function of the Messiah to reveal and establish the Divine sovereignty among men; but that sovereignty was in itself independent of and prior to the Messianic reign. Hence the phrase might be used in quite a spiritual sense, as when the writer of the Wisdom of Solomon says that Wisdom showed to Jacob "the kingdom of God, and gave him a knowledge of holy things."[1] Here the expressions are parallel, so that seeing the kingdom of God is equivalent to receiving a knowledge of holy things; it is, in short, to apprehend the reality and meaning of the Divine rule in oneself and in mankind.

The equivalent phrase, the Kingdom of Heaven, which is preferred by Matthew, is of frequent occurrence in the Rabbinical writers, by whom it is used in a spiritual sense to denote " the inward love and fear of God."[2] Men were said to take upon themselves " the yoke of the kingdom of heaven and the yoke of the Law," or to " shake off from themselves the kingdom of heaven." Such expressions point to a present spiritual condition, and not to a future external

[1] x. 10.
[2] Lightfoot, *Heb. et Talm. Exerc.*, Matt. iii. 2.

institution. The Messiah was no doubt expected to establish this reign of God within the heart, and its universal prevalence would result in the constitution of an ideal society; but these ideas are not included in the primary sense of the phrase, and there is no evidence that when the kingdom of heaven was announced the people could think only of the visible reign of the Messiah, with all the accompaniments of earthly glory which an unspiritual fancy could suggest.[1]

It appears, then, that Jesus would not have been guilty of paltering with the established meaning of a familiar term if by the kingdom of heaven he meant in the first instance the inward love and fear of God,

---

[1] See the author's *The Jewish Messiah*, pp. 319 sqq. The use of the term is investigated by Prof. Schürer in an article, "Der Begriff des Himmelreiches aus jüdischen Quellen erläutert," in the *Jahrbücher f. prot. Theol.*, Vol. II. 1876, pp. 166 sqq. The article is especially useful in showing that "heaven" is only used by a reverent metonymy for "God." He treats it as accidental that the phrase is used only in its abstract sense in the Rabbinical literature. Still he declares it to be certain that the formula in the New Testament must be understood in the abstract sense of "Herrshaft;" but then, by an apparent inconsistency, treats it through the rest of his article in the concrete sense of "Reich." The former may involve the latter, but it is important to keep the primary idea in mind.

the hidden power of religion in the heart. He may have meant, and have been understood to mean, an invisible and spiritual rule, the ideal condition of the individual or of society in which God is reverenced and obeyed as the supreme Lord of life; and then in regard to the laws and constitution of this kingdom he may have announced views of his own which differed widely from those commonly entertained. He may, therefore, have referred to that which alone is eternal and true among men, and not, as is so often supposed, either to the evanescent dreams of a suffering and intolerant people, or to the visible organization of the Christian Church. Whether this is so we have now to inquire.

The classical saying of Christ's upon this subject is contained in his answer to the Pharisees, who asked him when the kingdom of God should come. He replied: "The kingdom of God cometh not with observation: neither shall they say, Lo here! or there! For lo, the kingdom of God is within you," or, as perhaps we ought to translate the words, "in the midst of you."[1] It is clear that the Pharisees expected some outward and visible advent of the

[1] Luke xvii. 20 sq.

Divine sovereignty, and they most probably connected that advent with the appearance of the Messiah, the chosen agent by whom the ideal rule was to be established. This kingdom was to be preceded by certain signs, a climax of misery and wickedness which would call for a Divine intervention; and the Pharisees by their question may have wished to ascertain how far Jesus agreed with the opinion of the schools respecting these "birth-pains" of the coming age. It was in answer to a very similar question on the part of his own disciples that he is said to have spoken that long apocalyptic discourse which is in such striking agreement with the popular view.[1] We have here two representations which are not easily reconciled; but so far as they are inconsistent, we can have no hesitation in preferring the profound and original reply to the Pharisees, and especially when we observe that there are some interesting traces of the same view even in the longer answer to the disciples. That answer begins with a warning, as though Jesus felt that the disciples were on a false track: "Take heed that no man lead you astray; for many shall come in my name, saying, I am Christ, and shall lead many

[1] Matt. xxiv.; Mark xiii.; Luke xxi. 5 sqq.

astray." Farther on, the warning is repeated: "Then if any man shall say unto you, Lo, here is the Christ, or, Here; believe it not. . . . If, therefore, they shall say unto you, Behold, he is in the wilderness; go not forth: Behold, he is in the inner chambers; believe it not." These words, taken by themselves, seem to point to a more silent and spiritual coming of the kingdom than the disciples anticipated; and sentences which bear a different character may be due to a natural misunderstanding of highly figurative expressions, such as Jesus frequently used. Be this as it may, the answer to the Pharisees is unmistakable. It declares that the kingdom of God is not to come like some earthly pageant, to be gazed at with the bodily eye; it is not to have its seat in any particular place; it is not some future institution of worldly grandeur, but is here now in the midst of you, discernible by every spiritual eye, commanding the homage of every consecrated heart. I suppose there is nothing which more excites the contempt of the mean religious mind than to be told that all this common world is interfused with Deity, and that common men and women, the hard-handed children of toil, are sons and daughters of God. We cynically ask for a sign from heaven, and shake our conceited heads with scornful satisfaction when it cannot be given; and lo, the kingdom of God is in some humble cottage, and angels are ascending and descending upon some poor son of man, and God's anointed stands before us unknown in one whose father and mother we know to be very common people. We need not go on a pilgrimage to Jerusalem or Mecca or Rome; we have only to open the eyes of the soul, and we shall see the kingdom of heaven all around us, as when some sweet landscape appears through the dissolving mist; we shall dwell already in the celestial city, and earth's sordid ways will be paved with sapphire and gold. Thus Jesus confronted the Pharisees with a present kingdom of God; but they could not see it, for their eyes were blinded.

We may briefly touch upon several other passages which point to a present kingdom of God. When the Pharisees charged Jesus with casting out demons by Beelzebub, he said in the course of his reply, "If I by the spirit of God[1] cast out the demons, then is the kingdom of God come upon you."[2] Of course, there

---

[1] In Luke, "the finger of God."

[2] Matt. xii. 28; Luke xi. 20. This saying is not given in the parallel passage in Mark iii. 22 sqq.

was not yet any "divine society," any Christian Church, any renovated earth. All things were going on as they had done since the foundation of the world, except that frenzied minds were growing calm under the subduing word of a soul filled with God. Jesus used no incantations or magical rites, such as were common at the time, but stilled the wild and passionate heart or the overwrought nerves by the simple authority of the Divine love within him; and that was sufficient proof that the reign of God was present. But religious prejudice could see only the power of Satan in the work of the Holy Spirit. Was it not a perception of this ever-present kingdom, and of the blindness of heart which separated from it, that suggested the commandment, "Seek ye first the kingdom of God and his righteousness"?[1] We cannot seek a distant institution, which is to come at some unknown period with portents which will shake the earth and heaven; but we can seek the inward love of God, the dominion of truth and purity, in the midst of which we walk, as in a paradise, though eyes dimmed with selfishness cannot see it, and hands paralyzed with sin cannot feel it. Accordingly, the kingdom of heaven

[1] Matt. vi. 33; Luke xii. 31, simply "his kingdom."

belongs now to the poor in spirit, and to those who have been persecuted for righteousness' sake,[1] because their understanding is no longer darkened, and their conversation is in heaven.[2]

Another very significant saying is given in answer to the question, "Who, then, is greatest in the kingdom of heaven?" The answer is, "Except ye turn, and become as little children, ye shall in no wise enter into the kingdom of heaven." And then, if we may venture to combine the narratives, he added: "If any man would be first, he shall be last of all, and minister of all;" and he took a little child in his arms, and

---

[1] Matt. v. 3, 10.

[2] It may be that the form of the Beatitudes in Luke is the more original. If so, we can hardly suppose Christ's meaning to be that the mere fact of poverty brought a man within the kingdom of God; for he must have known perfectly well that there were bad poor men as well as bad rich men. But the poor who were shut out from earthly rule and power had free access to the heavenly kingdom, and their robe of virtue was more splendid than the imperial purple. Their poverty, moreover, which kept them low in worldly position, was a help rather than a hindrance in the spiritual realm. If the altered words in Matthew are a gloss upon the original Beatitudes, still they are a very early and very genuine utterance of the Christian spirit; and some of the sayings which have no parallel in Luke must, I cannot but think, have come direct from Christ himself.

said: "Whosoever, therefore, shall humble himself as this little child, the same is the greatest in the kingdom of heaven."[1] Here, again, the kingdom of heaven is something present; and it is evident that we are dealing with spiritual relations, and not with times and places. Very unchildlike people may enter a society, and one seems to have heard of some of this kind occupying high places within the Christian Church. But the desire for earthly greatness, the taint of earthly ambition, shuts us out of the kingdom of consecrated affections and crucified self-will. The mere question of the disciples, with its suggestion of rivalry and vainglory, proved that they had not yet entered; but they had not to go to another place, or wait on the slow march of events, but to be themselves changed, and return to the simplicity of childhood. Not to wear the trappings of earthly grandeur, and be waited on by obsequious crowds, but in humblest guise to do the greatest service, betokens the heavenly temper; and if we have not that temper, and cannot discern its dignity and beauty, it is only by being born from above that we can see it or enter into it.

The doctrine of a present kingdom, which men

[1] Matt. xviii. 1 sqq.; Mark ix. 33 sqq.; Luke ix. 46 sqq.

enter or leave in accordance with their spiritual disposition, was taught on another occasion, when some people brought their children to Jesus that he might put his hands on them and pray. The disciples, moved apparently by false notions of the greatness of their Master, would have kept them away; whereupon, according to Mark, Jesus was moved with indignation, and, calling the children to him, said: "Of such is (not will be) the kingdom of God. Verily I say unto you, whosoever shall not receive the kingdom of God as a little child, he shall in no wise enter therein."[1] Such words are true of the invisible empire of truth and righteousness, but they have never yet been true of any earthly institution.

The same lesson is taught by another saying which excited amazement at the time, and has ceased to astonish us only because we are so accustomed to it, and have learnt to attach so little weight to the words of the speaker: "How hardly shall they that have riches enter into the kingdom of God! ... It is easier for a camel to go through a needle's eye than for a rich man to enter into the kingdom of God."[2]

[1] Mark x. 13 sqq.; Matt. xix. 13 sqq.; Luke xviii. 15 sqq.
[2] Mark x. 23 sqq.; Matt. xix. 23 sq.; Luke xviii. 24 sq.

As a rule, nothing is easier than for a rich man to enter the Christian Church; and even when the Epistle of James was written, it had become necessary to complain of the undue deference which was paid to wealth. There have indeed been notable instances in which the door of the Church has been closed in the face of riches and power which came in the company of sin; but generally the golden key can unlock the most forbidding gates. But no bribes will avail with the guardians of the spiritual kingdom. Riches do not help us to enter there, but rather disqualify us by drawing away our hearts, and rendering us averse to the necessary sacrifices. We cannot serve God and mammon, though we have not yet given up trying to do so. To enter the Divine service is to enter the kingdom of God; and that kingdom is not afar off, so that neither rich nor poor can enter it, but its boundary-line is ever at our feet, as it was at the feet of the young ruler when the momentous choice was offered to him, and it needs only a firm and consecrated resolve to cross the border.

We can now understand how the Scribes or lawyers could shut the kingdom of heaven against men, and neither enter themselves nor suffer them that were entering in to enter.[1] Such words apply only to a kingdom which is already here, and includes some and excludes others within the same physical space, thus proving that we are engaged with spiritual ideas, and not with anything subject to the limitations of place and time. In confirmation of this, it deserves remark that, instead of, "Ye shut the kingdom of heaven," Luke has, "Ye took away the key of knowledge." Whichever may have been the original, we may fairly use one expression to interpret the other. What, then, was the error of these lawyers? The key of Divine knowledge is, as we shall see, purity of heart; and by substituting for the living action of the Spirit of God a superstitious regard for the letter of Scripture and mechanical rules of interpretation, they kept men bound in the heavy fetters of legalism, and did not allow the soul to rise on free wings into present communion with God. And when any caught glimpses of this higher realm, and began to move towards it, they were borne down by the weight of authority, and terrified by charges of blasphemy and infidelity; but the real infidelity was in the Scribes and their empty formalism.

[1] Matt. xxiii. 13; Luke xi. 52.

At an earlier period of Christ's ministry we meet with a saying which is far more hopeful in its tone. Towards the close of his career the forces of the opposition seemed to be triumphant, and the determined resistance of the Scribes and Pharisees was turning back even willing listeners from the new teaching. But in the happier days in Galilee, when crowds hung upon his lips, it seemed to Jesus that men were storming their way into the kingdom of heaven: it "suffereth violence, and men of violence take it by force,"[1] so ardent was their desire to hear and appropriate his words. The expression, which is the hyperbole of exalted hope, may be compared with the enraptured declaration, "I beheld Satan falling as lightning from heaven."[2] But what is meant by this pressing into the kingdom of heaven? It is generally assumed as a matter of course that the reference is to the Messianic kingdom. This, however, can hardly be the case; for even the disciples did not believe that Jesus was then and there establishing the kingdom of the Messiah, whatever expectations they may have had

[1] Matt. xi. 12; Luke xvi. 16. I follow here the chronology of Matthew.

[2] Luke x. 18.

that he would do so in the future; and in regard to the popular belief they could only say that some thought he was "John the Baptist; some, Elijah; and others, Jeremiah or one of the Prophets."[1] We are therefore driven by critical reasons to seek for another interpretation, and it is suggested by the remarks already made. Men were awakened to a more vivid consciousness of the reality and presence of God, and their old conventional religion was yielding to that baptism of the Holy Spirit which John anticipated, but was not able to administer. The veil between earth and heaven was rent, and it seemed for a time as though that love which is more than burnt-offerings and sacrifices would establish its throne among men.

This interpretation, however, may appear to be inconsistent with a curious saying by which the words on which we have been commenting are preceded: "Among them that are born of women, there hath not arisen a greater than John the Baptist: yet he that is less in the kingdom of heaven is greater than he."[2] Was not John himself in the kingdom of heaven, if we

---

[1] Matt. xvi. 14; Mark viii. 28; Luke ix. 19.
[2] Matt. xi. 11; Luke vii. 28.

give to this phrase a purely spiritual meaning? He was, and he was not. Under the Law and the Prophets men could receive the kingdom of heaven, and in this sense John undoubtedly belonged to it; yet he himself anticipated something higher that was still to come, and the higher must always be the kingdom of heaven, to which the lower must yield up its ancient prerogative. The Law and the Prophets cease to be the supreme and ideal rule as soon as Grace and Truth have come. Now Jesus, we cannot doubt, was fully conscious that he was proclaiming a new spiritual life, and was not walking in the beaten ways. He had a profound respect for John; else he would not have gone to his baptism, and spoken of him as he did. But still with calm confidence he departed entirely from his conception of a religious life, and succeeded in combining with an enlarged humanity a deeper sense of the Divine presence and communion: having come after him, he had got before him, for his nature was the grander of the two. In this higher sense, then, the kingdom of heaven was unknown to John, and men of far inferior gifts, who truly apprehended it, were greater than he.

This view is confirmed by another saying: "The

kingdom of God shall be taken away from you, and shall be given to a nation bringing forth the fruits thereof."[1] This implies that the Jews were already in possession of the kingdom of God, but were about to lose it through their unworthiness. We gather this meaning not only from the form of words, but from the context. They follow the parable of the vineyard, from which they are an inference. In this parable the vineyard represents the kingdom of God. The Jews had been its custodians, but had shamefully abused their trust; and therefore the vineyard was to be taken from them, and let out to other husbandmen, who would render the fruits in their seasons. In more modern language, the Jews failed to rise to their opportunities, and consequently would lose their place as leaders of the world's religious progress. And so it proved. As in so many other cases, the very ardour of religious zeal created a blind conservatism, which could not discern the signs of the times, and the Jews became mere obstructives in the movement which they ought to have led.

We may conclude this portion of our subject by referring to an incident which, as recorded by Mark,[2]

[1] Matt. xxi. 43. [2] xii. 28 sqq.

is very suggestive. After the discomfiture of the Sadducees, a Scribe asked Jesus, "What commandment is the first of all? Jesus answered, The first is, Hear, O Israel; the Lord our God, the Lord is one;" and he then added the two commandments, to love God and our neighbour. The Scribe rejoined: "Of a truth, Master, thou hast well said that he is one; and there is none other but he: and to love him with all the heart, and with all the understanding, and with all the strength, and to love his neighbour as himself, is much more than all whole burnt-offerings and sacrifices. And when Jesus saw that he answered discreetly, he said unto him, Thou art not far from the kingdom of God." It is clear that the Scribe's nearness to it was a spiritual nearness, and that men, therefore, are nearer or farther away, within it or without, according to their state of mind. Now it is interesting to observe that one of the passages which Jesus quotes from the Old Testament was particularly associated with the kingdom of heaven. A Rabbinical passage which illustrates this is cited by Wetstein:[1] "When any one prays while walking, it is necessary for him to take up the kingdom of heaven standing.

[1] *Nov. Test.*, Matt. iii. 2.

What is that kingdom of heaven? The Lord our God is one God." This was the great confession of faith among the Jews, and it would appear that its repetition was what was meant by taking on oneself the kingdom of heaven. Jesus accepts the confession, but could not feel that by itself it was adequate. He combines with it the commandment which, in its original connection, it was used to enforce. The unity of God involves the obligation of supreme love towards him; and this, again, includes love to his children. The mere repetition of "Hear, O Israel," might beget bigotry and pride instead of faith and love; but one who admitted, even though with conviction still imperfect, all that was spiritually involved in it, was really not far from the kingdom of heaven, and it might at least be hoped that he would join the forward movement, and commit himself to the present leading of the Spirit.

The foregoing remarks sufficiently illustrate the spirituality of Christ's conception of the kingdom of God; and we must now turn to some other aspects of the subject. Although the phrase under consideration does not in the first instance denote a society or a Church, nevertheless a kingdom implies a community over whom the king exercises his rule, and the reign of God implies the existence of men whose minds are governed by the Divine will. These are "the sons of the kingdom,"[1] or, in more figurative language, the labourers engaged to work in the vineyard;[2] the servants who make a faithful use of the talents entrusted to them;[3] the guests who are entertained at the marriage-feast.[4] It does not, however, follow that even in this sense of a community the kingdom of God is a kingdom of this world, occupying certain countries, controlled by a definite organization, and having its head-quarters in a certain city.[5] From what we have learnt of its spiritual nature we should expect it to be quite indeterminate, and recognizable, not by the professions, but only by the character, of its citizens. This has certainly not been the ordinary Christian view. Christians have aimed at making the Church

[1] Matt. xiii. 38.   [2] Matt. xx. 1 sqq.

[3] Matt. xxv. 14 sqq.; cf. ·Luke xix. 12 sqq.

[4] Matt. xxii. 2 sqq.; Luke xiv. 16 sqq.; Matt. xxv. 1 sqq.

[5] In saying this, I do not mean (as is evident from what follows) that the kingdom of God is to be found only in heaven. A kingdom may be on earth, and yet "not of this world;" and Christ'r doctrine of a kingdom of God among men does not involve chiliastic dreams as a necessary part of it.

coincident with the kingdom of God; and as long as the kingdom of God is an ideal which attracts to itself the aspirations of the Church, no aim can be more noble. But the moment we identify the two, and insist that, though there may be unworthy members within the Church, there can be no kingdom of God outside it, we depress our ideal, and prepare the way for false and intolerant judgments. Nevertheless, a confusion of this kind is so easily made, and is in such apparent harmony with the deepest experiences of some of the greatest souls (for instance, of Augustine), that we are not obliged to regard it as inherent in Christian faith without bringing to it the test of the Master's teaching. Did he sanction a view which has caused so much bitterness and strife, and spilled so much precious blood upon the earth, or did he inculcate principles which are in direct opposition to it? This question has already been answered by implication; but we must now view it a little more distinctly.

We may begin our inquiry with the declaration made in the Sermon on the Mount: "Not every one that saith unto me, Lord, Lord, shall enter into the kingdom of heaven; but he that doeth the will of my

Father who is in heaven. Many will say to me in that day, Lord, Lord, did we not prophesy by thy name, and by thy name cast out demons, and by thy name do many mighty works? And then will I profess unto them, I never knew you; depart from me, ye that work iniquity."[1] These are solemn words which Christendom has never yet taken to heart. It seems that the loud professions and miraculous zeal, which are just the qualities to ensure a man's worldly advancement, constitute no title to the kingdom of heaven. It is only by doing the will of God that men can find themselves within it; by iniquity, although they may occupy the highest place in the Church, they are, *ipso facto*, excluded. We must not evade the force of this impressive declaration by saying that no one does the will of God perfectly, and therefore there must be some other principle of admission in the background. Such pleas are only an irreverent evasion of Christ's teaching. It is not his habit to go into minute distinctions, but he speaks in the large and generous sense which is intelligible to the common understanding. In this sense men do the will of God, who, in spite of imperfections and failings, deliberately

[1] Matt. vii. 21 sqq.; cf. Luke vi. 46, xiii. 25 sqq.

make it the law of their lives; and if we remember the spirituality of the kingdom of heaven, we may say that just in proportion as a man does the will of God, he is within that kingdom; just in proportion as he works iniquity, he is remote from it.

With this saying we may combine another, which teaches in effect that one may be outside the Church and yet inside the kingdom of heaven. When Jesus was told that his mother and his brethren were seeking him, he said: "Whosoever shall do the will of my Father which is in heaven, he is my brother, and sister, and mother."[1] Here, it is true, the kingdom of heaven is not mentioned; but we may fairly suppose that Christ would have included within it those whom he acknowledged as his own spiritual kindred. It is true also that the remark was made in immediate relation to his own disciples, who were before him; but in itself it is quite unlimited, and lays down a universal principle. We may compare this enlargement of its immediate application with Paul's use of a verse in Joel:[2] "Whosoever shall call upon the name of the Lord shall be saved." This was said in imme-

---

[1] Matt. xii. 50; Mark iii. 35; Luke viii. 21.
[2] ii. 32.

diate reference to Mount Zion and Jerusalem; but Paul infers from it that "there is no distinction between Jew and Greek: for the same Lord is Lord of all, and is rich unto all that call upon him."[1] This was interpreting the Prophet in the spirit, and not in the letter; but we do not, I think, go beyond the letter of Christ's teaching when we say that we are to look for his spiritual kindred not only within the Christian Church, but among barbarians and Scythians, Indians and Chinese, the only test being whether they do the will of God.[2] This is precisely the test that was laid down in the Sermon on the Mount; and from these two sayings combined we learn that the kingdom of heaven and the Christian Church are not coincident, but rather resemble two intersecting circles. Christians in seeking, like the Jews of old, to monopolize the gift of God, are simply blinding themselves to the larger movements of his Spirit, and, by not rising to the height of their Master's thought, they will fail to

[1] Rom. x. 12.

[2] This larger view was not forgotten in the second century. Justin Martyr says: οἱ μετὰ λόγου βιώσαντες Χριστιανοί εἰσι, κἂν ἄθεοι ἐνομίσθησαν, οἷον ἐν Ἕλλησι μὲν Σωκράτης καὶ Ἡράκλειτος καὶ οἱ ὅμοιοι αὐτοῖς. He includes men of his own time, οἱ δὲ μετὰ λόγου βιώσαντες καὶ βιοῦντες Χριστιανοὶ... ὑπάρχουσι. Apol. I. 46.

recognize the heavenly kingdom when it comes with some new and glorious manifestation upon the earth.

The same lesson is taught, though without reference to the kingdom, by a little incident recorded by Luke. On one occasion a woman in the crowd lifted up her voice, and said, "Blessed is the womb that bare thee, and the breasts which thou didst suck." But he said, "Yea rather, blessed are they that hear the word of God, and keep it."[1] By these words Jesus brushes aside mere adventitious distinctions, and shows how spontaneously his thoughts reverted to the one test, fidelity to the word (or uttered will) of God. We may refer also to the figurative account of the final judgment,[2] when all nations appear before the Son of Man. Here the sole test is the practice of simple and self-denying love. Those who have that distinction are the blessed of the Father, who are called to inherit the kingdom; those who have it not are sternly rejected, in spite of their plea that they never lost an opportunity of ministering to the Judge himself. Not a syllable is said of the requirements on which theologians delight to insist; nationality, religion, church, and creed, are disregarded, and the Son of Man applies

[1] xi. 27 sq. [2] Matt. xxv. 31 sqq.

a universal human test. For a swift moment Christendom apprehended the truth and saw that God was no respecter of persons, but in every nation he that feared him and worked righteousness was accepted of him;[1] but soon a cloud of pride and intolerance obscured the splendid vision, and to this day, in the reading of the New Testament, a veil lies upon the heart of Christians. And so men shall come from east and west, and north and south, and shall sit down with Christ and his Apostles in the kingdom of God; and there are last who shall be first, and first who shall be last.

From the principles thus laid down, we may infer that the subjects of the kingdom of God form an indeterminate community scattered over the world, whose members are to be discovered only by spiritual, and not by theological, tests. But the same view is presented by Christ even more directly. In the parable of the Tares[2] two things seem to be laid down very distinctly. First, the wheat and the tares, the righteous and those that do iniquity, are represented as scattered over the whole field. The field, we are expressly told, represents "the world;" and this is what we should expect, for the "vineyard" is chosen

[1] Acts x. 34 sq.   [2] Matt. xiii. 24 sqq., 37 sqq.

to represent the more special province of the elect. The parable, therefore, tells us that the "sons of the kingdom," the followers of the "Son of Man," who as such possess a true humanity, are to be found in every region of the world, and are not limited to some fenced enclosure; and similarly that there is no sacred spot where no sons of the Evil One can intrude. And secondly, these two classes of men cannot be distinguished by any artificial test. By their fruits they are known, and only the final outcome of the life can justify a sharp separation. Thus beneath the eye of God our conventional distinctions disappear. There are children of the Devil within the Church; there are children of God outside it. All round the world the kingdoms of good and evil are indissolubly blended, and the one eternal distinction is that between the "righteous" and "them that do iniquity."

The parable of the Good Samaritan[1] is equally explicit. The object of the parable is not to show that "our neighbour is the suffering man," but that he is the good man, even though he be a heretic and an alien. The Priest and the Levite represent the purest blood of Israel, the conventional neighbours of the

[1] Luke x. 30 sqq.

wounded man; but their cowardly selfishness deprives them of that honourable title. The Samaritan represents what was religiously and nationally odious; but then he was so good that the lawyer, who would not even name such a creature, has to confess that the man who showed mercy was the real neighbour. Jesus winds up the conversation by saying, "Go, and do thou likewise;" that is, if you wish to inherit eternal life (for this was the subject of discussion), imitate the goodness of a Samaritan. If we wish to appreciate the full force of this teaching, and to apply it to ourselves, let us substitute for Priest and Levite, Priest and Deacon, and for Samaritan, Buddhist or Mohammedan. Love is the only bond of union which is recognized in the courts of heaven; and wherever we find love, though it be in stranger or infidel, we find one on whom the approving eye of Christ would rest.

If we inquire into the conditions upon which men would be admitted to the kingdom of God, we find only casual answers; but they are in entire conformity with the foregoing view, and, if brief, are deeply suggestive. We have seen that the prime qualification was doing the will of God; and that wherever Christ perceived a devout endeavour to do this will, he recognized a spiritual brother. In this sense we may believe that many of those who were conscientiously opposed to him were included within the kingdom. But then the kingdom of God always means the highest that is known; and in the mind of Jesus it expressed an ideal larger and higher than anything he saw in the religious character and institutions around him. The time had come for an onward movement into a spiritual faith, which should be of a world-wide comprehensiveness. His adversaries, blinded by an inveterate prejudice, could not see the signs of the times. They wanted a miraculous portent from Heaven to guarantee the worth and authority of a teacher, and could not discern the seething thoughts and struggling aspirations which were breaking down the ancient superstitions, and were preparing the way for a religion which should bind together men of various races and of various culture in the communion of spiritual worship. But, for those who saw it, the new idea dimmed the ancient glories, and, as the heavenly radiance faded from the face of Moses, the kingdom of God passed from the Jewish Law and ritual, and became a new covenant of grace between the Divine Father and his human children. From this point of view, even John the Baptist, with his grand reforming zeal, with his anticipation of one who would sweep clean the threshing-floor of Israel, and with his hatred of wickedness in high and low, was nevertheless excluded from the kingdom, owing to a want of intellectual breadth and enlarged spiritual discernment; and if for a moment he beheld in Jesus the conquering Son of God, he afterwards found the wide and genial humanity of the new Teacher so unlike the mighty one of his imagination, with winnowing fan of judgment, and unquenchable fire for the chaff, that he never cast in his lot with him, but died in doubt whether his prophetic dreams were on the eve of fulfilment. Who, then, would listen to the call, and enter on the untrodden ways? Not the wealthy; for the self-denial was too severe, and treasure in heaven too intangible in comparison with present luxury and ease.[1] Not the priests and rabbis; for in an ancient and established order the grooves of thought are cut too deep to allow a ready transference from the beaten road, and the voice of nature is stifled by the strict rules of conventionality. For such as these the ascetic severity of an austere righteousness is a proof of

[1] Matt. xix. 16 sqq.; Mark x. 17 sqq.; Luke xviii. 18 sqq.

insanity; the wide and natural freedom of an innocent and tender humanity is fit only for a glutton and a wine-bibber. So they neither repented at the preaching of John, who simply emphasized the moral requirements of their own system, nor gave heed to the new teaching, which would have altered fundamentally their conception of life and duty. Who, then, would listen? The publicans and the harlots, whom sin indeed had led astray, but whom self-righteousness had not made deaf to the word of God, when it came to them in accents of sympathy and love.[1] To such as these the kingdom of heaven presented itself unexpectedly, like a treasure which a man accidentally finds in a field; and therefore it so filled them with joy that they were willing to part with everything else to secure it.[2] They had not sought it; but it, in the person of Jesus, had come to seek and save them, convincing them that they too might have forgiveness and hope. In their case the condition of entrance was a recipient mind, conscious of its need, and open to the natural claims of pity and goodness. Other men of different character sought for it, like a

[1] Matt. xxi. 31. Cf. Luke vii. 29 sqq.; Matt. xi. 16 sqq.
[2] Matt. xiii. 44.

merchant seeking for goodly pearls.[1] These were conscious of the higher demands of truth and righteousness, and, knowing the limitations of human thought, kept their minds open heavenward, and were willing to sacrifice all for the most precious thing that they could find. The self-devotion of their search placed them already within the kingdom,[2] for the pure self-abandonment of a heart seeking after God and his righteousness raises man into the eternal realm, and makes him apprehend the light when some dividing truth rises newly upon the world.

Christ, however, had no wish that disciples should join him rashly. If sometimes he gave a sudden invitation to follow him, at other times he discouraged those who volunteered their discipleship. All that was involved was first to be clearly understood. He was going on the way of self-denial, and the foxes and the birds were better off than he.[3] Those who wanted to follow him must be prepared to sever the natural ties of affection, and to take up a daily cross; and it was mere folly not to sit down, and count the

[1] Matt. xiii. 45 sq.
[2] "The kingdom of heaven is like a man *seeking*."
[3] Matt. viii. 20; Luke ix. 58.

cost, and take the measure of their moral strength, before casting in their lot with a homeless wanderer.[1] Those who put their hand to the plough, and looked back, were not fit for the kingdom of God;[2] and those who, from a timid regard to current practices, were ashamed of what was highest and most progressive in their own age, would be without honour in its victorious advent.[3]

Deliberation and resolve may be within our own power; but a change in our point of view which will open before us the vision of a new world, is not a matter of will or of intellectual honesty. This depends on spiritual forces which are not under our direct control; and if they work by some secret law of their own, it is a law which is incalculable by us. Spiritual susceptibility, delicacy of spiritual perception, are indispensable conditions of any profound alteration in our inward life; and why these exist in so much larger measure in some than in others we cannot tell. The early Christians, who were most clearly aware of the contrast between their present and their past, felt that a new principle of life had taken possession of them;

---

[1] Luke xiv. 25 sqq.   [2] Luke ix. 62.
[3] Matt. x. 32 sq.; Mark viii. 38; Luke ix. 26, xii. 8 sq.

and this was so different from all that they had known before, that they could describe it only as a new birth. Jesus himself is reported to have said: "Except ye turn, and become as little children, ye shall in no wise enter into the kingdom of heaven;"[1] and, in speech yet more searching, "Except a man be born from above, he cannot see the kingdom of God."[2] We can teach doctrines and prescribe commandments to every man of ordinary intelligence; but "the vision and the faculty divine" we cannot shut up in a creed or a law, and hand on like a parcel to the unprepared, nor, when the eye of the soul is asleep, can we paint the heavenly glories on its retina. These thoughts give rise to many questionings on which we cannot enter now. We must be content with noting the fact that entering the kingdom of God implies, in the Christian view, the perception of a spiritual scene, as full of marvel, and beauty, and hope, as this material world when it reveals itself to the freshly-opened eyes and dawning intelligence of a child.

The preceding remarks will enable us to understand how it is that a kingdom which is present in men's hearts is nevertheless spoken of as future. The pro-

[1] Matt. xviii. 3.   [2] John iii. 3.

clamation, "The kingdom of God is at hand," with which Jesus began his preaching,[1] and which he handed on to his disciples;[2] the prayer, "Thy kingdom come;" the warning to watch, for we know not the day nor the hour,[3]—point to something unfulfilled, some future crisis of our fate, which may come at any moment and find us unprepared. And so it is with all our ideals. They are here, but they are not yet realized. They are working powerfully among little groups, but centuries may elapse before they have permeated society and changed the face of the world. They may come as the lightning flash or as the trumpet's note, revealing to us new possibilities of nobleness, and summoning us to some new service of God, and find us unprepared, owing to the indolence of habit or the cowardice of self-indulgence. And then the high advantages and long laziness of culture shut us out, while fresh and buoyant life comes from east and west and north and south to take our forfeited place.[4]

[1] Mark i. 14 sq.; Matt. iv. 17.
[2] Matt. x. 7; Luke x. 9, 11.
[3] Matt. xxv. 13; Luke xii. 40.
[4] Matt. viii. 11 sq.; Luke xiii. 28 sq.

The advent of the ideal time is described in the earliest Christian teaching as a coming of the Son of Man, who is to appear on the clouds, in the glory of the Father, and attended by a retinue of angels, to judge the world and establish his kingdom.[1] This coming belongs to the eschatology of which I spoke in an earlier part of this Lecture, and is encrusted with the Messianic idea of the Jews. This is not the place to enter into a critical examination of the passages where the coming of the Son of Man is alluded to; but I may be permitted to observe that, to a large extent, they are expressed in the style of Oriental imagery, and readily lend themselves to poetical interpretation. We may look upon them as the pictorial drapery of aspiration and faith; and we must not, owing to the altered figures of our own speech, forget the central thought which no accessories have obliterated from the vision of Daniel. Whatever else the coming of the Son of Man may have suggested, it

[1] See Matt. x. 23, xiii. 41, xvi. 27 sq.; Matt. xix. 28, Luke xxii. 28; Matt. xxiv. 30, Mark xiii. 26; Matt. xxiv. 37 sqq., Luke xvii. 22 sqq.; Matt. xxv. 13, 31; Matt. xxvi. 64, Mark xiv. 62, Luke xxii. 69; Mark viii. 38, Luke ix. 26, xii. 8; Luke xii. 40, xviii. 8, xxi. 27 sqq.; Matt. xx. 20 sqq., Mark x. 35 sqq. Cf. Matt. xxvi. 29, Mark xiv. 25, Luke xxii. 18.

implied the advent of a true and divine humanity, and the final suppression of the inhuman and brutal forces under which the world has groaned so long. And what if the reign of righteousness and truth is coming with the soft steps and silent splendours of a summer's dawn, and not with the rustling of angel's wings and the blare of trumpets in the sky? Is it less real or sublime? The glory of the Father is all around us in earth and heaven, and we are encompassed by his angels, the men and women who serve the world in love, and bring messages of brotherly kindness to our selfishness and strife. If we will receive it, the Son of Man has come, and the throne of his glory is the human heart.

But turning from the language of Jewish Apocalypse, we find the deliberate thought of Jesus expressed in parables, in which he clearly recognizes the slow and silent methods of Divine Providence, and the analogy which exists in this respect between the material and the spiritual creations. The kingdom of God is as if a man should fling his seed upon the ground, and sleep and rise night and day, and the seed should spring up and grow, he knows not how. For the ground bears fruit spontaneously; first the blade, then the ear, then the full corn in the ear.[1] Or it is like a grain of mustard-seed, which grows from such small beginnings into a great shrub.[2] Or, again, it is like leaven, which a woman took and hid in three measures of meal, until it was all leavened.[3] Such language is unmistakable in its meaning, and is wholly inconsistent with the pageantry of a Messianic advent, with its procession of angels, and fearful portents in earth and sky. It accords with our experience of spiritual forces, which come not in the earthquake and the storm, but as the soft breath of evening, whispering messages of love within the soul. Steadfastly they work within the recesses of the heart, slowly ripening the character of individuals, and bringing society, step by step, from its state of animal hatred and warfare into the peace and mutual kindness which mark a brotherhood of the children of God. The things which God has prepared for those who love him are not for the carnal eye and ear; and if we would see his kingdom and his righteousness, we need not the heavens to be rent, but the eye of the spirit to be opened.

---

[1] Mark iv. 26 sqq.
[2] Matt. xiii. 31 sq.; Mark iv. 31 sq.; Luke xiii. 19.
[3] Matt. xiii. 33; Luke xiii. 21.

Thus the Christian prayer, "Thy kingdom come," when interpreted in accordance with the mind of Christ, is not a prayer for the outward pomp of a victorious Church, or for preternatural appearances in the startled heavens, but for the ever-growing realization, in ourselves and in the world, of the ideal kingdom of holiness, justice and love, those high attributes which, from their dwelling in the bosom of God, have been manifested upon earth, and constitute the eternal life of men.

LECTURE V.
THE CHRISTIAN DOCTRINE OF GOD.

LECTURE V.

THE CHRISTIAN DOCTRINE OF GOD.

FROM the kingdom of God we pass naturally to its Ruler, and enter on a consideration of the Christian doctrine of God. In doing so we must endeavour to forget for a time the elaborate metaphysical systems which theologians have reared as a splendid sepulchre for the teaching of Christ, and have recourse to the spiritual experience of the early Christians, and the recorded utterances of Christ himself. Nor are we to confine ourselves to what we may deem distinctive of Christianity: for Jesus was not one of those who preferred originality to truth, but brought forth out of his treasure things old as well as new, only imparting to ancient truth the vivifying power of his own personal thought and life. We must remember, moreover, that it is exceedingly difficult to determine how far any idea is really an advance upon everything that has gone before. It may have been anticipated by a few great thinkers, who nevertheless were unable to impress it upon the world; or the word in which it is expressed may have been used, but in a far inferior sense; or the elements of which it is composed may have been vaguely present in men's minds, and waiting only for a touch of inspiration to fuse them together, and send them forth as a clear and life-giving faith.

Bearing these qualifications in mind, we may say that the fundamental and characteristic idea of Christianity on this subject is that God is our Father. This word is of course figurative, being derived from one of our human relations; but it is on that account better adapted for religious purposes, being capable at once of the deepest significance and of the utmost latitude of application, simple enough for the heart of a child, and yet transcending the highest thought of a man. The Christian idea, however, while remaining sufficiently large and vague to adapt itself to a variety of culture, nevertheless has a distinctive complexion of its own which we must endeavour to disengage and understand.

First, then, the Fatherhood of God does not imply merely that he is the Author of our being. On this point a comparison of the New Testament with the writings of Philo is eminently instructive. Philo speaks of the relation between man and God, and of the indwelling of God in man, in language which might almost seem to anticipate Christianity;[1] but this poetical and spiritual philosophy does not seem to create in him any sense of personal communion and love, as between a Father and his child; and when he uses, as he frequently does, the term "Father," he follows his Greek training, and extends the relationship to the entire cosmos. Thus God is the Father simply as the ultimate cause and supreme Ruler of the universe. Now this philosophical language is absent from the New Testament,[2] while, on the other hand, the term "Father" becomes the constant expression of the personal relationship between God and man. This difference in the habitual use of the same word must be indicative of a deep-seated difference of sentiment; and I believe the difference lies in the vividness

[1] See my *Philo Judæus*, II. pp. 262, 280 sqq.

[2] The only apparent exception is James i. 17, ἀπὸ τοῦ πατρὸς τῶν φώτων, which does not, I think, afford a real parallel.

of personal experience, and the realization of what is involved spiritually in the notion of Fatherhood. When Paul says, "Ye received the spirit of adoption, in which we cry, 'Abba, Father.' The Spirit itself bears witness with our spirit that we are children of God;"[1] "because ye are sons, God sent forth the spirit of his Son into our hearts, crying, Abba, Father;"[2] and when John says, "Behold what manner of love the Father has given us that we should be called children of God;"[3] it seems clear that the writers are referring to some new experience, which had imparted to their minds a holy exaltation, and awakened within them the consciousness of a hitherto unacknowledged relationship. The semi-pantheistic absorption of the soul in the essence of God had become the conscious intercommunion of Father and child; philosophy had turned into faith; and to become a perfect son of God was not only the intellectual ideal, but the operative aim and purpose of life.

The Old Testament agrees with the New in opposition to Philo, in reserving the term "Father" for the personal relation between God and man. Not only,

[1] Rom. viii. 15 sq. [2] Gal. iv. 6. [3] 1 John iii. 1.

however, is the word much less frequently employed, but it never occurs as the accepted name by which God is referred to or addressed. It expresses undoubtedly a close and endearing relation; but, though not without exceptions, it is used in reference to the nation or its representative rather than its individual members, and is found in rhetorical appeal, and not as the expression of a universal and governing sentiment.[1]

[1] The following are the passages where the term is used or implied:

Exodus iv. 22, 23. "Thus saith the Lord, Israel is my son, my first-born: and I have said unto thee, Let my son go, that he may serve me."

Deuteronomy xiv. 1, 2. "Ye are the children of the Lord your God: ye shall not cut yourselves . . . for thou art a holy people unto the Lord thy God, and the Lord hath chosen thee to be a peculiar people unto himself, above all peoples that are upon the face of the earth."

xxxii. 5, 6. "They have dealt corruptly with him, they are not his children, it is their blemish; they are a perverse and crooked generation. Do ye thus requite the Lord, O foolish people and unwise? Is not he thy Father that hath bought thee? He hath made thee, and established thee." 9. "Jacob is the lot of his inheritance." 18, 19. "Of the Rock that begat thee thou art unmindful, and hast forgotten God that gave thee birth. And the Lord saw it, and abhorred them, because of the provocation of his sons and his daughters."

2 Samuel vii. 14, 15. "I will be his [Solomon's] father, and he shall be my son: if he commit iniquity I will chasten him . . . but my mercy shall not depart from him." [Parallel in 1 Chron. xvii. 13, and xxii. 10.]

Here, as in so many other subjects, we have foreshadowings of the larger truth that was to be, and

> Psalms lxviii. 5. "A father of the fatherless, and a judge of the widows."
> lxxxix. 26 sqq. "He [David] shall cry unto me, Thou art my Father, my God, and the rock of my salvation. I also will make him my first-born, the highest of the kings of the earth.... My covenant shall stand fast with him."
> Isaiah i. 2. "I have nourished and brought up children, and they have rebelled against me."
> lxiii. 16. "For thou art our Father, though Abraham knoweth us not, and Israel doth not acknowledge us: thou, O Lord, art our Father; our Redeemer from everlasting is thy name."
> lxiv. 8. "But now, O Lord, thou art our Father; we are the clay, and thou our potter; and we all are the work of thy hand." (Cf. Jer. ii. 27, "Which say to a stock, Thou art my father; and to a stone, Thou hast brought me forth.")
> Jeremiah iii. 4. "Wilt thou not from this time cry unto me, My Father, thou art the guide of my youth?" 19. "I said, Ye shall call me My Father; and shall not turn away from following me."
> xxxi. 9. "I will cause them to walk by rivers of waters, in a straight way, wherein they shall not stumble: for I am a Father to Israel, and Ephraim is my first-born."
> xxxi. 20. "Is Ephraim my dear son? Is he a pleasant child?"
> Hosea i. 10. "In the place where it was said unto them, Ye are not my people, it shall be said unto them, Ye are the sons of the living God."
> xi. 1. "When Israel was a child, then I loved him, and called my son out of Egypt."
> Malachi i. 6. "A son honoureth his father, and a servant his master: if, then, I be a Father, where is mine honour? and if I be

it is impossible for us to decide how far a few gifted minds may have seized the deeper significance of those prophetic utterances which seem to anticipate the more spiritual thought of a later time; but it is clear that Paul, who was brought up in the Rabbinical

a Master, where is my fear? saith the LORD of hosts unto you, O priests, that despise my name."

ii. 10. "Have we not all one Father? Hath not one God created us? Why do we deal treacherously every man against his brother, profaning the covenant of our fathers?"

The closest resemblance to the Christian view is found in the Wisdom of Solomon, ii. 16—18, in the reproaches uttered by the wicked against the just: ἀλαζονεύεται πατέρα θεόν. . . . εἰ γάρ ἐστιν ὁ δίκαιος υἱὸς θεοῦ, ἀντιλήψεται αὐτοῦ.

The following table gives the number of times it is used in the writings of the New Testament:

Gospels: Matthew	43
Mark	4
Luke	16
John	122
	185
Acts	3
Pauline Epistles	43
Hebrews	2
James	3
1 Peter	3
2 Peter	1
1 John	13
2 John	4
Jude	1
Revelation	5
	263

schools, felt that the idea of sonship was something new, and that before his conversion "a veil" had hidden from him the profounder "spirit" of those ancient Scriptures whose "letter" he knew so well. Was it not that he saw in the person of Jesus the manifested ideal of sonship, and beheld, as by a flash of revelation, all the vast possibilities of spiritual light and communion which were involved in that ideal? The new meaning gave a new direction to his life, and awakened new hopes for mankind.

What, then, is the essential character of this Christian ideal? It is fundamentally a moral and spiritual relation between the soul and God, which is realized by an inward experience of renewal and communion. Any metaphysical implications which this religious experience may contain are evolved by subsequent reflection, and belong to the province of the theologian rather than the inspired teacher. One who is lost in the new consciousness of a Divine relationship, a child who has found its Father, is too much absorbed in the communion itself to ask for its explanation, or to seek for the new elements which it has introduced into the world of thought. Accordingly, the Christian Scriptures hardly enter upon these high philosophical themes, and are content to assume, as belonging to the very essence of the religious experience, that there is a spirit in man akin to the Divine; that he may become "partaker of the Divine nature,"[1] and share "the fellowship of the Holy Spirit;"[2] and that God may abide in him, and he in God.[3] It is this indwelling of the heavenly life, of "the life of God,"[4] that constitutes man a son of God. Paul applies this view to Jesus himself: "Sprung from the seed of David according to the flesh, appointed Son of God in power according to the spirit of holiness."[5] This shows, I think, that whatever may have been his precise view of the person of Christ, it was the spiritual relation, the indwelling power of divine life, that struck him as fundamental. It was this, accordingly, that determined his view of human capacity and destiny: "As many as are led by the Spirit of God, these are sons of God."[6] Jesus was "the first-born among many brothers;"[7] and the end and aim of the natural world was "the revelation of the sons of

[1] 2 Peter i. 4.   [2] 2 Cor. xiii. 13.
[3] 1 John iv. 15 sq.   [4] Eph. iv. 18.
[5] Rom. i. 3 sq.   [6] Rom. viii. 14; cf. Eph. v. 1, 2.
[7] Rom. viii. 29.

God," of men who walked according to the mind of the Spirit, and found therein "life and peace."[1] This idea is not confined to Paul, as though it were his private thought, but, though very differently expressed, is no less luminous in the First Epistle of John. With the writer of this Epistle the fundamental Christian fact is the manifestation of the "eternal life which was with the Father,"[2] and this was a life of light and love. The followers of Christ, then, were required to walk in light and love, and, owing to God's love resting upon them, were called, and were, children of God.[3] God had given them of his Spirit; and, as God in his very essence was love, he that loved was born of God, and knew God;[4] and he that was born of God became incapable of sin, owing to the seed of Divine life abiding in him.[5] The thought which is thus common to the two disciples is found in the teaching of Jesus himself: "Blessed are the peacemakers, for they shall be called sons of God;"[6] "I say unto you, love your enemies, and pray for those who persecute you, that ye may become sons of your Father who is in heaven, because he makes his sun to

---

[1] Rom. viii. 19, 6.   [2] i. 2.   [3] i. 7, iii. 1, v. 13, &c.
[4] iv. 7 sqq.   [5] iii. 9.   [6] Matt. v. 9.

rise on the evil and the good, and sends rain on the just and on the unjust."[1] Our love constitutes our sonship; not the earthly love, which only responds to the attraction of its object, but the divine love which flows from the deep fountains of life within, and blesses friend and foe.

It is, then, from this relation of spiritual sonship that the term "Father" derives its distinctive meaning in Christianity. God is thought of as one who enters into communion with the soul of man, as the Source and Giver of that spirit of holiness and love which alone is eternal life. He is sometimes called specially "the God and Father of our Lord Jesus Christ," because it was Jesus, the first-born in the new community of the sons of God, who made this idea of sonship a living reality among men; for in fullest measure he dwelt in God, and God in him, and he showed forth among men that life of love which is for ever in the bosom of God. It was on account of this richness in its spiritual contents that such importance was attached to the confession that Jesus was the Son of God. This was an acknowledgment that earth and

[1] Matt. v. 44 sq. The language in Luke vi. 35 is different, but essentially the same in meaning.

heaven had met, and that man might rise out of his earthly and animal nature, and become conscious of a divine power within him, strengthening and shaping him to highest ends. The heart which was dead to spiritual things denied it; but those whom the spirit of Christ had touched with its healing virtue, and who had become conscious of a new life with God, confessed it with that grateful and exalted joy which a newly kindled faith never fails to awaken. In those days the acknowledgment sprang from spiritual apprehension, and not from mere intellectual speculation, or the inheritance of a formal creed, which often makes confession as empty and heartless as denial.

Agreeable to the doctrine of the Divine Fatherhood is that of the way in which God may be known. This way was not intellectual, but religious. In the New Testament the existence of God is assumed as an admitted reality, and no attempt is made to establish it upon philosophical grounds. Paul, indeed, makes a momentary allusion to the evidence which the works of nature had always afforded of "his eternal power and Godhead;"[1] but it was by a more inward and spiritual method that he became known to the hearts

[1] Rom. i. 20.

of Christians. In the beautiful story of the baptism, which is related with the picturesqueness of Oriental imagery, it is while Jesus is praying that the heaven is opened, and the Holy Spirit descends upon him, and the heavenly voice greets him as the Beloved Son.[1] It was therefore in accordance with his own experience that he said, "Blessed are the pure in heart, for they shall see God,"[2] and with a profound sense of inward revelation, which might be shared by the simplest, and lay quite apart from the speculations of the learned, that he exclaimed, "I thank thee, O Father, Lord of heaven and earth, that thou hast hid these things from the wise and prudent, and revealed them unto babes."[3] A claim like this was naturally a subject for scorn among the heathen philosophers; for how absurd it was to suppose that ignorant peasants could know more of God than philosophers who had spent their lives in thought and study, and found little but baffling mystery at the end of their labours? Yet the reason for this assumption on the part of Christianity is very plain. The knowledge of God which it seeks is a knowledge of his character and

[1] Luke iii. 21 sq.   [2] Matt. v. 8.
[3] Matt. xi. 25; Luke x. 21.

will, and these can be known only through an inward experience. Righteousness, holiness, and love, can never be found through the most ardent intellectual pursuit; but when they come and take up their abode within, they instantly reveal themselves, and proclaim, in tones that cannot be mistaken, their divine beauty and power. As the inward qualities of man can be revealed only in our human consciousness, so none but the Spirit of God can know the things of God; and therefore it is only through his Spirit that they can be revealed to us.[1] But in order that this revelation may take place, the Spirit must dwell in our consciousness, and become incorporated as it were with our personality; and thus it is only as children of God, in the sense already explained, that we are able to know him.

But how, it may be asked, was it possible to distinguish this higher Spirit from that which was merely human and personal? In the first place, it was felt to be a gift, which had been "received" at a certain definite time.[2] It had not been slowly wrought out by moral effort or exhausting study; but it had come

[1] 1 Cor. ii. 10 sqq.
[2] See, for instance, Rom. viii. 15; 1 Cor. ii. 12.

athwart the old belief and practice, and presented itself as a challenge and incentive to a new life. Then, secondly, it was felt to bear its own authentication as divine. "Love is of God." It has no need to prove its heavenly birth, for it is full of life and light, while its opposite is darkness and death. The sense of an indwelling love, which had slain the natural enmities, enabled the disciple to exclaim, "I know:" "We know that we have passed out of death into life, because we love the brothers;"[1] "We know that he abides in us, from the Spirit which he gave us;"[2] "We know that we abide in him, and he in us, because he has given us of his Spirit."[3]

But while this internal experience was indispensable for the apprehension of God, and bore witness to an immediate relation between God and the soul, it could be called into activity by an external manifestation, and, generally speaking, was dependent on external appeal. One who lived in the spirit of sonship could awaken the dormant consciousness, by showing forth in word and deed the Divine love that dwelt within, and making it pass, through the contagion of sympathy, into minds fitted to receive it. From the earliest times

[1] 1 John iii. 14.   [2] Ibid. 24.   [3] Ibid. iv. 13.

the claim has been made that this illumination of the deep mysteries of our being came into the world in Christ; that therefore he was more than a teacher and example, and that he was a revealer, in seeing whom we looked beyond himself into the bosom of that Father by whose Spirit he lived. Thus Paul exclaims, in the ardour of his faith: "God has shined in our hearts, to give the light of the knowledge of the glory of God in the face of Christ."[1] Here the inward and the outward are combined in one act of revelation, the light within rising to meet the light without, the consciousness of the Divine Spirit in the heart newly kindled by and interpreting the glory of that Spirit in the person of Christ. This, I suppose, is the primary experience out of which all the weary controversies about the nature of Christ have sprung. The disciples saw and felt in Jesus the presence and power of a love and holiness which carried their thoughts beyond the known limits of humanity, and betokened the indwelling of Divine life. Thus they were brought near to God, and were made aware that the same Divine life was stirring in themselves, and that the ideal of their being was to lose the life of

[1] 2 Cor. iv. 6.

self in the life of God, and so become the expressive organs of his character and will. The theologians endeavoured to press this experience into a system of thought, and to interpret it through the forms of Greek philosophy; and while I am far from denying the legitimacy of such attempts, or the grandeur of some of their results, we ought never to confound the spiritual fact with the intellectual interpretation, for too often, in the strife of tongues, the experience, which alone is vital, is dishonoured and destroyed for the maintenance of dogmas which necessarily share the uncertainty of all human speculation. We need for a time to revert to the simple, heartfelt faith which walks in light, and is so absorbed in the contemplation of the beauty and love which it beholds that it forgets to question, and declines to raise a cloud of intellectual theory around the pure visions of the soul.

How far Jesus anticipated the feelings of his disciples, and announced himself as the revealer of the Father, involves a difficult question of criticism, and the answer must depend largely on the degree of authenticity which we attach to several of the sayings in the Fourth Gospel—a problem on which it is impossible for us to enter here. But one or two general observations bearing on the spiritual aspects of the subject may be permitted. From one point of view, a claim of this kind on the part of Jesus would be regarded as an evidence of extravagant presumption and self-conceit. This charge seems to me to depend for its validity on the conception of man as an individual complete in himself, cut off from the universal life, and drawing all his greatness and goodness from certain resources of his own. If a man take this view, and then proclaim his own splendid character and ability, he is undoubtedly a boaster, for his thoughts are centred on himself, and he is seeking his own glory. But supposing that Jesus took a different view, and felt that man's true life was found only in the inflowing of the universal and eternal Life,—supposing that the consciousness of the Divine Spirit in his heart had reached an unexampled clearness and power—that the words and tones which thrilled the multitudes surprised and awed his own soul—that the love which he felt for the sinful and the sad seemed to flood his inward being from a source other than himself,—could he refrain from telling his disciples, at once with glowing faith and with unaffected humility, that he could do nothing of himself; that the love in which they rested their weary hearts was the love of God; that the righteousness which they revered was the righteousness of God; in a word, that in proportion as they saw what was deepest and most commanding in him, they saw, not the transient frailty of a mortal, but the eternal life of God? If we cannot penetrate thus far into the consciousness of Jesus, I fear that the meaning and power of his life are beyond our ken.

But, however this may be, we cannot fail to observe that Christ treats all human goodness as divine in its character, for he argues from the imperfect goodness in man to the higher goodness in God. "Ask," he says, "and it shall be given you. . . . What man is there of you who, if his son shall ask him for a loaf, will give him a stone; or if he shall ask for a fish, will give him a serpent? If ye, then, being evil, know how to give good gifts unto your children, how much more shall your Father which is in heaven give good things to them that ask him?"[1] A similar lesson is taught under the similitude of the shepherd seeking for the lost sheep: "Even so it is not the will of your Father which is in heaven that one of these little ones should perish."[2] Other parables, notably that of the

[1] Matt. vii. 7 sqq.; Luke xi. 9 sqq.   [2] Matt. xviii. 12 sqq.

Prodigal Son, might be cited in evidence of the same line of thought. It is clear that Jesus had no suspicion that goodness in God was something totally different from goodness in man, but looked upon the sweet charities of life, and those natural gleams of kindness which irradiate the path even of the sinful, as imperfect reflections of the Divine benignity.

Again, Christ reasons from the action of God in nature. He feeds the birds, and clothes the lilies with a beauty that the grandeur of kings cannot rival; and therefore we ought to trust him in the care which he takes of his children.[1] Again, "He makes his sun to rise on the evil and the good, and sends rain on the just and the unjust."[2] What a horrible indifference to moral distinctions is exhibited by Providence! exclaims this discontented and luxurious age. What a wonderful love, thought Christ, that pours itself forth, asking for no return, but finding its blessedness in blessing. Thus the children of God must love their enemies, and give, asking for nothing again.

It is clear that these inferences from man and nature are not formal arguments, addressed to the reason, and

---

[1] Matt. vi. 25 sqq.; Luke xii. 22 sqq.
[2] Matt. v. 45; cf. Luke vi. 35.

they can find no response unless the Divine Spirit is already revealed within. The only reply which Christ offers to our scepticism is his appeal to our slumbering consciousness of a deeper life within, and of holier demands upon us, than we ordinarily acknowledge.

We must now pass to some details of the Christian representation of God. In doing so, we must first make the general remark that Christ's direct teaching about God occupies a surprisingly small part of his recorded utterances. There is, indeed, always the implication that human life and duty rest on a divine ground. Jesus assumes a few great doctrines, as he was entitled to do among those whom he addressed; but he introduces them in answer to questions, or by way of moral and spiritual appeal, and not as a teacher of theology. Nothing can be more unlike his method than that which prevailed among the dogmatists of a later time; nothing more remote from what he laid down as essential than that which controversialists bound as a yoke upon the intellect; nothing more contrary to his spirit than the enforcement of metaphysical confessions by penal statutes. With the subtilties which have plunged the Church into schism, persecution and bloodshed, he had nothing to do; and things which have been held up as fundamental dogmas of Christianity are conspicuously absent from his teaching. Bearing this in mind, we may notice the grand ideas which he assumes, or on which he insists.

He takes for granted the great Jewish doctrine of the Unity of God. When asked by one of the Scribes which was the first commandment of all, he answered: "Hear, O Israel; the Lord our God, the Lord is one; and thou shalt love the Lord thy God with all thy heart."[1] In this grand utterance of the ancient Law the Unity of God ceases to be a matter of abstract speculation, and becomes the basis for an undivided moral allegiance. It is this which secures it such a fundamental place in the teachings of primitive Christianity. No man can serve two masters;[2] and polytheism not only involved a want of due reverence towards the Creator, but broke the moral unity of man, and gave a sort of religious sanction to the foulest practices.[3] The Unity of God implied for the individual the "single eye," which gazed at the simplicity of truth and righteousness; for the Church,

[1] Mark xii. 28 sqq.   [2] Matt. vi. 24; Luke xvi. 13.
[3] Rom. i. 18 sqq.

THE DIVINE UNITY. 191

the possession of one spirit, pervading its multifarious operations, and binding its various members into "one body;"[1] for the nations, the acknowledgment of a human brotherhood, since the one God must be God of Jew and Gentile alike.[2]

We must further observe that this doctrine of the Divine Unity is nowhere qualified or guarded against the interpretation which a Jew, or indeed any plain man, would have put upon it. It is impossible within our limits to discuss the ecclesiastical dogma of the Trinity. We need not necessarily regard that doctrine as false, even if we fail to find it in the primitive records of Christianity, for certain implications of spiritual truth might require centuries to impart to them the clear outlines of an intellectual system. But if we attempt to judge the New Testament as we would the original documents of any other religion, we cannot but be struck with the fact that the very phraseology which is necessary to express the doctrine of the Trinity is absent, that such statements as that "there is one God and Father of all"[3] are made

[1] 1 Cor. xii. 4 sqq.; Eph. iv. 3 sqq.
[2] Acts xvii. 26; Rom. iii. 29 sq.
[3] Eph. iv. 6.

without any reserve or explanation, and that at most there are a few passages which might be explained as references to this doctrine if we knew upon other grounds that it existed when these writings were composed; and we are forced to the conclusion that, whether it be true or not, it formed no essential part of the primitive Gospel, and that in its whole form and complexion it stands in marked opposition to the kind of teaching which Jesus himself preferred. But there is hardly anything which official Christendom has valued less than the teaching of its Master.

As God is one, he is the "Lord of heaven and earth," in whose will men ought devoutly to acquiesce.[1] "Of him, and through him, and unto him, are all things," and he works out his great designs in human history according to the counsels of his own wisdom.[2] Here it is worth noticing that Paul, from whom the last quotation is made, although he is compelled by the exigencies of controversy, and by mental habit and training, to be far more theological than Jesus, nevertheless does not forget the latter's practical aim. After his vindication of the sole sovereignty of God,

[1] Matt. xi. 25 sq.; Luke x. 21; Matt. xxvi. 39, and parallels.
[2] Rom. xi. 33 sqq.

and the burst of praise with which he concludes his argument, he at once proceeds to an exhortation founded on the intimacy of communion between man and God, and the mercy of the Sovereign Ruler towards his erring children: "Present your bodies a living sacrifice," and follow "the perfect will of God."[1] The same ethical tendency is apparent when Christ alludes to God's omnipotence. "All things," he says, "are possible with God," and therefore he is able to effect a moral renewal which, to mere human strength, might seem impossible.[2]

The doctrines of the Divine omnipresence and omniscience are more impressive in their bearing upon human conduct. God is Father of each man, whom he sees in secret; and he knows the deed of charity, which hardly betrays itself even to the consciousness of the doer, the silent prayer which is offered in the lonely chamber, the contrition of heart which assumes before men a cheerful countenance. Therefore men ought to be perfectly simple in their actions, hiding them from human praise, and receiving no reward but that which the Father gives in the secret consciousness

---

[1] Rom. xii. 1 sqq.

[2] Mark x. 27; Matt. xix. 26; Luke xviii. 27; with the context.

of pleasing him.¹ This simple independence of human applause must also give courage when men are hostile. Not a sparrow falls to the ground without God, and the very hairs of our head are all numbered; so that instead of being afraid of men, with their limited power, we should rather fear him on whom we entirely depend, and who, though he cares even for the sparrow, cannot receive the faithless.² The same doctrine is taught by the disciples. Without any pantheistic confusion, they still assert in the strongest way the nearness of God to man, and the intimate blending of the Divine life with ours. "He is not far from any one of us; for in him we live, and move, and have our being."³ He is "above all, and through all, and in us all."⁴ The forces of nature, then, are God's perennial activity. The laws that guide the sparrow's fall keep suns and planets in their course. The light that glistens in the dewdrop trembles across immeasurable space, and makes one glory in the universe. The

---

[1] Matt. vi. 1 sqq. The objection that Christ here teaches men to work selfishly, for the sake of a reward in heaven, seems to me to rest on an extraordinary perversion of the general tenor of the passage.

[2] Matt. x. 28 sqq.; Luke xii. 4 sqq.

[3] Acts xvii. 27 sq.   [4] Eph. iv. 6.

powers which knit together this corporeal frame into a home for a conscious spirit bespeak the living energy of the ever-present God. We miss God because we seek him amid cold abstractions, and think the universe is undivine: Christ beheld him in bird and flower, in rain and sunshine, and in the beating heart of man.

As ever present and knowing all things, God is the hearer of prayer. This is universally assumed in the faith and practice of the early Christians. God sees in secret, when the chamber-door is shut, and needs no words to interpret the silent prayer of the heart.[1] He requires not the temple of Samaritan or Jew, but seeks those who will worship him in spirit and in truth.[2] He regards not the distinctions of race, but is "rich unto all who call upon him."[3] The subject of prayer will be further considered when we deal with Christian ethics, and have to view it upon its human side. On the Divine side, Christian doctrine and practice rest upon the statement that "God is Spirit," and therefore, in order to be acceptable to him, prayer, worship, sacrifice, must be spiritual.

The answer to prayer and the reward of well-doing

[1] Matt. vi. 6 sqq.   [2] John iv. 21 sqq.
[3] Rom. x. 12.

come from God's free bounty, and not from any claim which his creatures can establish upon him. He is "the Giver," who bestows the heavenly wisdom, which is pure, and peaceful, and just.[1] Eternal life is his gracious gift.[2] All the blessings of the Gospel originated in his love, and that love is freely poured out in men's hearts, filling them with hope and a triumphant gladness.[3] In the parable of the Labourers the employer bestows the full remuneration on those who had come last into the vineyard, and defends himself on the plea that it is lawful for him to do what he will with his own.[4] This plea has often been used by the selfish, who, disregarding the connection in which the words are used, are pleased to find so high a sanction for their cupidity. But in the parable the words are a plea for generosity, and a rebuke to those who think that their own superior merits should procure them a richer measure of Heaven's favour. Men may shut themselves up in dark caves of faithlessness and sin; but the moment they emerge, the sun pours upon them the light and warmth which others have never left,

---

[1] James i. 5, iii. 17. [2] Rom. vi. 23.
[3] John iii. 16; Rom. v. 5 sqq.; 1 John iv. 10, 19.
[4] Matt. xx. 1 sqq.

and too often have never learned to value. So the love of God sheds its beams with a perennial glory; and hearts that waken from the sleep of sin revive under its kindling welcome, while too often those who have enjoyed it longest know it least, and murmur at the freedom of its gifts.

This unfailing love implies forgiveness. Love has no resentment, and is not bound by an inexorable law, which can judge only the outward deeds, and knows nothing of the affections of the heart. With this message, Christianity went into the foul places of the world's sin; and wherever men embraced the new faith, they felt that they were forgiven, and, having left the old life behind, had entered into a new life of communion with God. The simple sense of need appeals to the Heavenly Father, and, when his children plead that they have nothing to pay, he frankly forgives them. It is thus that they are taught to love him; and wherever, in Christian history, men have "loved much," they have a profound consciousness of that Divine love which has sought and forgiven them.[1] Forgiveness, however, is not unconditional. Sin is a state of alienation from God, and therefore repentance

[1] Luke vii. 40 sqq.

is indispensable. So long as the prodigal is content with his riotous living, he can know nothing of the sweet and calm delights of home; and with broken and contrite heart he must turn his face homewards before he can receive the welcome of his Father's kiss. There is joy in heaven over one sinner that repents.[1] There is another condition, however, which Christ lays down very emphatically: men must forgive as they hope to be forgiven,[2] and the measure with which they mete to others will be applied to themselves.[3] The reason is very clear. Hatred and resentment cannot have communion with forgiveness and love. These belong to antagonistic realms, and the dark passions of men encompass them with a cloud which keeps out the light of God.

But though the earliest Christian writers dwell so much on the Divine love, and on the freedom with which Divine gifts are bestowed, they never forget that sense of responsibility which had been so deeply implanted in the conscience by the Jewish Law. The eternal law of righteousness was never abrogated, in

[1] Matt. xviii. 13; Luke xv.
[2] Matt. vi. 14 sq., xviii. 35.
[3] Matt. vii. 2; Mark iv. 24; Luke vi. 38.

the sense that men might disregard it, and go upon their own way. They might, through faith, lay hold of a spiritual and transforming power, and rise, through the fulness of the life of God within them, above the Law, freely discharging its obligations in the spontaneous expression of inward holiness. But they could not escape from the Law by sinking beneath it, or screen their wickedness from its condemnation under the pretext of spirituality. Such an attempt was a mockery of God, whose law that men should reap as they sowed must remain for ever inviolable.[1] The great Judge of all would act according to truth, and render to every man according to his works;[2] and those who practised the evil deeds which a carnal mind suggested, should not inherit the kingdom of God.[3] Thus the power of resisting the higher will is presupposed, and the disciples are continually exhorted to show forth in their conduct the new spirit of which they had become conscious. At times, indeed, the grace of God may have seemed to come with such overwhelming force as to suspend the power of choice, and lead men to what was good even against their will; but he in whom the sense of communion with God was

[1] Gal. vi. 7 sq. [2] Rom. ii. 2, 6. [3] Gal. v. 19 sqq.

calmest and most perennial, knew that there were "tides of the Spirit," and that with most men the times of revealing are succeeded by periods when God seems to withdraw, and leave the soul to work out for itself the new responsibilities of a momentary inspiration. Paul himself was not always in the third heaven. Faith was not yet the equivalent of sight; and it was possible to exchange the religious rapture, which turned all duty into a grateful sacrifice of love, for the dull routine of daily service, when God seemed to be far off, and to impose upon men a solitary task.[1] Thus God, while freely communicating of his own life, and raising man into the dignity of a son, does not destroy his responsibility, but leaves him in partial independence to work out his own career amid the dangers and temptations of the world. And this is what we should expect. The world is far more terrible when we have to confront it with wisdom and virtue which we must exercise through an effort of our own, and train through the hard discipline of failure and suffering; but this position of trust is infinitely grander than if

---

[1] See the parable of the Vineyard, Matt. xxi. 33 sqq.; Mark xii. 1 sqq.; Luke xx. 9 sqq.; and the parable of the Talents, Matt. xxv. 14 sqq.

we were swayed by an irresistible instinct, however Divine might be the power of which we were the passive instruments. The slave may never err in the task which is imposed, and may have abundance for his animal comfort; but he is not the son and heir. The son must have in himself something of the freedom of the Father's life, and go forth in loving and reverential duty to bear, if need be, the scourge and crown of thorns, and in unconstrained obedience to his Father's will to lay down his life for his brethren.

Such, then, are the leading features in the Christian doctrine of God. We must, in conclusion, notice two developments, one on the practical, the other on the intellectual side.

The relation of Father and Son, being purely spiritual, was universal. In its presence, national and ecclesiastical distinctions vanished. God loved the *world*, and had no respect of persons. Sin and righteousness alone sorted men into opposing classes; and Jew and Gentile, male and female, bond and free, became one in the possession of the same filial spirit. This principle is involved throughout the teaching and practice of Christ; but the necessity for asserting its practical application did not arise till after his departure from the world. It was not to be expected that every one would see with equal clearness what a revolution in thought and practice it implicitly contained; and when the question arose, what should be done with Gentile proselytes, it was Paul who seized most firmly the meaning of the new movement, and insisted on carrying it forward to its legitimate results. It was a fact of experience that in Christ God was reconciling the world to himself, and that the heart of the Gentile responded even more readily than the heart of the Jew to the appeal of his love. Through the inworking of the spirit of Christ the point of view was entirely changed; and those who, while accepting him as the Messiah, failed to perceive this, were left behind, and, lingering in the old paths of legal obligation, dropped into the position of a sect holding an imperfect Christianity. The importance of this practical development when the Gospel started on its career can hardly be exaggerated. Its victory turned Christianity into a religion universal in its principles; but when the practical necessity was met, the more spiritual teaching gradually sunk into abeyance, and the vast range of its implicit contents has not yet become familiar to the consciousness of Christendom.

I have already alluded to the doctrine of the Trinity, and showed how Christ avoided the discussion of metaphysical questions. We must, however, observe that there were certain elements in Christian experience which, when taken up and interpreted by Greek philosophy, necessarily resulted in this doctrine; and though we may believe that the form and the terminology of the doctrine were derived from a foreign source, we may nevertheless admit the reality of fundamental Christian facts which imparted to it all its religious vitality. The Love of God was the original source of the new religion, and occupied the central place in the Christian consciousness. But it was in Christ that this love was revealed; in him the word of God to man had spoken with unexampled clearness and power. He was felt to be the beloved Son, the elder brother, the leader and inspirer of the whole movement. In him, as filled with the life of God, many a weary and doubting soul found rest, and rose out of the darkness and sin of earth into the heavenly light and love. Words of comfort dropped upon the oppressed heart, and divine thoughts stole, as with the footsteps of angels, into the troubled mind; and at length that Reason which had come in partial flashes of truth to sage and prophet, seemed to have risen with its full-orbed splendour. Faith in the sonship of man rested upon the sonship of him who had manifested, and brought home to human consciousness, the eternal life which was, and is, for ever with God. But when this life passed into the hearts of believers, and bound them together in a holy community, it was recognized as the Spirit of God, spreading as a diffused breath among the brotherhood, and, like the vital air, kindling and sustaining the life of the soul. This common life which wrought within the several members of the Church was felt, not to be a mere attribute of man, but an indwelling of God, who distributed spiritual gifts, and shaped the organism of the society according to his own good pleasure. These deep experiences gave a three-fold direction to Christian veneration. Love, Reason, Holiness, were all alike divine, and yet to human thought were all distinct from one another. In the old philosophy they were conceived as essences in which men might participate, thereby becoming marked with the corresponding qualities. But God, so far from participating in them, was the fount of their being; for, in the language of Augustine, "He is what he has." What we are apt to describe as attributes belonged to the very substance of his being, and in that substance found their unity. We cannot follow the long controversy to which the metaphysical interpretation of religious experience gave rise. It marks a daring flight of human reason; and it may be that the various positions maintained from time to time by the majority in the Church were necessary correctives of one-sided tendencies or of rash speculations. But the interpretation which required centuries to reach its final form is not part of the primitive religion. It belongs to philosophy rather than to faith, and has stood in the way of the very experiences on which it was originally founded; for the majestic ideas of Greek philosophy which gave it shape have, to a large extent, died out of our modern thought, and to the great mass of Christians are simply unintelligible. Theology has its rightful place, and the uplifting power of sublime speculations cannot be denied. But the great Teacher himself chose another path; and the humble Christian may find life and strength in his faith in God as the loving Father of mankind; in Jesus Christ as the Beloved Son, the first-born among many brothers; and in the Holy Spirit of God, whereby the hearts of men are sanctified and drawn together in a unity which leaves untouched the free and beautiful play of diverse tendencies and gifts. God is Spirit; God is Light; God is Love—these are the fruitful truths which surpass all the ecclesiastical creeds, and their day is yet to come.

LECTURE VI.
ETHICS.—I.

4

LECTURE VI.

ETHICS.—I.

CHRISTIANITY is a religion which, in all its forms, is profoundly ethical. A very large proportion of the teaching of Christ is devoted to moral questions. He sets before men the highest standard of conduct, and makes the most imperative demands upon their faithfulness. Whatever doctrines may be assumed as the spiritual roots of morality, Jesus never passes judgment on a man on account of his speculative belief, but it is invariably conduct which calls forth his approval or his rebuke. It is necessary to insist upon this point, because in later times this order of judgment has frequently been reversed, and men have been condemned and tortured for their carefully formed and conscientious belief, while vice and crime have been leniently condoned. Though this false and cruel judgment has unhappily been one of the marked features of Christendom, nothing could be more contrary to the teaching and spirit of the Master; and we must regard it as one of those lower and alien elements which fastened themselves upon Christianity, and succeeded in utilizing some of its vital force for the nourishment of their own corrupt life. But in spite of such malignant influences, the holy exaltation of Christian character has never perished from the world; and one can always turn with refreshment from the disputes and violence which have disfigured the history of the Church, to the quiet retreats of piety and love, where the Spirit of Christ has carried the soul into communion with God, and ministered through the hands of disciples to human want and pain. It is now our task to analyze and describe this ethical life, as it appears in the earliest records of our religion.

The conception of the ideal end, or highest moral good, rests upon the doctrine of the Divine Fatherhood, which we considered in the last Lecture. Man, as a child of God, is to aspire to be in all respects worthy of his birthright. He is to share the spiritual nature of God, to be led by the Spirit of God, to dwell in God and have God dwelling in him, to be perfect as the

Heavenly Father is perfect. This, it will be observed, is in a certain sense a very vague standard, depending for its application upon each man's power of spiritual apprehension. From one point of view this constitutes a weakness. So high and impalpable a standard can make no appeal to men who understand nothing but definite precepts, and have no consciousness of a divine life working in the depth of their souls. But once let this consciousness be wakened, and though the ideal may be vague, it has the vagueness of an infinite and entrancing beauty, which woos the soul on from height to height of holiness, and still exhibits something more divine than past attainments. Even if its form were utterly undefined, still the sense of grandeur which it awakens would give an elevation to the aims and a disinterestedness to the conduct, which must in time colour the whole life, and draw forth all the hidden nobility of the man.

This idea of the supreme good determines the place of Christian ethics in systems of philosophy. Though, as we shall see, Christianity lays the greatest stress upon the exercise of benevolence, it does not estimate character by the tendency of actions to produce happiness either for the individual or for society. Not pleasure or happiness or utility, but spiritual perfection is its end and aim; and the quality of this perfection cannot be ascertained by any study of precepts or any calculation of resulting delights, but only by the inward experience of the diviner life taking captive the lower and personal life, and calling it from the pettiness of self-absorption to what is universal and eternal.

In accordance with this view of the highest good, Christ never stops with the outward manifestations, but passes on to the inward reality of moral life. The searching words of the Sermon on the Mount have been often dwelt on. The angry feeling, the impure desire, are open to condemnation; and it is not enough that we refrain from taking vengeance on our enemies, we must love them. So also the disciple says, "Every one that hateth his brother is a murderer, and ye know that no murderer has eternal life abiding in him;"[1] for hatred only waits its opportunity to inflict the most destructive ill, and is most remote from the Spirit of God. It is needless to quote passages to prove that love, the inward benevolence and devotion of the heart, is placed in a supreme position; for the

[1] 1 John iii. 15.

insistence upon it runs like a refrain through the New Testament, and must be familiar to every reader; but I may remind you of a few sayings which further emphasize the inwardness of real righteousness. Christ says men shall be known by their fruits; does not this, it may be asked, throw us back upon conduct as the one thing needful? Not so; for the conduct is regarded simply as a sign of the inward condition. It affords the same evidence of a man's interior character as the fruit yields of the soundness or decay of a tree; and we must argue back from the actions which we can see to the good or evil treasure in the heart, which can only reveal itself through tokens that owe all their moral worth to the nature of their source.[1] Yet it was possible to assume a fair exterior, and to go through a formal routine of religious observances, which were not the fruit of inward holiness, but only stuck on, as it were, to deceive the careless eyes of men, while the real character was to be seen through the irreverence towards parents, the cruelty to widows, the casuistic evasion of duty, and the ostentation which turned even religion into an act of self-display. The outside was conformed to the letter of the Law, as interpreted by

[1] Matt. vii. 16 sqq., xii. 33 sqq.; Luke vi. 43 sqq.

the highest authorities, but the inside was full of hypocrisy and lawlessness, and therefore exposed to the severest moral condemnation.[1] Even more impressive is the pregnant saying: "Not that which enters into the mouth vulgarizes the man; but that which proceeds out of the mouth, this vulgarizes the man." This assertion ran too directly counter to the prejudices of the disciples to be at once intelligible; and Jesus was obliged to explain that moral evil alone can make a man common, and that moral evil has its seat in the heart.[2] By this great utterance he swept away with indignant scorn the whole system of legalism, which placed ritual before morals, and through scrupulosity in regard to outward ceremonial overlooked the corroding ill within. Yet he did not despise a useless ceremony, if it too came from the heart. I may refer to the touching incident of the poor widow casting her two mites into the treasury. Probably no eye but Christ's looked with reverence upon that humble woman in the midst of the ostentatious crowd; but he declared that she had cast in more than they all, for he cared not for the size of the gift, but for the gene-

[1] Matt. xxiii.; Luke xi. 39 sqq.
[2] Matt. xv. 1 sqq.; Mark vii. 1 sqq

rosity and devotion with which it was offered.[1] We have reached, then, this position—that morality or goodness, primarily, is a condition of the inward life, in which the feelings, desires and impulses, are conformed to real righteousness, or, in other words, to the Spirit of God; and that only secondarily does it consist of the actions whereby that inward life is expressed.

Certain important deductions readily follow from this fundamental principle. The Pauline view of the abrogation of the Law was involved in it. The immediate purpose of the Apostle was to relieve the Gentiles from the burden of the Levitical Law; but in securing this end he was led to enunciate principles which go far beyond the limits of a temporary controversy As one trained in the Rabbinical schools, he naturally used arguments which make but little appeal to our modern thought, and with these we are not at present concerned. But the substance of his contention is this: that righteousness in the sight of God did not consist in formal obedience to an external code of morals, but in the presence of the eternal spirit of righteousness, the righteousness of God, within the heart. When the very fountain of law was operative

[1] Mark xii. 41 sqq.; Luke xxi. 1 sqq.

within, the external commandment, however divine, passed out of view; and the study of particular precepts was superseded by the energy of the divine life in the soul. "Thou shalt not steal;" "Thou shalt not commit adultery," are injunctions of permanent and universal obligation; but to the honest and pure man they are futile,—nay more, they never receive their perfect and ideal fulfilment till they have ceased to present themselves as a binding law without, and have become a spontaneous and inevitable expression of inward sanctity. And so throughout the whole range of moral obligation. The Law which correctly defines and imposes it is divine, and confronts us with imperative commands; and yet for him in whom the Spirit of God abides, it melts away, and becomes simply the intellectual expression of his own deepest love and devotion.

If real righteousness be thus inward, sin must be so no less. "Out of the heart proceed evil thoughts," with all their dreadful train of vice and crime.[1] Sin, accordingly, is an estrangement of the inward life from the life of God.[2] It is indeed a state of "lawlessness,"[3]

---

[1] Mark vii. 21 sqq., with the parallels.
[2] See Eph. iv. 18.   [3] 1 John iii. 4.

and expresses itself through transgressions of the commandments; but the most perfect mechanical obedience to the moral law would not purge away sin so long as the heart was deformed and foul, and the brute-life sat upon the throne of God in the divine palace of the soul. It is in consequence of this spiritual fact that the later theology has distinguished two kinds of sin, original and actual. We cannot here discuss the forms which this distinction has assumed, or the effect which scientific and historical inquiry must have upon them; the simple facts of Christian consciousness alone concern us. To the moralist and legislator transgression, the saying or doing of something wrong, is sin. This is actual, presenting itself in the world as a thing that we can judge and punish. If, on the other hand, there is no transgression, man must stand aside, and the law cannot interfere. But he whom the word of Christ has reached cannot be satisfied with this external innocence. To him impure thoughts, covetousness, worldliness, envy, hatred, malice, selfishness, anger and resentment, are sin, even if, like wild beasts, they are kept within their cage, and never allowed to give vent to their savage nature. The man may feel that he has not created these things, and that therefore their presence does not involve moral guilt so long as he wages war against them; but still he regards them as evils which belong, not to the physical, but to the moral realm. Opposed as they are to the divine ideal of humanity, they separate him from the beauty of holiness, and deny him the peace of a cleansed and reconciled heart.

Hence arises the necessity for conversion, which is primarily a change in the inward principle of life. Jesus began his preaching by taking up the warning cry of the Baptist: "Repent, for the kingdom of heaven is at hand;" and this word "repent" implies, not only a change of conduct, but a change of mind. He demanded of the Pharisees that they should cleanse the inside of the cup and platter; in other words, that they should cherish inward purity and truth, to which the outward life would spontaneously conform, whereas the most diligent outward cleansing would not remove the inward selfishness and intemperance.[1] On another occasion he made the emphatic declaration: "Verily I say unto you, unless ye be converted, and become as little children, ye shall not enter into the kingdom of heaven."[2] This was said in immediate reference to

---

[1] Matt. xxiii. 25 sqq.; Luke xi. 39 sqq.   [2] Matt. xviii. 3.

the ambitious views of the disciples; but it is susceptible of a much wider application. Men whose thoughts were bent upon their own aggrandizement were *ipso facto* outside the spiritual realm, and could enter it only by a change to the simplicity and self-renunciation of love; and so, in general, it is only the sweet and heavenly disposition that can make one a subject of that kingdom where God is the sole sovereign of the heart. The deepest saying upon this subject is that which was addressed to Nicodemus: "Verily, verily, I say unto thee, unless a man be born from above, he cannot see the kingdom of God."[1] Different views are taken, which we cannot pause to discuss, as to the historical character of the narrative where these words occur; but whether they were literally addressed to a "ruler of the Jews," or were spoken in the spirit to the heart of a disciple, they are equally true as an expression of the mind of Christ, and sum up in one profound phrase the purport of a large part of his teaching. If the pure in heart shall see God, it is equally true that the impure cannot see him. Spiritual things are spiritually discerned; and no striving of the senses and the intellect, no enforce-

[1] John iii. 3.

ment of duty by the determined will, can ever discover that which is revealed only in visitations of the Spirit. The filial mind, the communion with God, the sense of Divine love and peace flooding our inward being, which are the essence of Christianity, cannot be created by strenuous endeavour any more than our own volition has created our physical frame: they must come as a birth from on high, opening our eyes to a new world of heavenly beauty, and ravishing our ears with the sound of angelic songs, and giving to the conscious soul a rapture which, at its entrance on the visible scene, it could not know.

But this, it might seem, does away with human responsibility; for many men appear to be incapable of these higher experiences, and no one can be justly blamed for not obtaining that which God alone can create. It rests with man, however, to be true to the highest which he knows, and not to bar out the Spirit of God by his pride and self-will. As a race, we are slowly climbing upward towards the appointed end, and we are variously endowed with spiritual gifts, that we may receive mutual help, and the glowing faith of one may kindle into the warmth of life the dormant soul of another. Nor does responsibility cease when we have passed from the carnal to the spiritual mind, even though there may be seasons when the Divine Spirit seems to supersede the efforts of the will, and all is gracious and beautiful within. To whom men have committed much, of him will they demand the more; and growing clearness of insight presents ever new and higher problems of duty. Ideally, he that is born of God cannot sin,[1] but becomes a perfect instrument and expression of the Divine righteousness. This lies before us, however, as a distant vision; and meanwhile the inward principle of our life may be spiritual, and yet without the vigilance of duty we may lapse, and offend against that love which has revealed itself amid our darkness.[2] In this world we can never dismiss the sentinel that guards the soul; and yet the storm and struggle of a protesting conscience die away as the life born from above grows and strengthens, and a peace which passes understanding rests upon the humble and grateful heart.

It is not surprising, therefore, that Jesus, who insisted on the necessity of inward righteousness, demanded with no less emphasis the corresponding

[1] 1 John iii. 9.   [2] See Gal. v. 25.

practice. Unless the inward life be taken up by the will, and embodied, through a deliberate effort, in the outward activity, it is apt to drift away into an aimless and feeble sentiment, wasting itself in excited talk, and trying to hide its weakness in the vehemence of its professions. It was not enough, therefore, to receive the word with joy;[1] it was not enough to have titles of honour on the lips, while there was no practical outcome of the assumed reverence; he only who did the things which the new teaching required built his character upon a rock, and would be found unshaken in the day of trial.[2] It is related that a rich man, touched apparently by some new sense of spiritual want, once came to Jesus, and asked what he should do to inherit eternal life. Jesus did not find fault with the question, or point out the need of something more inward, but referred to the great moral commandments. These the man had probably never been tempted to violate; and he intimated that the answer hardly met his case. Jesus then exhorted him to do something which he well knew could be done only under the suasion of heartfelt faith and love, to give

---

[1] Matt. xiii. 20 sq.; Mark iv. 16 sq.; Luke viii. 13.
[2] Matt. vii. 21 sqq.; Luke vi. 46 sqq.; cf. Luke xiii. 25 sqq.

up his pleasures and gains and worldly position, and devote himself to the good of his fellow-men. An admonition to love his neighbours would probably have met with an eager response; the demand that he should *do* something commensurate with an entire love and self-devotion sent him away in sorrow; and thus Christ may have revealed to him the inward poverty which his untempted comfort had hidden from his conscience.[1] Amid the various aspects under which primitive Christianity presents itself, this feature in the teaching of Jesus is never forgotten. The regenerated inward life required a reformed code of morals; and the necessity for good works is insisted upon by the speculative Paul and the mystical John as strongly as by the practical James. For each and all, good works were the only satisfying evidence of inward sincerity and faithfulness.

This allegiance to duty involves the most strenuous effort and self-denial. Only as men who struggle through a narrow door and along a narrow path can we hope to secure our true life.[2] The follower of Jesus must take up his cross, the symbol of self-

[1] Mark x. 17 sqq.; Matt. xix. 16 sqq.; Luke xviii. 18 sqq.
[2] Matt. vii. 13 sq.; Luke xiii. 24.

renunciation, not wearing it as a trinket on his breast, but showing its marks in a life of self-sacrifice, even as the Son of Man came not to be ministered unto, but to minister, and to give his life a ransom for many. The love of parents and children must not stand in the way of discipleship. Hand and foot and eye must be parted with sooner than yield to the seductions of sin. Only thus is our true life preserved. It dies under the chill of selfishness when it would sit at home, nursing its own sweet musings, and shrinking from the labour and the strife without. It grows by the law of self-sacrifice. In imparting itself it becomes richer; and in self-forgetting service, which in the completeness of love would give up all it has, it attains its fullest beauty and power.[1] In this practice of "good works," while we are to shrink from all self-display,[2] we are no less to avoid all unworthy concealment. We must not be ashamed of the principles upon which we act, but allow men to see, and to glorify God for, the beautiful deeds which they pro-

---

[1] Mark viii. 34 sqq.; Matt. xvi. 24 sqq.; Luke ix. 23 sqq.; Matt. x. 37 sqq.; Luke xiv. 26 sq., xvii. 33; Matt. xx. 28, Mark x. 45; Mark ix. 43 sqq., Matt. v. 29 sq., xviii. 8 sq.

[2] Matt. vi. 1 sqq.

duce.[1] Thus, with braced and resolute will, we must act in the loving simplicity of an honest and good heart.

We must pass now from this more general consideration of principles, to notice the more important details of Christian virtue. From the nature of Christ's ethical principles, as well as from the popular method of his teaching, we might expect to find a complete want of system in his presentation of the various duties of life. He did not endeavour to construct either the logically developed theory of a philosophical thinker, or the classified code and definite injunctions of a legislator. The Spirit has, no doubt, a law—that is, a permanent order and authority—of its own, as was clearly recognized even by Paul;[2] but still there is no real analogy between an external law, which prescribes or prohibits certain defined and unvarying modes of activity, and the free and spontaneous movements of a "spirit of life," which unfolds itself with infinite variety amid the ceaseless changes of circumstance and opportunity. Jesus, therefore, would have been acting in contravention of his own profoundest teaching if he

[1] Matt. v. 14 sqq.
[2] See, for instance, Rom. viii. 2.

had attempted to lay down a new law which should be binding on the judgment and the conscience of his disciples. He attempted, however, nothing of the kind. The Sermon on the Mount is not a moral code, but a description and enforcement of broad principles of action, illustrated by examples which are not all applicable to our modern life; and it is easy for a literalist, proud of his shallow sagacity, to ridicule some of its precepts, and point merrily to the fact that no Christian ever dreams of observing them. This kind of objection mistakes altogether the nature and purpose of the teaching; and it is even possible that Jesus may have used exaggerated language, not only from the Oriental inclination to hyperbole, but in order that men might clearly understand that he was not laying down rules to be followed with a slavish exactness, but seeking to arouse pure and noble motives, which would direct the conduct in accordance with the interior law of their own life. And I may venture to remark in passing that this explains why Christianity has to a certain extent failed in comparison with lower forms of religion. It addresses itself to the manhood of the soul, and would commit the free children of God to the leading of the Spirit;

and when they fail to rise to this elevation, it does not offer as a substitute any precise rules which they can obey mechanically as a religious duty. The genuine Christian cannot be known by particular professions or practices, but only by the heavenly spirit of his life; and if a man is never radiant with the light which shone in the face of the Son of God, in his case Christianity has failed.

In accordance with these principles, Jesus summed up the teaching of the Old Testament in the two great commandments, to love God with all the heart, and soul, and mind, and strength, and to love one's neighbour as oneself. As reported in Mark,[1] he added: "There is no other commandment greater than these;" while Matthew reports the stronger expression: "On these two commandments hang all the Law and the Prophets."[2] The Apostle Paul presents the same view. Speaking in reference to social duty, he declares that all the Law is fulfilled in one precept: "Thou

---

[1] xii. 28 sqq.

[2] Matt. xxii. 35 sqq. Cf. Matt. vii. 12, and Luke x. 25 sqq., where love to one's neighbour receives the beautiful illustration of the good Samaritan, and an act of neighbourly love is used to prove that an alien and a heretic may be a neighbour in the highest sense.

shalt love thy neighbour as thyself;"[1] doing so on the ground that "love works no ill to a neighbour," and therefore renders all the prohibitions of the second table superfluous.[2] James, without speaking of it as a summary, describes it as a "royal law," which is violated by "respect of persons" as truly as by adultery or murder.[3] I need only allude to the emphatic way in which John dwells upon love, not only as indispensable to the Christian character, but communicating the fulness of life and divine knowledge. In this the various types of primitive Christian thought are at one, applying in their several ways, and according to the measure of their spiritual understanding, the same great truth promulgated by the Master himself.

In order, however, that we may estimate the value of these utterances, we must notice the kind of application which they were intended to have; for Christendom in its public capacity has, through a large part of its history, acted in flat contradiction of the teaching of its Founder, unless the obvious meaning of that teaching is explained away as soon as it is brought into the arena of action.

[1] Gal. v. 14.   [2] Rom. xiii. 8 sqq.
[3] James ii. 8 sqq.

We must notice first the virtues which ought to be exercised in our immediate relations with God.

Allegiance to God must be complete and undivided. There must be no seeking for worldly pomp and power through any subservience to the spirit of evil. Jesus is represented as repelling the allurements of ambition by appealing to the ancient words: "Thou shalt worship the Lord thy God, and him only shalt thou serve;"[1] and whatever interpretation we may give to the narrative, there can be no doubt that the reply which he is said to have made to the tempter expresses his own definite and irreversible choice. He saw that "no man can serve two masters," and it was necessary to choose between the world and God. The eye which is distracted between duty and gain must lose its clearness of vision; and only when it is "single," steadily directed to one object, does it enable us to form a luminous judgment.[2] Men are therefore forbidden to be anxious even about the necessaries of life. Our eagerness to secure these must not draw our hearts away from God, or lead us to doubt the kindness of his providence. He knows our needs, and we must

[1] Matt. iv. 10; Luke iv. 8.
[2] Matt. vi. 22 sqq.; Luke xvi. 13.

seek their legitimate satisfaction along the lines of duty, and never lose sight of our paramount end, the kingdom of God and his righteousness, amid a vain ostentation or the greedy accumulation of unprofitable wealth.[1] John repeats the lesson in his own words: "If any man love the world, the love of the Father is not in him;"[2] and Paul in his: "Be not conformed to this world, but be ye transformed by the renewing of your mind, that ye may prove what is the good and acceptable and perfect will of God."[3]

This absolute trust in God, this spirit of faith, ought not only to remove all anxiety about worldly possessions, but to make men calm and fearless, alike amid the waves of the stormy sea and before the threatenings of the persecutor.[4] Jesus insists again and again upon the practical power of faith. It is a victorious force in the soul of man, before which all obstacles give way. It is the persuasive power in prayer, evoking the blessing which is denied to the timid and the doubting. "All things are possible to

---

[1] Matt. vi. 25 sqq.; Luke xii. 22 sqq.
[2] 1 John ii. 15. [3] Rom. xii. 2.
[4] Matt. viii. 24 sqq., Mark iv. 36 sqq., Luke viii. 23 sqq.; Matt. x. 26, Luke xii. 4, 32.

him who has faith." To use the bold Eastern imagery, he can command a tree to be plucked up by the roots, or a mountain to be lifted from its base and cast into the sea, and it will obey him.[1] Such expressions may give us some idea of the triumphant sense of power and joy with which Jesus carried on his work, at least before the clouds of seeming failure gathered thick around him. The faith which he felt in himself he commended in others, and we are repeatedly told that he ascribed the cure, not only of moral, but of physical maladies to the faith of those who sought his help.[2] Faith, however, though it may and does remove mountains, sometimes removes them very slowly; and, as its severest trials come, as its noblest qualities shine forth, in the presence of opposition and disaster. It is not when we see Satan falling like lightning from heaven that the steadfastness of our heart is proved, but when the transient glow of the lightning darkens into

[1] Matt. xvii. 20, xxi. 21 sq.; Mark ix. 23, xi. 22 sqq.; Luke xvii. 6.

[2] Luke vii. 50; Mark v. 34, Matt. ix. 22, Luke viii. 48; Matt. xv. 28 (the faith not mentioned in Mark vii. 29); Mark ix. 23 (cf. Matt. xvii. 17, and Luke ix. 41); Matt. ix. 29; Mark x. 52, Luke xviii. 42 (faith omitted in Matt. xx. 29 sqq.); Matt. viii. 10, 13, Luke vii. 9; Luke xvii. 19.

the form of a cross, and he who in the vastness of his compassion would be the Saviour becomes the despised and rejected of men. Then faith fills the soul with heavenly peace;[1] and, in the calm assurance that even through pain and discomfiture and death God will work out his own blessed purposes, it takes the bitter cup and drinks it. So the disciple says it is our faith that has conquered the world.[2] I need only refer to the prominent place which is assigned to faith in the teaching of Paul. To discuss the meaning which the word bears in Pauline theology would require an essay, and I must here content myself with the briefest suggestions. For both Paul and John faith meant ultimately that same absolute trust in God, and surrender of the heart and will to him, which it meant for Christ. Paul's gospel is briefly this: have Christ's faith, and then without any law you will conquer sin and death. Still for the disciple there necessarily arose a further idea, which could not have existed for the Master. Faith in God was associated with faith in him through whom it had come, and who had first stirred the soul to its depths. But faith in him was not mere belief in anything that he had said or done,

[1] See John xiv. 27. [2] 1 John v. 4.

but a peaceful confidence in his spirit of life as indeed divine, the eternal life which by its indwelling raises men into sons of God. It was thus a moral and spiritual force, which commanded the soul with all the power of a religious conviction, and blended inseparably with its highest experiences, so that it became quite natural to speak indifferently of the indwelling of the Spirit of God, of the Spirit of Christ, and of Christ himself.[1] All these expressions point alike to that high communion which was being given to the world in Christ; and in those days the belief that Jesus was the Son of God was not a theological form, but a glowing conviction of the heart, which had discovered in Christ that filial life which shall alone abide when the false ambition and greatness of the world shall have sunk into decay. If so, the appropriation of the Spirit of God is the measure of Christian faith.

From faith follows faithfulness, which is an essential Christian virtue. "No man, having put his hand to the plough, and looking back, is fit for the kingdom of God."[2] It is only when men forget God, or think him far off, that they forsake the path of duty, and turn to their own pleasures instead. Whatever our

---

[1] See Rom. viii. 9 sq.   [2] Luke ix. 62.

talents may be, they are to be accepted and used as a sacred trust; and he who shrinks from the irksomeness of duty and the strain of high endeavour, can only look forward to spiritual darkness and the loss of his most precious gifts. But fidelity brings its own blessing in the shape of augmented power and growing fulness of life.[1] It is the faithful steward who is appointed over the household;[2] and in the apocalyptic letter to the church at Smyrna it is to him who is faithful unto death that the crown of life is promised.[3] Here there is no distinction of small and great, for character expresses itself alike in each: "He that is faithful in the least is faithful also in much, and he that is unrighteous in the least is unrighteous also in much."[4]

To maintain this constant faithfulness, vigilance is necessary. The disciples were required to be like virgins waiting for the coming of the bridegroom at a marriage-feast,[5] or like servants waiting for their master, and not knowing at what hour he would come.[6]

---

[1] Matt. xxv. 14 sqq.; Luke xix. 12 sqq.
[2] Luke xii. 42; Matt. xxiv. 45.   [3] Rev. ii. 10.
[4] Luke xvi. 10.   [5] Matt. xxv. 1 sqq.
[6] Matt. xxiv. 42 sqq.; Mark xiii. 35; Luke xii. 36 sqq., xxi. 36.

The exhortations to vigilance are connected with the anticipated coming of the Son of Man,—a subject to which we have already referred, and in regard to which we cannot be confident that we have a correct report of Christ's own language. But at all events it was a true interpretation of his spirit which, in view of this expected crisis in the history of the world, urged men to a constant readiness for such a momentous change; and it is easy to generalize the moral requirement which is presented to us with this particular application. Not only is the time of his death utterly unknown to each man, but fresh duties or unexpected trials may come at any moment, and find us unprepared. To watch for such events with anxiety and fear would be inconsistent with the trust in God which is placed so high among Christian virtues; but men should watch for every intimation of the Higher Will, and commit themselves trustfully to the absolute disposal of God, and then they would not be surprised or overwhelmed when their accustomed ways were broken up, and they were forced to address themselves to new problems, whether of activity or of patience.

Sincerity is another virtue on which the greatest stress was laid by Jesus. His opposition to the

Pharisees was grounded on their hypocrisy; and by hypocrisy he seems to have meant, not merely the conscious acting of a part, but the deeper and more incorrigible mischief of possessing a spurious instead of a genuine religiousness, which blinded the eyes and perverted the judgment of the Pharisee himself as much as it misled the undiscerning crowd who applauded him for his sanctity. He warned his disciples against this evil leaven,[1] and exhorted them to cultivate the utmost simplicity in their religious practices, veiling them from the eyes of men, and, as far as possible, even from themselves.[2]

Sincerity of conduct is closely connected with humility, a readiness to perceive our own ill-desert and the immeasurable claims which God has upon our service, and a willingness to take what is esteemed the lowest place among men. In obeying every commandment of God, men do no more than their duty; and the fulfilment of duty does not entitle them to

---

[1] Luke xii. 1. In Matt. xvi. 6 sqq., and Mark viii. 15 sqq., the explanation, "which is hypocrisy," is not given; but we can hardly doubt that the explanation in Luke is correct.

[2] Matt. vi. 1 sqq.: "Let not thy left hand know what thy right hand doeth."

boast of their merit.[1] The Pharisee, proud of his good deeds, returns from his prayers full of self-satisfaction, and utterly blind to the real relations between himself and God; but the publican, smitten with sorrow for his sins, feels the blessedness of God's pardoning love, and is justified rather than the other. This parable illustrates a general principle, which Christ seems to have been fond of repeating: "Every one that exalteth himself shall be humbled, and he that humbleth himself shall be exalted."[2] Conceit brings with it spiritual poverty; for it involves a radical falsity, and is in essence a worship of self instead of God. Humility is attended by spiritual elevation, because it removes the false estimates which hide the truth from us, and places us in our true relation towards God. "Blessed are the poor in spirit, for theirs is the kingdom of heaven;"[3] for in that kingdom he is greatest who loves and serves most.[4]

[1] Luke xvii. 10.

[2] Luke xviii. 14. Also Luke xiv. 11, and, in a different connection, Matt. xxiii. 12.

[3] Matt. v. 3.

[4] Matt. xviii. 4, xx. 25 sqq., xxiii. 11; Mark ix. 35, x. 42 sqq.; Luke ix. 48, xxii. 25 sqq. Cf. John xiii. 1 sqq.

All this seems to inculcate a perfect simplicity of character, which takes no thought for its own greatness or distinction, but cheerfully turns to the very humblest tasks that benevolence may require. But we must in fairness notice an anecdote preserved by Luke, which, as it stands, conveys a very different lesson. Jesus is there represented as advising men, when they are invited to a marriage, to take the lowest seat, in order that they may be invited to go up higher, and have glory in the eyes of those who sit down with them.[1] This seems to recommend a mock humility for the sake of the greater distinction which it will procure for us. Such conduct would be only to outwit the Pharisee in his own arts. It is difficult to suppose that the Evangelist himself can have intended this, and it is certainly opposed to the general tenor of Christ's teaching. But a very slight change would remove this injurious impression, and it is possible that in the course of transmission an illustration has been turned into a precept. Jesus may have observed at some banquet the humiliation of a pretentious guest, and the distinction accorded to one who had modestly taken the bottom place; and then he may

---

[1] Luke xiv. 7 sqq.

have used this incident to illustrate his favourite maxim, and show how, in the spiritual realm, true elevation and greatness of character are the direct offspring of humility.

Man's sense of need, and of dependence upon God, expresses itself in prayer; and prayer accordingly occupies a very prominent place in the Christian religion. It enters into every form of public worship; it has continually nourished the secret springs of private devotion. We are told far less than we should like to know of Christ's own habits and mode of expression in his communion with God through prayer, but what we are told is deeply significant. It is clear that he avoided all those prolonged austerities of worship which attract the gaze of the vulgar, and maintained the reverent reserve which he recommended to his disciples. Of his daily practice we know nothing; but we can hardly doubt that he knelt often in his lonely chamber, and opened his heart to Him who sees in secret. We hear, however, of his withdrawing into the wilderness, or climbing the mountain, that he might pray amid the solitude of nature; and his teaching shows how real and uplifting he felt this communion to be.[1] He asserts in the most positive way that there was a genuine answer to prayer: "Ask, and it shall be given you; seek, and ye shall find; knock, and it shall be opened to you."[2] Prayer, however, must be earnest and persevering, and men are not to abandon themselves to faintness and despair because there is no immediate response.[3] But it is not to be long, or full of vain repetitions; for God knows what we have need of before we ask him, and much speaking is apt to degenerate into pretence.[4] So averse was Jesus to every kind of display in connection with religion, that he directed his disciples, when they prayed, to enter their private chamber, and shut the door, so that none might witness their devotions but the Father who sees in secret.[5] This, literally

---

[1] For the prayers of Jesus, see Luke iii. 21; Mark i. 35, Luke v. 16; Luke vi. 12; Mark vi. 46, Matt. xiv. 23; Luke ix. 18, 28; Matt. xi. 25, Luke x. 21; Luke xxii. 32, xxiii. 34. I must refer also to John xi. 41 sq., xii. 27 sq., and xvii., though I am unable to assign the same *historical* value to these passages as to those in the Synoptics.

[2] Matt. vii. 7; Luke xi. 9.

[3] Luke xi. 5 sqq., xviii. 1 sqq.

[4] Matt. vi. 7 sq.; Mark xii. 40, Matt. xxiii. 13, Luke xx. 47.

[5] Matt. vi. 6.

construed, amounts to a prohibition of public worship; but probably it was intended to refer only to prayers which, although private, were at that time frequently offered in public places. Still it is a remarkable instance of the way in which Jesus trusted to the free working of the Spirit, that he nowhere refers to the obligation of attending public worship, and lays down no regulations for its observance, but leaves it to his disciples to follow their own bent, and frame their own rules, as their spiritual needs may from time to time suggest. In regard to private prayers, too, he says nothing as to their frequency or the hours of the day when they should be offered, but only requires real privacy and simplicity, that they may be a true communion between the soul and God. There is one other condition which must not be forgotten. The heart must be at peace with men, if it is to find peace with God. We must forgive if we hope to be forgiven; for bitterness and resentment shut out the Spirit of God, and refuse the blessing which he is waiting to bestow.[1]

On the proper objects of prayer little is said. Sayings, indeed, are recorded which remove every limit

[1] Matt. vi. 14 sq., Mark xi. 25 sq. Cf. Matt. xviii. 35.

both from the range and from the power of prayer. All things, whatsoever men ask in prayer, if they have faith, it is said, they will receive;[1] and again, if two disciples agree upon earth about anything that they shall ask, it shall be done.[2] These expressions, however, like so many others, must be limited by the occasion, and by the end in view. Jesus felt confident that the highest aspirations of the prayerful man would surely be fulfilled, and that all obstacles must yield before his faith; and he desired to infuse this confidence into the minds of his disciples. But he cannot have believed that men might pray for things which he did not regard as proper objects for human desire and effort, or that prayers for such things would be granted. The interpretation of the disciple is probably correct, "If we ask anything according to his will, he hears us."[3] So Jesus himself, in his hour of agony, clothed in words the spirit of all genuine prayer, "Not as I will, but as thou wilt."[4] We are nowhere told that he drew any sharp distinction between prayers for

[1] Mark xi. 24; Matt. xxi. 22.
[2] Matt. xviii. 19. Cf. John xvi. 22, and xv. 16.
[3] 1 John v. 14.
[4] Matt. xxvi. 39; Mark xiv. 36; Luke xxii. 42.

outward and for inward blessings; but we should observe that in the Lord's Prayer there is only one petition for the former, and that is limited to the prime necessary of life, our daily bread. Paul exhorts the Philippians in everything by prayer and supplication to let their requests be made known unto God; but he does not say they will be granted. He knew that his own thorn in the flesh had not been taken away in answer to his prayer. But still there is an answer, blessed above all others, the peace of God within the heart.[1]

[1] Philip. iv. 6 sq

LECTURE VII.
ETHICS.—II.

LECTURE VII.

ETHICS.—II.

In the last Lecture we briefly reviewed the ethical principles of Christianity, and then proceeded to consider the type of character involved in the two great commandments of love to God and love to man. Our time only permitted us to dwell on the former of these commandments, and we must now pass on to notice the leading points connected with the latter. Love, as we have seen, is the supreme term in the social ethics of Christianity. Even Paul, the Apostle of faith, places it not only before the gift of angelic speech or prophetic power, but above hope and faith. A man may have the very faith which Christ so highly commended, and be able to remove mountains, and yet, without love, he is nothing.[1] This, then, is the

[1] 1 Cor. xiii. 2.

standard by which a professing Christian is to judge himself. If in his dealings with his fellow-men his ruling principle is self-interest, and he cares not who suffers provided he himself gets on, his profession of Christianity is a hollow pretence; and when he boasts of his faith in Christ, he only insults the Master whose teaching he despises and disobeys. It is only through the spirit of love pervading and transforming our whole inward being that we *know* that we have passed out of death into life.[1] This spirit is the Spirit of God, who is Love, and without it we cannot be his. He that hates his brother is in the dark;[2] but when all our hatred is driven out by love, we know the light, and see clearly, even as we distinguish the splendours of the dawn from the darkness in which we groped. Faith and hope belong only to the finite and imperfect being, and help us to lay hold of that which is life indeed; but love is of God, the infinite and perfect, and is itself the eternal life, which was manifested in Christ, and takes up its abode in all who are his.

This view of love, as an abounding life within, might relieve us of the question why we should love

[1] 1 John iii. 14. [2] 1 John ii. 9.

man. Still Christianity has a special answer to this question; for when it first penetrates the mind, it completely revolutionizes the sentiments with which we regard mankind. For the first time we truly apprehend that they are our own brethren, and see them clothed with an indescribable dignity. Behind the meanest raiment, and the coarsest features, and even the ravages of sin, we behold the hidden child of God, and revere a nature which is gifted with such vast possibilities, and called to be a temple of the Holy Spirit. Hence we "honour all men;" and the crimes and vices which defile the temple not only excite our indignation, but waken our pitying sorrow, and our longing to print once more the lost ideal on the soul. Thus love to man rests on a special ground, and is indeed involved in our love to God; for he that honours not the child honours not the Father, and if a man love not his brother whom he has seen, how can he love God whom he has not seen?

But independently of the particular sentiments towards mankind which are evoked by Christian faith, the life of love is in its own essence one of spontaneous and overflowing goodwill. Hence there are no limits to its exercise. It is not like the natural affections, which are called forth only by pleasing objects, and adapted to the temporary purposes of life, but, like the sun, pours its energy abroad, to give light and warmth wherever its beams may fall. It pervades and glorifies the natural affections, lifting them into the eternal realm, and filling them with a divine constancy and power. But it goes further. It befriends the stranger, and ministers to the needy in their pain and sorrow.[1] Nay, it extends itself to our enemies. It does not return insult for insult, or blow for blow. Blessing, and only blessing, can issue from its lips; and, instead of meeting evil with evil, it overcomes evil with good.[2] These things are summed up by Jesus in the universal precept, "All things whatsoever ye would that men should do to you, do ye even so to them."[3] This precept, however, must be interpreted by the spirit of love, and not be slavishly followed; for we might desire wrong or foolish things for ourselves. It is a rule of practical sympathy, and requires

[1] Matt. xxv. 34 sqq.; Luke x. 30 sqq.; James i. 27; 1 John ii. 17.

[2] Matt. v. 38 sqq., Luke vi. 27 sqq.; Rom. xii. 14, 17 sqq.; 1 Peter iii. 9.

[3] Matt. vii. 12; Luke vi. 31.

us to correct our judgments by placing ourselves with loving imagination in the circumstances of others, instead of seeing our duties towards them through a mist of selfishness. Christian love is always clear-eyed, seeing into the heart of human relations, and, through its surrender to the Divine Will, forming a just judgment.

It goes without saying that all injurious conduct is forbidden, for "love works no ill to its neighbour."[1] The prohibitions, therefore, of the second table are confirmed.[2] Every man must speak truth with his neighbour, because we are members one of another. The former thief must steal no more, but rather labour, working with his hands that which is good, that he may have something to communicate to him who has need. All bitterness, and wrath, and anger, and clamour, and evil-speaking, must be put away, and give place to mutual kindness and compassion.[3] The rivalry of ambition and faction must be laid aside; for in the kingdom of heaven he is greatest who

---

[1] Rom. xiii. 10.

[2] Mark x. 19; Matt. xix. 18; Luke xviii. 20.

[3] Matt. v. 21 sqq.; Eph. iv. 25 sqq.; Luke x. 37.

renders the humblest service.[1] We are not to judge one another, and sharply search out another's faults, while we are blind to our own, but rather restore the erring in a spirit of meekness, and help him to bear the heavy burden of his contrition, remembering that we too may be tempted, and we have a load of our own to carry.[2] Offences against ourselves must be forgiven with unwearying patience and forbearance;[3] and in all our dealings we must be on the side of peace, and endeavour by our calmness and impartiality to still the waters of strife.[4]

A few words must be said about the duty of giving.

[1] See before, p. 237 ; Gal. v. 15, 20 ; 1 Cor. i. 11 sqq., iii. 3 sqq. ; James iii. 14 sqq.

[2] Matt. vii. 1 sqq., Luke vi. 37; Gal. vi. 1 sqq. ; Rom. xiv. 4, 10 sqq.; James iv. 11 sq., v. 9, 19 sq. Cf. Mark ix. 42, Matt. xviii. 6 sq., Luke xvii. 1 sq.

[3] Matt. vi. 14 sq., xviii. 15 sqq. (which seems hardly consistent with the more absolute injunction farther on; but the point is that we are not to cast off an offending brother till we have done everything in our power to win him back), 21 sqq.; Luke xvii. 3 sq. ; Eph. iv. 32 (though the word is much wider than simple forgiveness). The clause in the Lord's Prayer is a perpetual reminder of this lesson, which is so difficult except to Christian love.

[4] Matt. v. 9 ; Mark ix. 50 ; Rom. xii. 18, xiv. 19 ; 1 Cor. xiv. 33 ; 2 Cor. xiii. 11 ; Eph. iv. 3 ; 1 Thess. v. 13 ; Heb. xii. 14 ; James iii. 17 sq.

According to Luke's report, Christ said to the Pharisees: "Give alms, and behold! all things are clean unto you;"[1] and directed the disciples to sell their goods and give alms.[2] These precepts, however, are confined to this Gospel, which, more than any of the others, dwells on the dangers of wealth, and extols the advantages of poverty; and we must, therefore, be careful not to form an exaggerated idea of the value attached to almsgiving by Jesus. In one of the passages referred to he is contrasting the giving of alms, which may at least relieve the sufferings of a fellow-creature, with mere ceremonial offerings, which were too often regarded as a substitute for moral duty; and in the other he is showing the superiority of the inward treasure, which is beyond the reach of thief and moth, to outward wealth, the love of which may be checked by spending it freely for the benefit of others. Here, as in so many instances, the precept is given with a breadth and force which drives it home, and is not burdened with the qualifications which the context suggests, and which necessarily arise in the practical arrangements of life. Elsewhere Christ refers to almsgiving only to enjoin simplicity in its exercise.[3]

[1] Luke xi. 41.   [2] Luke xii. 33.   [3] Matt. vi. 1 sqq.

The duty of giving, however, is universally recognized in Christian teaching. Christ himself says: "Give to him that asketh thee, and from him that would borrow from thee turn not thou away."[1] All such precepts are illustrations of the law of love. To give, and to deny ourselves in order to give something towards the alleviation of human woe, is a primary duty in the social ethics of Christianity. But love requires that we should give, as far as possible, with judgment and knowledge, the object being, not to relieve ourselves of an uneasy conscience, but to do the greatest amount of good. We are warned in modern times against the casual alms, which are proved by experience only to foster the evils which we wish to cure; but we must be careful that we do not shut up our compassion, or cloak our selfishness under the plea of enlightenment. The field of wise philanthropy lies open; let us pour our treasure into it.

In this connection we must not overlook the duty of combating the moral evil in the world, and bestowing on men some sort of spiritual gift. On this subject we have no very precise precepts; but Jesus himself came "to seek and save the lost,"[2] and appointed a

---
[1] Matt. vi. 42.   [2] Luke xix. 10.

chosen band of disciples to carry on and extend his work. It is a universal Christian prayer that the kingdom of God may come, and every one who utters this prayer sincerely must desire to do his part in helping the advent of righteousness. But each man must determine for himself, by a consideration of circumstances and of his own endowments, in what way he can be of most service; for the kingdom of God is not spread merely by the direct action of the Church through its appointed agents, but by all the influences that go forth from honourable and God-loving men in their daily transactions in the world. The man of scrupulous honour on the Stock Exchange bears witness to a higher rule than that of covetousness, and in that particular line his witness has a higher authority than that of any preacher. And so in every calling the true Christian is a minister of God, and with a modest sincerity displays that benign and healing spirit which sweetens the fountains of human life, and makes men feel the reality of things divine. The Church, however, as a society, has a collective duty in this respect. Where the whole organism is healthy, a sufficient number will hear a call to the special exercise of missionary or ministerial activity; and the general body will gladly devote its best—its wealth, its culture, its intellect—to the spiritual service of mankind. Where the supply of men set apart and dedicated to the work is inadequate or of inferior quality, there must be some blight which is wasting the religious force of the community, and the distinctive spirit of Christianity is giving way before the attractions of the world.

Such, then, are general indications of the way in which Christian love operates. They are but indications; for the circumstances of life are infinitely varied, and a living spirit meets them as they arise with its own free activity. The knowledge of love must come through our own consciousness, and we cannot see this part of the kingdom of heaven till we have learnt in our own experience what it is to love an enemy, and to have our natural and earthly antipathies transfigured by a heavenly benignity which is boundless as its source. Yet an outward appeal may help to bring our own dim and struggling ideas and aspirations into clearness and order; and he who would understand the social ethics of Christianity cannot do better than read Paul's grand description of love, and meditate upon it till his own heart feels the glow, and intellect and will bow down before this sovereign principle of good.

It is in accordance with the general spirit of Christian ethics that there are very few precise rules affecting the special relations of life. The conduct of husband and wife, of parents and children, of masters and servants, of older and younger, of strong and weak, of subjects and rulers, must be regulated by the law of mutual love and reverence. There is, however, an exception in the case of marriage; for here Jesus set himself in direct antagonism to the loose practice of his time. To him marriage was a holy relation, instituted in the beginning by the Creator himself, and therefore possessing all the permanence of a Divine law; and accordingly nothing could justify divorce except a complete violation of the marriage contract. "What God has joined together, let not man put asunder," is the grand rule by which he raises marriage far above considerations of mere social utility, or temporary contracts to be maintained during convenience.[1] Christian love transmutes the passion which draws man and woman together, and converts it into an inviolable bond; for though passion is fitful and

[1] See Matt. v. 31 sq., xix. 3 sqq.; Mark x. 2 sqq.; Luke xvi. 18.

capricious, love is of eternity, and partakes of the changelessness of God. All true marriage, therefore, is entered upon with a solemn sense of the Divine leading, and is felt to be far more than an earthly and arbitrary tie; and to the Christian conscience the notion which is sometimes put forward, that it is a mere legal contract which, like a partnership in business, ought to be dissoluble at will, is simply revolting, and seems worthy only of a community of beasts. From this sentiment of the divine sanctity of marriage has sprung the practice of monogamy. Christianity spontaneously accepted this practice, and confirmed it by the exalted view which it took of the marriage union.

Before quitting the subject of love, we must ask whether Christianity recognizes any duties towards the inferior animal creation. As is well known, the Jewish Law lays down some distinct regulations requiring the exercise of humanity towards the brutes, one or two which show even a remarkable tenderness of sympathy towards their possible sufferings; and it may fairly be said that Christianity, in adopting the Old Testament, with whatever reservations, incorporated such precepts as these. Still it cannot be denied that professing Christians have often shown an extraordinary callousness in this respect, and the New Testament is strangely silent as to that whole realm of barbarity in which creation has groaned under the tyranny of man. Indeed, Paul expressly repudiates the idea that God can care for oxen, and changes one of the generous provisions of the Law into an allegory for the benefit of Christian missionaries.[1] Even the great Apostle had his limitations, and he was so absorbed in contemplating the relations between God and the human soul that all else seems to pass out of view, and we cannot find that the beauty of the scenery through which he passed, or the varied and winning life of beast and bird, had any charm for him. But in this I do not think he reflects the spirit of the Master. It is true we are not told of any particular precepts which Christ laid down as to the treatment of animals; but we get some interesting glimpses into his way of regarding both the animate and the inanimate world around him. His teaching abounds in references to the familiar scenes of his native land, showing that he had observed them with a loving eye, and he refers especially to the beauteous vesture of

[1] 1 Cor. ix. 9 sq.

the flowers, saying that Solomon in all his glory was not arrayed like one of these.[1] Instead of thinking that God did not care for oxen, he taught that our Heavenly Father fed the birds,[2] and that not a single sparrow fell to the ground without God, or was forgotten before him.[3] In repelling a charge of violating the Sabbath, he affirms, with evident approval, that there was not a man among his opponents who would not pull a sheep or an ox or an ass out of a pit on the Sabbath-day, and is only indignant that they will not go on to the universal principle that it is allowable to do good on the Sabbath-day.[4] According to this teaching, it is a good deed to relieve the distress of a sheep or an ass, and one which justifies us in setting aside the pedantic scruples of an external piety. But apart from these particular illustrations of Christ's spirit, we may say that Christian love is intrinsically opposed to all cruelty, and must regard the brute creation with a sympathizing friendliness. How far our power over the animals may be legitimately exercised it is difficult

---

[1] Matt. vi. 28 sqq.; Luke xii. 27 sq.
[2] Matt. vi. 26; Luke xii. 24.
[3] Matt. x. 29; Luke xii. 6.
[4] Matt. xii. 11 sq.; Luke xiv. 5.

to determine with precision, and it is impossible now to enter into the problems and controversies which the question suggests. In our general practice we are necessarily guided by a sort of rude common sense; but we may safely lay down the rule that Christian love includes the whole sentient creation within its embrace, and will not wantonly limit that measure of happiness which the Creator has designed for it.

We must now leave the virtues which spring out of our love to God and man, and speak of the duties which, however they may affect others indirectly, terminate immediately in oneself. Here also we are confined to general principles, and meet with no rules of self-discipline; but every man is left free to form his own rules, to suit his own particular requirements. It is expected that of ourselves we shall form a just judgment, and keep ourselves free from the blinding influence of prejudice.[1] We are to be like merchantmen seeking goodly pearls;[2] and we are not to pay a conventional honour to the prophets of the olden time, while we persecute the prophets of to-day, at once closing our ears against the new truth which comes to prove the hearts of men, and burying the old beneath

[1] Luke xii. 54 sqq.   [2] Matt. xiii. 45.

a sepulchre of artificial and unappreciative respect.[1] Nevertheless, we are to be on our guard against false prophets, and not rush after every novelty, assuming that a man is great and good because he abuses his neighbours, and attacks their time-honoured convictions. We must judge them by those ethical rules which furnish the nearest and most certain ground of discrimination, for bad fruit does not come from a good tree, nor are deeds of beneficence and moral healing prompted by Beelzebub.[2]

Christianity requires the strictest personal purity—purity of thought and feeling as well as of deed.[3] It also, as we have seen, demands constant vigilance and self-denial. Nevertheless, it is opposed to asceticism. This may seem a questionable statement, considering how largely asceticism has entered into Christian history, and how deeply it has coloured the idea of the Christian saint. But the spirit of Christ himself is the standard of his religion; and though he denied

---

[1] Matt. xxiii. 29 sqq.; Luke xi. 47 sq.

[2] Matt. vii. 15 sqq.; xii. 24 sqq., Mark iii. 22 sqq., Luke xi. 15 sqq.

[3] Matt. v. 8, 27 sqq.; Rom. vi. 13; 1 Cor. v. vi. 13 sqq.; James i. 27.

himself to the uttermost in obedience to the voice of
God within him, asceticism is precisely the characteristic which he seizes on as distinguishing John
the Baptist from himself. "John came neither eating
nor drinking, and they say, he has a demon; the
Son of Man came eating and drinking, and they
say, behold a gluttonous man and a winebibber, a
friend of publicans and sinners."[1] These words show
that by the freedom of his living he offended the religious people of his time, who thought that holiness
consisted in bodily privations; and throughout his life
there is not a trace of those austerities which captivate
the vulgar imagination and attract the fame of superior
sanctity. There is always the same quiet and reverent
moderation, the same spontaneous and exalted purity;
and if on one side scandal has left his character unsullied, on the other side not even legend has tricked
him out with the adventitious glories of an external
holiness.[2]

Nevertheless, Christ seems to have given some sanction to religious abstinence in what he is reported to

[1] Matt. xi. 18 sq.; Luke vii. 33 sq.

[2] We may contrast with this the account which Hegesippus gives
of James, the Lord's brother

have said about fasting. On a certain occasion he was asked why the disciples of John and the Pharisees fasted, while his disciples refrained from doing so. He replied that they would fast when the bridegroom was taken from them, and added the illustration of a patch on an old garment, and of new wine in old wineskins.[1] The purport of the two answers is the same. The old practice of formal and stated fasts, under the pressure of a supposed religious obligation, was inconsistent with the new religion. When Christ's disciples fasted, they would do so naturally and spontaneously, under the stress of heartfelt sorrow. In the Sermon on the Mount he assumes that his disciples will fast; but he does not inculcate the practice, or lay down any rules as to its frequency or its character. Here, as in everything else, he leaves the judgment free, and only enjoins privacy, lest the religious exercise should engender spiritual pride and hypocrisy.[2] It may be that in our imperfect state some bodily discipline may be needed to subdue our self-indulgence and give firmness to the will, and each man must decide for himself what will be beneficial. For my

---

[1] Matt. ix. 14 sqq.; Mark ii. 18 sqq.; Luke v. 33 sqq.
[2] Matt. vi. 16 sqq.

own part, I believe that the true outcome of the mind of Christ is to place no reliance upon artificial acts of self-denial, but to remember always that the body is "the temple of the Holy Spirit," and to treat it always with the reverence due to a consecrated shrine. Here Christianity set itself in direct opposition to the highest wisdom of the ancient world, which looked on the body as a prison or a tomb, and thought that the only way to God was to trample on its rights, and seek the spiritual, not in and through the natural, but by waging war against it. Paul, indeed, knew full well the foulness of a mind enslaved to the flesh; but then the body was the organ of the mind, and might be used for righteousness as well as for sin, and it will be shielded from all abuse, and transfigured as on the mount of heavenly vision, when we know that it is a house built by God for the indwelling and operation of his own Spirit.

Connected with personal purity is the injunction not to swear,[1] for this too rests ultimately upon reverence towards Him to whom the oath appeals. The name of God may indeed be avoided, but everything created by him should share the reverence which we profess

[1] Matt. v. 33 sqq.; James v. 12.

to feel towards the Creator. It seems most probable that Jesus referred to the hasty oaths of common conversation, and would inculcate that simple purity of speech which a sense of the Divine presence inevitably begets. But the principle laid down is fairly applicable to judicial oaths. It may not be obligatory to refuse these, when made with a due feeling of their solemnity; but in themselves they come of evil, and imply the legitimacy of falsehood when our statements are not confirmed in this way. To the honest man they make not a particle of difference, and all his serious words are spoken as in the presence of God. It would, therefore, I think, be more in accordance with the mind of Christ to abolish these oaths entirely, and to enforce the speaking of truth by adequate penalties for false testimony. This, however, is a question which affects most men to a very limited extent, and what they need is to remember always to preserve a reverent simplicity of speech, and never to sully their lips with language which can offend the Holy One.

Finally, a few words must be said about the possession and accumulation of riches. In some of his teaching Jesus seems at first sight to attach a special merit to poverty, and to condemn the possession of wealth. For instance, in the parable of the Rich Man and Lazarus we are told nothing of the characters of the two men, but only of the contrast between the luxury of the one and the penury of the other.[1] But we must correct this first impression by some other considerations. To have insisted on a life of poverty as in itself meritorious would have been opposed to the view which he maintained in regard to asceticism; and it does not appear that even in the earliest times the Church demanded a renunciation of wealth as a condition of membership. The point of the parable referred to seems to be simply this: that the relative position of men may be completely reversed in a world whither we cannot carry our material riches. It is one illustration of the statement that there are last who shall be first, and first who shall be last, and of the truth that the conventional judgments of earth are widely different from the judgments of God. It is nevertheless undeniable that Jesus recognized a spiritual danger in the possession of wealth. Then, as now, it sometimes alienated brothers, making the possessor hard and selfish, and exciting the covetousness of the needy;

[1] Luke xvi. 19 sqq.

and yet it is no lasting property, but at any moment death may invade the lordly mansion, and carry off the naked soul to the land where only spiritual wealth is reckoned.[1] And, again, abundance of this world's ease and comfort is apt to soften the mind, and make it indisposed to encounter hardship and self-denial for the sake of others. "How hardly shall they that have riches enter into the kingdom of God!" and yet with God's help it is possible,[2] and many rich men have entered and rendered invaluable service. But does not Jesus expressly forbid his disciples to lay up treasure on earth?[3] Yes; and the reason given for the injunction will explain it: "Where your treasure is, there will your heart be also." Wealth is a relative term, and it is largely its possession that distinguishes the civilized man from the savage. All the arts of life, the cultivation of the mind, and the progress of society, are dependent upon it. If we seek the kingdom of God, it will be added to us, and we shall

---

[1] Luke xii. 13 sqq. It deserves especial notice here that Christ does not say a word against the brother who had the inheritance, but rebukes the covetousness of the one who thought he had been wronged.

[2] Mark x. 23 sqq.; Matt. xix. 23 sqq.; Luke xviii. 24 sqq.

[3] Matt. vi. 19 sqq.; Luke xii. 33 sq.

gather around us an organization suited to our advanced intelligence, and expressive of the higher and ideal elements of our thought. Nevertheless, it is not to be our primary object, but to come in, as it were, by the way, so as to minister to our inward growth, and afford larger opportunities for our beneficent activity. The man whose only passion is to be rich is among the meanest of his kind, and is often tempted on to deeds of rapacity and cruelty that make the conduct of a footpad respectable by comparison. But so long as the mind enlarges in due proportion to the increase of riches, and the heart's treasure is felt to be the intellectual and moral power which no thief can steal or moth destroy, then, if in the pursuit of our duty wealth accumulate, we shall use it as a holy trust from God, and be grateful for the increase of opportunity which it brings.

We have now sketched, in the barest outline, the principles of Christian ethics, and the nature of the duties which result from these principles. In conclusion, we must refer to the doctrine of a future life, and its law of retribution. On this subject the earliest teaching maintains a reverent reserve, and does not profess to describe with any minuteness what passes behind the veil. The imagination is indeed appealed to through bold and striking figures; but it is obvious that these are only the popular symbols of what eye has not seen or ear heard, and we must be content to fall back on a few great principles, which are enunciated with unmistakable clearness.

That Christianity proclaimed the doctrine of immortality with extraordinary power is a familiar fact. Even to those who had already accepted that doctrine, it seemed that the Gospel had brought life and immortality to light, through the confidence that Jesus himself had passed into the eternal realm, and was there the known centre of affection and hope, the embodiment and norm of that life with God which his disciples aspired to attain. That future life, however, was not severed from all connection with the present, but carried the aims and efforts of this world to their legitimate result. The inwardness of real righteousness did not abrogate the obligations of duty or put an end to responsibility, but rather made more evident the consequences of virtue and vice, and changed punishment from an arbitrary infliction into the inevitable result of evil choice. The destruction of the soul's highest powers was itself the direst penalty of sin; fulness of life was itself the best reward of virtue. This law of retribution is most clearly enunciated by Paul: "God is not mocked; for whatsoever a man soweth, that shall he also reap. For he that soweth to his own flesh, shall of the flesh reap corruption; but he that soweth to the spirit, shall of the spirit reap life eternal."[1] And elsewhere he says: "The wages of sin is death, but the gracious gift of God is life eternal."[2] I need only allude to the way in which eternal life is represented as the highest goal of human destiny in the Johannine writings; and the Epistle of James refers to "the crown of life" as the promised reward of a faithful and enduring love.[3] Jesus himself, in the synoptical account, fully recognizes the fact of retribution. In the passages in the Sermon on the Mount, where he cautions his disciples against seeking for human applause, and declares that their Father, who sees in secret, will reward them, we need not suppose that he is pointing to the future life, as it is not mentioned. He is rather laying down the universal and ever-present law of consequences. Those who live for human praise will get it, and with it a polished mockery of virtue. Those, on the other hand, who

[1] Gal. vi. 7 sq.   [2] Rom. vi. 23.   [3] i. 12.

act from the simple impulses of goodness, and shrink from the ostentation of righteousness, will receive from their Father that on which their heart is set, a fuller inpouring of the Spirit of God. Elsewhere, however, he alludes clearly to the judgments of a future time. Accepting to a certain extent the Messianic ideas of the Jews, he anticipates a great crisis in human affairs, when the present probationary age of mingled good and ill will be consummated, and a final separation take place between the righteous and the wicked.[1] How much of this expressed his deliberate thought, how much was only popular and figurative, intended to reach the conscience through the accepted language of the time, it is difficult to say; but I think we may feel assured that the spiritual truth was uppermost in his mind, and that the drapery of Messianic expectation, even if regarded as answering to reality, occupied only a secondary place. For he abstains from following the Jewish imagery in its detail, and contents himself with large and bold outlines in his description of the future state of mankind. The righteous shall go into "life eternal,"[2] and "shall

---

[1] Matt. xiii. 40 sq., 49, xxv. 32 sq.
[2] Matt. xxv. 46.

shine forth as the sun in the kingdom of their Father."[1] The punishment of the wicked is described in language which is purely figurative, and partly borrowed from the old prophetic imagery. Now they shall be cast into "the outer darkness," and again into "the furnace of fire," where shall be "weeping and gnashing of teeth;"[2] or, yet again, they shall "go off into the valley of Hinnom, into the unquenchable fire, where their worm dieth not, and the fire is not quenched."[3] Strong images these of suffering and despair; but still images with a spiritual meaning, placing before us the loathsomeness and the fell consequences of sin. The experience of history and the growing spirituality of thought have dispelled the earthly splendours and gloom of the Messianic dream, and we no longer look for a gathering of all the nations before the judgment-seat of the Son of Man. But the divine ideal of humanity, presented in living form before the eyes of men, is for ever passing a silent judgment—a judgment far other than that which is conventionally exercised by priests and churches; and behold! there are last who shall be first, and first who shall be last,

[1] Matt. xiii. 43.   [2] Matt. xxv. 30, xiii. 42.
[3] Mark ix. 43 sqq.   Cf. Matt. v. 29 sq., xviii. 8 sq.

T

when this judgment is ratified by the verdict that awaits us all beyond the grave.

The question has been keenly debated whether the judgments of eternity pronounce an unalterable doom. It has undoubtedly been the prevalent Christian doctrine that this life affords the only period of probation, that after death the separation between the righteous and the wicked will be everlasting, and that the latter will be consigned to a hideous and hopeless torment. Some professing Christians gloat over the horrors of hell, which they always reserve for their neighbours; but some, of greater humanity and modesty, have been driven to distraction by the appalling conception. Did Christ proclaim this doctrine of almost universal damnation, and call it a "Gospel," good tidings of great joy? It is impossible in our limits to discuss a subject on which volumes have been written. I can only state my own belief that Christ, the preacher of good-will, the herald of a Father who cared even for a sparrow's fall, can never have intended to teach a doctrine which could justify the malignant ferocity of the Inquisition, and make the universe seem like a desert of woe, of which the burning horrors were only rendered more appalling by the contrast of a little oasis of selfish bliss. Such a doctrine would run counter to the whole tenor of his most authentic teaching, and ought not to be thrust upon him without the most conclusive evidence. But, in fact, his allusions to the punishments of another world are few, and are largely expressed in figurative and borrowed language; and there is a complete absence of those revolting and detailed descriptions which fill the mind with terror, and tend to drive the spirit of a son back into the spirit of a slave. It may well be doubted whether the notion of everlastingness, as we so clearly conceive it, was present in the mind at all. The distinction between righteousness and wickedness, and the different nature of their consequences, were seen to be profound and unalterable. A great crisis was expected when men would take their places according to their own chosen path, and receive according to what they had done in the body, whether it were good or evil; and there on the threshold of the eternal world the curtain falls. The rewards and punishments, as distinguished from the imperfect and seemingly capricious judgments of the present, belong to the eternal realm, where every disguise is stripped off, and every sentence is according to truth; but no attempt is made to penetrate the mysteries of the far future, or to draw aside the veil from the all-embracing counsels of the Divine Wisdom. We must allude, however, to one remarkable passage which is opposed to the unlimited nature of punishment, and lays down the principle that punishment will be proportioned to guilt: "That slave who knew the will of his Lord, and did not prepare, or do according to his will, shall be beaten with many stripes; but he that knew not, and did things worthy of stripes, shall be beaten with few stripes."[1] These great principles, then, remain: that righteousness receives its own reward of ever-growing life; that sin entails inevitable suffering; that punishment varies with guilt; and that God is love: and with these we may be content to prepare for the great revealing when our mortal eyes are closed in death, and we may trustfully commit even the erring and sinful to the care of that Father who may be forgotten, but who cannot forget or cease to love.

One other point of great importance is involved in what has already been said; but it must receive a moment's separate attention. The future judgment is

[1] Luke xii. 47 sq.

invariably represented as based upon moral distinctions; and the later barbarity of condemning men for supposed intellectual errors is one of the strangest examples which history affords of the departure of professed disciples from the teaching of their Master. In the grand vision of the judgment of all nations, the men who are accepted are those who ministered lovingly to the wants of the needy; those who are condemned are the men who selfishly neglected the duties of benevolence.[1] The slave who is cast into outer darkness is the one who failed to make a diligent use of his talent;[2] and another slave who called down his lord's displeasure was a drunken tyrant.[3] It is those who work iniquity that Christ declares that he will reject, however they may have called him Lord, Lord, and professed to prophesy and work miracles in his name.[4] Even when he speaks (according to the words ascribed to him) of confessing or denying himself before men, he is clearly assuming the presence of belief in him; and what he commends is the moral courage which dares to avow an unpopular faith, what he condemns is the moral

[1] Matt. xxv. 31 sqq.   [2] Matt. xxv. 14 sqq.
[3] Matt. xxiv. 48 sqq. ; Luke xii. 45 sq.
[4] Matt. vii. 21 sqq.

cowardice which conceals its convictions through fear of worldly consequences.[1] And so Christianity remained, a moral and spiritual movement, an organized brotherhood of holy living, till it was corrupted by philosophy and vain deceit, after the traditions of men, and not after Christ.

In following this outline of Christian ethics, we can hardly fail to have been struck with the identity of moral conception pervading the several writings of the New Testament. Our limits have not permitted us to treat this subject in detail; but sufficient has been said to suggest the predominance of one controlling mind, whose moral teaching reappears in spiritual unity amid great variety of expression. Critics have correctly laid stress on the diverse types of doctrine presented by different writers; but all the more remarkable is the extent of their agreement, all the stronger is the proof that the devious channels of thought flowed from a single fountain-head. Paul and James are probably the most remote from one another, and represent quite different orders of intellect. The latter is without the fiery energy, the speculative genius, the profound insight, of the former, and what

---

[1] Matt. x. 32 sq.; Luke xii. 8 sqq.

we may venture to call their ethical philosophy does not move upon the same lines. Nevertheless, both insist on that great commandment of love to one's neighbour which Christ selected as the groundwork of social morality; James is full of reminiscences of Christ's teaching; and Paul, who is sometimes said not to have known, or cared to know, anything of that teaching, reproduces it, in his own words indeed, but with an identity of principle, and a depth and clearness of intelligence, which are very surprising if he drew them altogether from his own imagination. The moral and spiritual force that came into the world in Christ, the grand conception of children of God, of men and women moving in loving obedience to the Father's will, and pouring forth his love upon the world, has remained through all the Christian centuries, the same luminous ideal amid changing modes of civilization, and in the darkest times of superstition and unbelief finding chosen souls to dwell in. And still it abides with us as the common life of all genuine disciples of Christ, caring nothing for the partition-walls which sects have built, withdrawing mournfully from the strife of factions, and at times choosing for its tabernacle the bosom of some sad protestor against the arrogant heathenism of professing Christians. But it has yet to come in all its conquering power, to subdue the brute empires, civil and spiritual, that have oppressed mankind with cruelty and war, and to establish the reign of a divine humanity. Meanwhile, amid the mist and confusion of ecclesiastical assumption, and wistful thought, and carping doubt, those who will may see light; for now, as ever, "abide faith, hope, love. and the greatest of these is love."

LECTURE VIII.
THE MOTIVE POWER OF CHRISTIANITY.

LECTURE VIII.

THE MOTIVE POWER OF CHRISTIANITY.

IN this our concluding Lecture we have to consider the motive power of Christianity. In the course of our inquiry we have seen that Christianity is not merely a moral law or a system of dogmatic truth, standing as an object of voluntary contemplation over against the conscience and the intellect of man, and throwing upon the human will the whole burden of obedience and reform. It is a religion of redemption, coming to seek and save the lost. It recognizes sin as the supreme evil, and proposes to cure it by regenerating human nature itself, and filling it with the life of God. How does it attempt to accomplish this vast purpose? In undertaking to describe some of the sources of its power, let us carefully distinguish the effect itself from our theory of the effect. It is possible to experience its inward energy, and have one's whole life changed and moulded by its influence, and yet interpret very imperfectly the force by which we have been swayed; and it may well be that it has many paths of approach to the human heart, and that no single experience can exhaust the wealth of its resources. The wind bloweth where it listeth, and we hear the sound of it, but know not whence it comes and whither it goes; so is every one that is born of the Spirit. We know its power; we know that, whereas we were blind, now we see, and that new aspirations, new dispositions, new aims, have captivated our minds; but the process may elude the grasp of our intellect, and we may be unable to tell the true story of that inward change. Still our intellect goes in search of knowledge, and would translate into terms of thought what has come to it in the form of spiritual impression; and thought, however inadequate, helps to retain and keep alive an impression which, if it touched only our emotions, might become evanescent. Bearing this limitation in mind, and remembering also the necessary brevity of a lecture, we may speak of some of the sources of regenerating power in Christianity.

First, then, it cannot be denied that ideas themselves, when embraced with hearty faith, possess a life-giving efficacy, and he who discovers or enforces some great spiritual truth, and makes it a reality within the minds of men, stands in the front rank of the world's benefactors. People sometimes, in their anxiety to do honour to Christ, speak as though it would reduce him to the level of mean and common men to regard him simply as a teacher, though that was his characteristic title when he was on earth. But if he was a solitary explorer in the realms of spirit, as Newton was in the realms of nature, and gathered up into a few grand announcements the partial truths of his predecessors, and if these announcements lived on, and became the bread of life to millions of souls, this alone would suffice to place him on a supreme eminence, and entitle him to the grateful veneration of mankind, even though the truth, when once proclaimed, assumed an independent energy, and took its place, like the law of gravitation, among the inalienable possessions of the world; and if it be said that this view would make him "a mere man," I must confess my inability to attach any precise, and still more any derogatory, meaning to that phrase, so undefined are the limits of human possibility, so akin is genius to divine creativeness, so intimately may the life of God blend with our humanity. In every man in whom the heavenly fire has been kindled, the two natures blend in the indissoluble harmony of a single person; and if the will were entirely surrendered, and never jarred against the will of God, the Divine Spirit would be continually manifested in the midst of human limitations, some divine thought would be expressed through the perennial activity of a human life. "A mere man," therefore, if we understand the phrase, not in some vulgar and irreverent fashion, but in the sense of pure and absolute man,—man, according to the Divine ideal of him,—is a being of unfathomable greatness, who, instead of dragging down our minds to what is earthly and common, lifts them to the Father from whom he has been born, and whose eternal life he manifests, even as the dewdrop may exhibit in its tiny sphere the splendour of the sun.

That Jesus himself attached the greatest importance to teaching, and to the truth which he uttered, is apparent not only from occasional sayings, but from the whole course of his public ministry, of which teaching was the principal part. The Sower was the sower of "the word," and it was the word that sprang up, and bore fruit according to the nature of the soil in which it was planted. It was those who listened to his words, and practised them, that were like a wise man who built his house upon a rock. The blessed are "those who hear the word of God and keep it." According to the report of the fourth Evangelist, Christ came into the world in order to bear witness to the truth.[1] The earliest disciples, although, as we shall see, they were swayed by another force, were not indifferent to this. Christianity is repeatedly referred to as "the word of God" or "of the Lord," "the word of the Gospel," "of salvation," "of reconciliation," or simply as "the word." Paul declares that Christ was "a minister on behalf of the truth of God."[2] He himself was most anxious to maintain "the truth of the Gospel."[3] It is said that the word of God's grace is able to build men up, and give them an inheritance among all those that are sanctified.[4] James declares that God has begotten us "by the word of truth," and that this word is able to save

[1] John xviii. 37.   [2] Rom. xv. 8.   [3] Gal. ii. 5, 14.
[4] In Paul's speech at Miletus, as recorded in Acts xx. 32.

the soul;[1] and Peter says we have been regenerated "through the word of God."[2]

It is apparent, then, that the truths or ideas which Christ impressed upon the world were felt to have in themselves a power of renewal and elevation, and to be capable of producing great individual and social changes. And how could it be otherwise when, in the name of God, Christianity placed itself in direct antagonism to the Jewish and heathen worlds amid which it took its rise? It is easy to collect an anthology of wise sayings, which will bear some superficial resemblance to Christianity; and the Christians themselves were not slow to recognize the inspiration of the Prophets of Israel, and the voice of eternal Reason in the finest utterances of the "divine Plato" and other philosophers of Greece. But that the faith contained something startlingly novel and revolutionary is evinced by the almost universal hatred with which it was regarded. And, indeed, it drove its ploughshare through the Jewish vineyard, and laid its axe to the old tree of heathen superstition. To step forth from the ancient enclosure, and feel that Jew and Gentile alike were members of the great

---

[1] James i. 18, 21.   [2] 1 Peter i. 23.

family of God; to renounce the sanguinary and exclusive worship of the temple in Jerusalem, and offer up spiritual sacrifices to the Father of all in the temple of the universe; to lay aside the venerable Law, which had been the hedge of monotheism and morality against the assaults of idolatry and sin, and to substitute for it a spirit within the heart, which might seem to the outsider an excuse for every kind of subjective caprice, though to the believer it expressed the immutable mind of God,—this was indeed a momentous change, and the idea of Divine sonship which brought it about was quick and powerful, alike from its newness and its grandeur. Still more thrilling must the truth have been to the heathen, when, from polytheism and idolatry, from degrading rites and low conceptions of morality, he came to believe in one holy God, the Father who had sought him with forgiving love, and claimed him as his child; and had nothing more been involved than beholding what manner of love the Father had bestowed upon him, that he should be a child of God, this faith alone would have enabled him to overcome the world, and to purify himself from its evil.

The intellectual side of Christianity, therefore, must

not be forgotten or undervalued. False views, which are the offspring of a perverted spiritual apprehension, tend to deteriorate the life; truth which has been discerned by a pure spiritual vision helps to restore and elevate it. So far it is a matter of no consequence by whom the truth was discovered, where or how it was first proclaimed; and if the origin of Christianity were buried in complete oblivion, the truth which was taught by Christ would remain unimpaired, just as the arts and sciences live on, though their beginnings are lost in the darkness of a pre-historic age, and only the greatest names have survived the ravages of time. We are indeed glad to remember and honour the names of great discoverers; but knowledge of the men in no way alters the effect of their discoveries. So, it may be said, we might have an historical interest in the Founder of Christianity; but if we had never heard of him, the truth which he announced would remain, and our religion would be uninjured. I am far from wishing to deny that there is a large element of truth in this view; and it is useful to remember it at a time when so many are shaken in their old faith by the uncertain results of historical and literary criticism. If it could be shown that we knew nothing of the origin of Christianity, that we did not know the authorship of a single book of the New Testament, still there would remain a noble moral system and grand spiritual ideals, which we might take to our hearts, and use as the nutriment of noble lives; or, as it is sometimes put, Christianity is the religion of Jesus, and we might have this religion though we were ignorant of Jesus himself.

I would speak with all respect of this view, and not call in question for a moment the genuine Christianity of those who hold it; for we all have imperfect experiences and imperfect thoughts, and the defect is now on this side and now on that. Nevertheless, I am sure that the great mass of believers would feel that it gave a very inadequate account, I do not say of ecclesiastical dogmas, which have been handed down for centuries, and do not always correspond to the present state of living conviction, but of what passed in their own souls when Christianity first took possession of them, and gave shape and colour to their lives, or of what has remained with them as its unrivalled and unique power. To them a Christianity without Christ would be something fundamentally different from that by which they have lived. He is bound up in their religious affections, and his is the quickening breath which turns into living creatures the cold forms of truth. He is more to them than all his teaching; his love has taken captive their hearts, and led them to the throne of God, and constrained them to all that is not unworthy and selfish in their conduct. Nor have they seen in him only Man ascending to the pinnacle of human goodness, but the grace and love of God coming down to reconcile and save an estranged and sorrowful world.

This experience is the spiritual root of the doctrine of Christ's person which slowly grew up and took shape under the influence of controversies which extended through several centuries. We enter here on the ground of polemical theology; and numerous questions start into view which it is impossible for me to discuss. It is commonly assumed that the ecclesiastical dogma, as it is found in the so-called Athanasian Creed, existed from the first, and that the very foundations of Christianity are the doctrines of the Trinity and of the Deity of Christ. This appears to me quite contrary to the historical evidence, and to the plain statements of the earliest documents. Generations had passed away before the very terms which were needed to express these doctrines were invented or adopted; and theology was wrought into clear and precise forms of thought and language only through the application of Greek metaphysics to interpret the deliverances of religious experience. But that, quite independently of erroneous Messianic ideas inherited from Jewish teaching, the disciples looked upon Jesus as much more than a sage, who happened to arise in Palestine, and had some good and useful things to communicate to the world, appears indisputable. "No man cometh unto the Father but by me;" "He that hath seen me hath seen the Father"—these words give utterance to a profound experience in the hearts of disciples; and, whatever view may be taken of the Gospel in which they are found, they seem fairly to express the general sentiment. They do not, however, lay down any doctrine of Christ's ontological rank, or the mode of his relation to the Father. They furnish rather the spiritual material out of which doctrines are fabricated; and it is quite possible that to one who held the later dogma, and boasted of his orthodoxy, they might be blank of meaning, while to another who did not care to push his imperfect reasoning into these transcendent realms, or to assert what he could not prove, they might be fraught with power and blessing. Nevertheless, in the highest order of mind, spirit and thought work harmoniously together; and the intellect, starting from the philosophy and vocabulary of the age, produces a system which serves, at least for the time being, to incorporate and explain the hidden life of the soul. Thus there inevitably arose, at an early period in the Church's history, a doctrine of Christ's person which placed him outside of all known categories of humanity, and sought to trace the source of that divine impression which he made upon the responsive heart, even while it insisted on the reality of his human nature, and made him the first in a new category of the sons of God. For this purpose the Greek doctrine of the Logos, falling in, as it did, with many expressions and descriptions in the Old Testament, appeared suitable; and it will not be without profit if I endeavour to illustrate the beginnings of Christian theology by sketching the salient features of a doctrine which has had such a remarkable development, and which contains truths that we cannot afford to lose.

The English student is placed at some disadvantage in this inquiry, not only in consequence of our complete departure from Greek modes of thinking, which makes it difficult to recover the exact point of view from which metaphysical questions were regarded, but owing to the want of any precise equivalent to the Greek term "Logos." The usual translation, "the Word," probably leaves most readers entirely in the dark as to its meaning, and they look upon it as a sort of proper name for the second Person in the Trinity. But in the ancient theology the term was never thus emptied of its proper signification; and indeed on this signification was based one of the most telling arguments of the orthodox writers. It was impossible to imagine a time when God was without thought, and therefore thought, although a product of the Divine Mind, must be eternal as God himself. This word "thought" is the best English representative of the Greek term; for it denotes, on the one hand, the faculty of reason, or the thought inwardly conceived in the mind, and, on the other hand, the thought as expressed outwardly through the vehicle of language. In the former sense, too, it has the same ambiguity as the Greek; for we may use it of reason in general, as when we speak of a man of thought, or of a single conception, as when we say, "That is a strange thought."

And, again, we use it in the plural as well as the singular, and a countless number of thoughts are comprehended in our one faculty of thought. It is equally common for us to detach the thought from the mind in which it originally resided, and speak of it as though it had an existence of its own. We may speak of a beautiful thought or a terrible thought without any reference to its authorship; and the term may even denote the permanent expression of the mind's work in the form of a book, as in the "Thoughts of Pascal," "Young's Night Thoughts." Even in this latter sense, therefore, thought is the best rendering; for the Greek term never denotes a single word, but only the verbal expression of a complete thought, whether that expression be a single proposition or an entire treatise. The division into two classes of signification thus indicated is natural enough; for language is the utterance of reason, and we generally reason within ourselves, and make our thoughts clear to our own consciousness, through the agency of an inward and silent language, so that the two ideas of thought and speech are indissolubly blended in our experience. The process of which we are conscious in ourselves was transferred at last to the universal Mind, and a distinction was drawn between the hidden thought of God which was with him from eternity, and belonged to the very essence of his being, and his uttered thought, which stepped forth, as it were, into time and space, and was revealed in nature or in man. Let us endeavour to trace the gradual evolution of a doctrine which, through a period of several centuries, engaged the keenest intellects of Greece and the profoundest religious meditation of the Hebrew people, and, prior to the use made of it by Christian writers, culminated in a strangely mingled structure of Eastern and Western ideas among the Jews of Alexandria.[1]

About five hundred years before the time of Christ, an inhabitant of Ephesus laid the first lines of a doctrine which has played so important a part in Christian theology, and which, according to tradition, the latest of the Evangelists incorporated in his Gospel in that very city. Heraclitus was known to the ancients as the dark or obscure philosopher, and to us he is even more obscure than to them, for only scattered frag-

[1] The following account is a mere sketch, though I hope it may prove suggestive. For a fuller treatment, I may refer to my work on Philo Judæus.

ments of his work survive; yet enough remains to disclose a profound and penetrating genius. At a time when science was in its infancy, and to the popular imagination capricious gods appeared to lurk in grove and stream, and to direct the affairs of earth and sky by a changeful and lawless fancy, he clearly perceived that the universe was one, and that all its multifarious changes were governed by a rational and unalterable law. To this law he gave the very name which is translated "Word" in our Gospel. To him, too, the Word or Thought was in the beginning. It was the eternal basis of the universe, pervading all its substance, and preserving in unity and order the perpetual drift and change which, with slower or faster movement, affects every object that we see. The unceasing flow and instability of phenomenal existence was described by the paradoxical saying that you could not enter the same river twice, for wave constantly succeeds to wave. Yet we call the river the same, though its waters are continually rushing past, and not a drop that reflected the sunset glow remains to welcome the dawn; and if we seek to interpret this usage, we must see that the sameness which is not to be found in the particles of liquid exists in the permanence of ideal relations. The river is determined by a thought, which is different from the thought of a mountain or a cloud, and without that thought would vanish with the material particles which for an instant compose it. So in the world at large there is an incessant play among its elements; yet the whole presents to the eye of reason a tissue of rational thought, which preserves even the sun from transgression, and maintains from age to age the same inviolable law.

Heraclitus and the Greek thinkers (chiefly of the Stoical school) who followed him did not pass beyond this rational principle, and ascribe it to an infinite Mind, of whom it was only a partial revelation, but looked upon the immanent Thought of the universe as itself God. How far God, thus conceived as the pervasive order and law of the universe within which he was confined, was regarded as personal, it is difficult to decide; for the notion of personality, however clear it seems to ourselves, was not sharply defined; and although language which is strictly applicable only to a person was naturally used of the universal Reason, I think it was viewed rather as the essence of personality to all who participated in it than as itself a person. It was only in finite beings that it became individualized, reason in any particular man being distinguished from the universal Reason by its incapacity for further division; and therefore we must presume that true personality emerged for the first time in finite and individual minds, for we cannot reconcile the capacity for endless division and distribution with that unity of consciousness which we ascribe to a person. In this philosophy, then, the world was regarded as a system of necessary and material, but nevertheless rational, evolution, an unfolding of the contents of universal Thought into their genera and species, that unbounded variety of thoughts or (to use the Platonic term) ideas which are embodied in the multifarious objects around us.

The Jew, when he began to visit the Museum at Alexandria, and strayed into the lovely gardens of Greek literature and philosophy, could not be satisfied with this materialistic pantheism. His conscience, nurtured by an ancestral faith, owned the reality of an infinite God, who was above and beyond the universe, who took up the isles as a very little thing, and had unfolded like a tent the starry magnificence of heaven. Nevertheless, a sort of spiritual necessity for the Greek views arose in his mind; for as his idea of the Divine transcendence became more exalted, God appeared to recede from the universe and man, and an empty gulf yawned between the Infinite and the finite. And yet the world did not appear less, but more divine—not the dead fabric of a distant God, but a tissue of living forces, an expression of the Eternal Mind. If it was inadequate, still all that the Greek had said of the universe was true. It was, indeed, pervaded from centre to circumference by Thought; it was the seat of inviolable law, and revealed a beautiful and well-ordered plan answering to the demands of reason in ourselves. Put these conceptions together, and it follows that the Reason manifest throughout the system of the world was not the ultimate Source of things, but the uttered Thought or Word of God. In accordance with the realism of the time, this Thought could be conceived only as an essence. As such, it was distinct indeed from God, inasmuch as Thought was less comprehensive than Being, and was made objective to God in the forms of the material world; and nevertheless it was so far identical with him that it belonged to the inmost recesses and eternal nature of the Divine Mind. Thus the chasm was bridged over which divided the Creator from the creation. It was through Thought becoming the Word that God passed from the loneliness and unity of his own infinite and unimaginable being into relations with the finite, and revealed himself in the profuse variety of created things. The sublime idea of an artist is bodied forth in the shape which he gives to the passive marble, and the soul of Phidias, though his cunning hand has mouldered in the dust of centuries, still looks upon us through the majestic forms which sprang from his creative genius. In some perfect cathedral, while we admire the multitudinous beauty of detail, and wonder at the amplitude of imaginative and constructive resource, we yet feel that every detail is subordinated to a single design, and that one all-controlling thought, the architect's word to mankind, is impressed on the entire fabric. So the creative power of God looks upon us through the solemn eyes of midnight, and in the vast temple of the world the impress of an all-uniting Thought images the mind of the Supreme. Or we may say that creation is a grand poem which gives definite shape to the Divine conception, and matter is the page on which the Creator has inscribed his everlasting Word.

But it was not only in the material world that

Divine Reason was manifest; it appeared consciously within the mind of man, and, according to the Stoical doctrine, was the universal light of the human race, to follow which, and so live "conformably to nature," was the highest wisdom. This doctrine also was accepted by the Jew. Vast as was the gulf which he placed between man and God, yet he did not regard the Divine Word as a soliloquy, or the song of the morning stars as chanted to a desolate and unintelligent space. When God spoke, he spoke to a responsive reason; and it was the share of the Divine Thought in man that interpreted that Thought in the universe. As a poet would vainly pour out his lyrics to an ape, so God would speak to us in vain if our being were wholly alien to his; and our power, whether of imaginative or of scientific interpretation of the world, proves that we no less than nature bear the impress of the Divine, and in rising to the apprehension of some universal law—it may be of gravitation or of the evolution of organic life—we think the thoughts of God, and so exercise a Divine faculty.

The essential features of this system of thought are discernible in those parts of the Old Testament which celebrate the praises of Wisdom, although they contain no evidence of borrowing from the Greeks. Wisdom appeared to the writers of these passages to be the mediating power between God and the universe, and between God and man; and this one word, descriptive as it was of the supreme attribute of God, summed up in itself the highest intellectual and moral excellence. But when the teaching of Moses was dressed in the phrases of Greek philosophy, and the sublime intuitions of the prophets were worked into a system of speculative thought, it was natural that the term Logos, which had been used by the Greek thinkers, should be preferred. "Wisdom" was more closely associated with conscious and responsible beings; and although we may say that it is apparent in the world as a whole, it is not so easily applied to separate and dissimilar objects, for "Wisdom" has no plural. But if we see the Thought of God in the world at large, we no less behold his separate thoughts in the various species of things, and the term readily adapts itself to the Platonic doctrine of ideas. Accordingly it plays the most prominent part in the writings of Philo, although "Wisdom" is still introduced upon suitable occasions.

To the Jews, however, the Thought or Word of

God had, in addition to the philosophical signification which was imported into it, a more special meaning suggested by the Scriptures. It was not only the cosmic thought which gave order to chaotic matter, or the common and ever-present light of reason; it was the particular command addressed to the conscience, the particular truth which in some moment of high inspiration was borne in upon the mind. Thus the Word had come to Moses and the Prophets, and they, as faithful witnesses, translated what they heard into human speech, and inscribed it in sacred writings. These writings acquired a traditional veneration, and, as the inspiration of Israel grew cold, were used no longer to stir the hidden fire of the soul, but to shape as with a mechanical rule the outward routine of life. To the Jews, therefore, the Word of God became more and more the mandate of their national Law, and by the stricter party was converted into dead tables of stone that lay with stiff oppression upon the heart. To themselves, however, this concentration of Divine wisdom in a book was like collecting the scattered beams of light into a focus; and the permanent fixing of revelation in Scripture is gratefully set forth by so sensible and religious a writer as the son of Sirach in a remarkable passage. Wisdom, he says, came forth from the mouth of the Most High. She covered the earth as a mist, and made her tabernacle in high places. She acquired a possession in all the earth, and in every people and nation. With all these she sought rest (apparently in vain). And then he who created her commanded her, and made her tabernacle to rest in Jacob. He settled her in the beloved city, and her authority was in Jerusalem. Then, after a figurative description of her excellence, the writer adds: "All these things are the book of the covenant of the Most High God, the Law which Moses commanded as an inheritance for the synagogues of Jacob."[1] Here there is a progressive limiting of the range of Wisdom. First it appears as a cosmic power. Then it comes to the human race, and visits every nation. Disappointed, it pitches its tent in Israel; in Israel it chooses Jerusalem for its seat, and finally it seems to be identified with the Law. The order of thought in this passage, and its leading ideas, are so closely parallel to those in the Proem of the Fourth Gospel that one cannot help conjecturing that the later writer, though using such different

[1] Ecclus. xxiv. 3—23.

language, and marching to such a different conclusion, was influenced by a reminiscence of the earlier; and indeed it is possible that his doctrine is set forth in conscious opposition to the older teaching.[1]

Be this as it may, the Evangelist wrote amid these surroundings of Hebrew and Greek thought. His Gospel, so far as I can judge, gives no evidence of his having been educated in Greek philosophy, the characteristic phraseology of the schools being entirely absent; and in spite of some general resemblances, it would be impossible to prove that he was acquainted with Philo's writings. The cast of his style and thought is entirely his own; and when he appropriates old ideas, he dresses them up in a new language, and sends them forth with a new pomp and power to conquer fresh realms, and to change and renovate the philosophy from which they are supposed

[1] There is little resemblance of language; but we may compare ἐν Ἰακὼβ κατασκήνωσον (Ecclus. xxiv. 8) with ἐσκήνωσεν ἐν ἡμῖν (John i. 14); also the allusions to the δόξα and to the νόμος. I cannot but notice also the contrast between Ecclus. xxiv. 21, οἱ ἐσθίοντές με ἔτι πεινάσουσι, καὶ οἱ πίνοντές με ἔτι διψήσουσιν, and John vi. 35, ὁ ἐρχόμενος πρός με οὐ μὴ πεινάσῃ· καὶ ὁ πιστεύων εἰς ἐμὲ οὐ μὴ διψήσῃ πώποτε, taken in connection with the language about eating Christ's flesh and drinking his blood.

to have been borrowed. It seems probable, then, that he had only an indirect knowledge of Greek ideas; but the philosophy of any period gradually permeates the whole of society, and affects the habits of thought even of those who have never read a philosophical work. In Ephesus it would have been impossible to reason continually on the verities of Christian faith as though philosophy had never been; and if Paul discoursed "in the school of one Tyrannus,"[1] John can hardly have failed to encounter some of the philosophical teachers, and may have been forced to consider the relation between his own doctrine and that of the more thoughtful portion of the Greek community. We may assume his familiarity with the sacred Scriptures of his own people; and thus both from Greeks and Jews he would hear of the Logos,— from the former, of Thought as the principle of reason in nature and in man; from the latter, of Thought enshrined as the Word of God in an inspired book. How were these related to one another, and to Christian truth?

As the Evangelist meditated on these things, he saw that the Word had become flesh. This was to him no

[1] Acts xix. 9.

idle and speculative dream, but a reality of experience; for the image of the Beloved had sunk into his heart, and changed his inmost being; and, as he gazed, the whole aspect of life, of truth, of duty, was transfigured. The Thought of God, his Thought or Word to mankind, had been graven in a human image, and had spoken in the pathetic and awful tones of a human life and death. But in proceeding to this further conception he did not deny any truth that had been already reached. For him, too, the creation bore the impress of Divine Thought, and without that Thought no single thing had been made. He does not dwell on this, for he is hastening to another theme; but how much is conveyed in the few words which he employs! Not only the mysterious pomp of heaven, marching with undeviating regularity from age to age, but each minutest flower, each insect that flitted its happy moment in the sunshine, was an expression of Divine power, and sprang into being in accordance with the laws of Eternal Reason. His spiritual ear caught a Divine melody as the waves of the Ægean broke at his feet, and heard amid the silence of the night the far-off music of the spheres; and when, leaving details, he saw all things united into one stupendous plan, he beheld, as in the speaking face of a statue, the cosmic Thought of the infinite Artist visibly portrayed. Yet this was not the Word of God which man most deeply craved. All was order and beauty without; but what of the disorder and vileness within? What of holiness and pity and love? How was their inner meaning to be revealed? How were God's tenderness and sympathy and forgivingness to be shed over the world, and made a living reality to the hearts of men? They could not be enshrined in mere material bulk; they could not gleam from the stony eyes of a mountain, or plead with us in the tempest's shriek. The heavens declare the *glory* of God, but to find his higher spiritual attributes you must see them in the expression of a holy face or the conduct of a devoted life. The Word made flesh, the Divine Thought for humanity making its tabernacle in the form of a Son of Man, satisfies our religious need as nature by itself can never do. In seeing nature we see the Creator, the unapproachable, many will say the unknowable, Cause; but in seeing Christ we see the Father, and "it sufficeth us," and our hearts are at rest.

Again, the Evangelist accepted the doctrine that

the Word of God, the utterance of the Eternal Reason, spoke directly to the soul. It was the light which gave light to every man. But how few in this dark world received and followed it! It needed special messengers from God to bear witness to it, and stir men's languid faith. This was the distinguishing duty of the Prophets of Israel, to cry aloud, "Thus saith the Lord," whether the people would hear or whether they would forbear. It was a long and noble band, worthily ended by John the Baptist, who, like his predecessors, gave his testimony to a higher revelation than he had received, and, having called on his countrymen to prepare for it by repentance, died a martyr's death. But the Word of God spoken by the Prophets was the particular message of the hour, and, when committed to writing, tended more and more, in accordance with the fundamental conception of Judaism, to become a rigid law, which might indeed prescribe duties and prohibit crimes, but could never reveal the inward nature of holiness. Law was the highest religious term among the Jews; God was the great Legislator; his word was a commandment; and human life was hedged round with restrictions which destroyed the free movement of the spirit. Hence the antithesis: "The Law was given through Moses; grace and truth came through Jesus Christ." For the Christian the Word of God had ceased to be an ancient law, and had become flesh. The Divine thought for humanity had ceased to be inscribed on parchment deeds, to be interpreted only by the skill and lore of the Rabbi, and had been wrought into the personality of a living, breathing man. "The life was the light of men." The holy and gracious spirit of sonship, which spoke and worked in Christ, passes into the heart, and becomes there an eternal life, which needs no witness but itself. "We know that he abideth in us by the spirit which he hath given us."

And now let us endeavour to see, if only with a hasty glance, some of the bearings of this doctrine. It indicates the method of Christian revelation, and sheds a light upon the nature both of God and man. The Word made flesh discloses to us, not some particular truth or requirement, but the very spirit and character of God, so far as we are able to apprehend it; for the Divine Thought is God himself passing into self-manifestation, just as our speech is our own personality entering into communication with others. When, therefore, the Christian, in his anxiety to know more of God, turns wistfully to his Master, he thinks not so much of what Christ has told as of what he has shown. This is the message which Christ has delivered to the world, that "God is love." But then, what is love? How can we know it, and enter into the depth and richness of its meaning, unless we see it, and feel its warmth upon our hearts, and are taken home, forgiven and reconciled, to its bosom? Had Christ merely spoken about it as a theologian's dream, while its power was absent from his life, we should have been little the wiser; but in the fulness of his communion with God he lived it, and proved its reality through uttermost self-sacrifice. It is thus that he has become the beloved Saviour and Comforter of souls which are conscious of sin, because this supreme Word of God to man has become flesh in him, and been manifested in the joys and sorrows, the struggles, the suffering, and the triumph of a human life.

Bnt if in this human image is portrayed the Divine Thought which returns into the bosom of the Father and declares his paternal love towards men, no less was Christ a tabernacle for God's Thought of what mankind, morally and religiously, should be. As a great artist fixes his ideal upon the canvas, and introduces through the eyes to responsive and interpreting minds an exalted beauty and a depth of spiritual expression that no description could ever convey through the ears, so God has set before us in Christ a spirit of life, revealing to us, in the unity of its manifold perfection, that Divine ideal of righteousness of which the most elaborate law can be nothing more than a description. In this way Christ is an end of the Law, for, having seen the Divine Word in him, we pass behind the word of the statute-book, and hold immediate communion with eternal righteousness; and God no longer imposes on us a commandment the letter of which we must obey, but sends into our hearts the spirit of his Son, and invites us to live out of the resources of that spirit. If we seek for a name for this spirit, it is the same as we have already found in the higher sphere. If love is the essential life of the Father, it ought to be the essential life of the children; and this is the Word which has not only been made flesh in Christ, but, though it is still waiting for an ampler realization, has been wrought through him into the fabric of human society. There is a legend that the Apostle John, when he had become too old and feeble to deliver a protracted discourse, used to come, supported by some of his disciples, into the congregation, and repeat the words, "My children, love one another." This was the sum and substance of his Gospel, and the glory of this Divine ideal of man he had seen in his Master and friend. In this supreme term there is an infinite wealth of meaning, and we may, with our busy and restless intellect, resolve it into beauteous dispositions, and apply it to the various ramifications of political, social, and domestic life; but when we wish to feel its central power, and to renew its sway over our own hearts, we kneel beside the Cross, and gaze into a beloved face where it is conquering the pains of death.

It is now apparent why the doctrine which I have attempted to unfold is the charter of our spiritual freedom. For the Jews the Word of God had become locked up in ancient documents and legal tradition. They searched the Scriptures, because they thought that they had eternal life in them; and in their devotion to the letter they missed the higher testimony of the Scriptures themselves, and would not come to the greatest of Israel's teachers that they might have life. But to those (they are still too few) to whose faith the Word has been made flesh, the chill rigidity of dogma and precept breaks into the warm movements of a living spirit. Unfettered by superstitious fears, they welcome the advance of knowledge, feeling assured that no science can ever turn to ugliness the divine beauty of holiness and love, or disprove what the Spirit says to the surrendered and faithful soul. The fragmentary records of Christ's life have little to satisfy an idle curiosity, and their artless and popular style and varying accounts invite the criticism of the learned; but all the more brightly do they reveal what we want to know, the character of a soul, and we receive from their perusal a distinct impression of a wonderful and exalted personality, which becomes ever after the haunting ideal of our lives. But this ideal can display itself through an endless variety of forms both of intellect and action, and instead of restraining any of our natural gifts, it pervades them all as with a breath of holy energy, and consecrates them to unselfish ends. Here, then, we rest: not primarily in the Church, nor in the letter of Scripture, but in the lowly Son of Man have we seen the Word of God, full of grace and truth; and hiding this Divine Thought in our hearts, we would make it the secret force of our activity, and, whatever may be our pursuits, rise into fellowship with Christ in the reverent worship of God and the loving service of mankind.

In conclusion, a word or two must be said about one other source of power in Christianity. The life which was "manifested" has lived on in the hearts of disciples; and in spite of all the unfaithfulness and blindness of the churches, it is a reality among us to-day, the most quickening and energetic of all the forces of civilization. Into the brotherhood of seeking and consecrated souls a man may enter, and find the strength of holy association, and the uplifting power of heavenward thought and purpose. It is easy to say that we can worship alone, and live the godly life out of our own solitary impulse. Undoubtedly this is possible, as it is possible to live among savages without losing the gentle and courteous ways of a civilized man. But to few is this strength given; and in cutting themselves off from religious communion with their fellows, men not only kill a natural yearning of the Christian heart, but separate themselves from a source of inward life and power. When the churches realize more fully their appointed end, to enshrine and perpetuate the life of Divine Sonship among men, and that

Spirit of which in these Lectures I have endeavoured to give some faint description is the animating principle of all their work, the nations will come to their light, the sinful and the doubting will find refuge in the revealing and life-giving energy of their love, and at last the Kingdom of God will be established upon earth.

INDICES.

INDICES.

I.
SUBJECTS.
SEE ALSO THE TABLE OF CONTENTS.

Alexandria, 297, 300.
Allegorical interpretation, 75, 76.
Almsgiving, 253 sq.
Anger, 212, 251.
Anxiety, 229, 235.
Asceticism, 262-265.
Assumption of Moses, 128.
Athanasian Creed, 292.
Athenagoras, 43.
Augustine, 101, 148, 204.
Authority, of the Bible, 119 sq.; in Christendom, 37 sq.; of competent students, 89; external and internal, 54, 58-59, 63, 71, 75; limits of, 96.

Baptism, 31.
Bartholomew, Massacre of St., 27.
Beatitudes, 136.
Bible, Doctrine of Church of England respecting, 45, 82 sq.; doctrine of Council of Trent, and of Westminster Confession, 45; historical claim of, 97; infallibility of, assumed, 44 sq., 81-83; influence of, in the early Church, 41-44; Jewish view of inspiration of, 47; modern view of, 45-47, 81 sqq.; modification in doctrine of infallibility of, 109.
Body, Christian view of the, 265.
Bruce, Professor A. B., 17.

Canon of Scripture in existence before the Christian Church, 41-44.
Carlyle, 101.
Christ: *see* Jesus Christ.
Christianity, Comparative failure of, 226 sq.; essence of, 10-12, 27; a missionary religion, 20-22; relation of, to its Founder, 12 sq.
Church, called "the Church of God," 23; organization of, 18 sq., 23, 28 sq.; origin of, 15-22; visible and invisible, 25.
Clement of Alexandria, 43.
Codex Bezæ, Interpolation in, 50.
Comparative Religion, 94.

Y

I. SUBJECTS.

Conceit, 237.
Consciousness, Christian, 104 sq.
Conversion, 161.
Copernicus, 86.
Council, General, 34; of Trent, decree of, about canonical Scriptures, 45.
Criticism, 84, 88 sqq., 94.
Cyprian, 11.

Development, Theological, 13-15, 33-35, 203-206.
Divorce, 60 sq., 65, 257.
Doctrine, Changes in, not destructive of Christianity, 9; not the essence of Christianity, 4, 26; formation of, 105-110; growth of, legitimate, 13-15, 33-35.
Drummond, James, The Jewish Messiah, 130; Philo Judæus, 297.

Emerson, 101.
Eschatological passages in the Gospels, 126, 132 sq., 163, 272-278.

Faith in Christ, 232 sq.
Fall, The, 86.
Fasting, 264.
Forbearance, 252.
Forgiving, a condition of being forgiven, 198, 241.

Galilee, 86.
Gardner, Professor Percy, 32.

Gentiles, Admission of, without the Law, 14, 201 sq.
Gore, Rev. Charles, 84, 93.

Hatch, Dr., 4, 18.
Hatred, 212.
Hegesippus, 263.
Heraclitus, 297-300.
Honesty, 251.
Hypocrisy, 236.

Imitatio Christi, 101.
Immortality, 270.
Inquisition, 27, 274.
Inspiration, 86, 89 sq., 93.

Jesus Christ, Consciousness of, that he revealed the Father, 185-187; not a critic, 47 sq.; ethical character of teaching of, 209; a Revealer, 184; spirit of, disclosed in the New Testament, 110 sq.; teaching of, not an exposition of Scripture, 49; want of system in the teaching of, 225 sq.
John the Baptist, 124, 142 sq., 157, 158, 263, 264, 311.
Judgment, Final, 152, 272 sq.; based on moral distinctions, 277.
Justin Martyr, 9, 43, 151.

Kingdom of God not identified with the Church, 17.

Law, Independence of, 14, 202, 215 sq., 232, 314; in what sense permanent, 66-69, 198 sq.

I. SUBJECTS. 323

Lightfoot, John, 129.
Lightfoot, J. B., 27.
Lock, Rev. W., 117.
Lord's Supper, 31 sq.
Lowe, Rev. W. H., 16, 53.

Man, Antiquity of, 86.
Marcion, 115 sq.
Martyrs, 21 sq., 37.
Messianic idea, in Christianity, 113-115, 126, 163, 165, 272, 293; among the Jews, 128-130, 131 sq.
Millennium, Belief in, 9.
Ministry, The Christian, 35-38, 255 sq.
Miracle and law, 87.
Missionary activity, 20-22, 254 sq.
Monogamy, 258.
Moore, Rev. Aubrey, 96.

Neander, 11.
New Testament, Unity in diversity in the teaching of, 111, 278 sq.
Nicene Creed, 123.

Oaths, 65, 266.

Parker, Theodore, 11.
Personality in Greek philosophy, 299 sq.
Philo, 171 sq., 304, 307.
Pilgrim's Progress, 101.
Poverty, 136.
Prayer, 195-197, 230, 239-243.

Prophets, Christ's use of the, 51-54; false, 262.
Psalms of Solomon, 128.
Ptolemaic System, 86.
Punishment, 270, 273; duration of future, 274-276.

Repentance, 197 sq., 218.
Responsibility, 198-201, 220 sq., 270.
Retaliation, 65.
Revenge, 212.
Riches, 138 sq., 253, 266-269.

Sabbath, Christ's view of the, 57-60, 260.
Sacerdotalism, 27 sq.
Sacraments, 31-33.
Sanday, Professor, 93, 95 sq., 117.
Sayce, Professor, 92.
Schürer, Professor, 130.
Science, in the Bible, 85-87; and Religion differently related to those who promulgated them, 11-13, 290-292.
Second coming of Christ, 9, 125.
Sibylline Oracles, 128.
Sin, original and actual, Doctrine of, 216-218.
Son of Man, Coming of the, 163 sq., 235, 280.
Spaniards in the Netherlands, 27.
Spirit, Holy, Communion of the, 19 sq.; how distinguished from the human and personal spirit, 182 sq.

Stoics, 28, 299, 303.

Tatian, 43.
Theophilus of Antioch, 43.
Trinity, Doctrine of the, 191 sq., 203-206, 292 sq., 295.
Truthfulness, 251, 266.
Tyler, T., 92.

Wealth, *see* Riches.

Westcott and Hort, 32.
Westminster Confession of Faith on the infallibility of Scripture, 45.
Wetstein, 145.
Wisdom in the Old Testament, 303 sq.; in Ecclesiasticus, 306 sq.
Works, Good, required, 221-223.
Worship, Public, 30, 241.

II.
PASSAGES OF THE BIBLE REFERRED TO.

Exodus.		Psalms.		Joel.	
iv. 22 sq.	173	xlii. 1	99	ii. 32	150
		xlix. 13	53		
Leviticus.		lxviii. 5	174	Malachi.	
xi.	64	lxxxiv. 12	100	i. 6	174
xxvii. 30	55	lxxxix. 26 sqq.	174	ii. 10	175
		ciii. 13	100	iv. 5	54
Deuteronomy.		cxxxvii. 9	93		
xiv. 1 sq.	173			Ecclesiasticus.	
xxiv. 1 sqq.	65	Isaiah.		xxiv. 3—23	306
xxxii. 5 sq.	173	i. 2	174	8	307
9	173	xl. 1	100	21	307
18 sq.	173	lxiii. 16	174	23	47
		lxiv. 8	174		
2 Samuel.				Wisdom of Solomon.	
vii. 14 sq.	173	Jeremiah.		ii. 16—18	175
		ii. 27	174	x. 10	129
1 Chronicles.		iii. 4	174	Matthew.	
xvii. 13	173	xxxi. 9	174	iv. 10	229
xxii. 10	173	20	174	17	124, 162
				23	124
Psalms.		Hosea.		v. 3	136, 237
xxv. 6	100	i. 10	174	7	112
xxvii. 1	99	vi. 6	59	8	99, 181, 262
xxxi. 5	99	xi. 1	174	9	178, 252

II. PASSAGES OF THE BIBLE REFERRED TO.

MATTHEW.		MATTHEW.		MATTHEW.	
v. 10	. . . 136	vii. 15 sqq.	. . 262	xiii. 3 sqq.	. . 18
14 sqq.	. . . 225	16 sqq.	. . 213	20 sq.	. . . 222
17 sq.	. . 66, 67	21	. . 7, 112	24 sqq.	. . 153
19	. . . 67	21 sqq.	149, 222	31 sq.	. . . 165
21 sqq.	. 64, 251	24 sqq.	. . 230	33	. . . 165
22	. . . 112	viii. 4	. . . 50	37 sqq.	. . 153
27 sqq.	. . . 262	10	. . . 231	38	. . . 147
29 sq.	224, 273	11 sq.	. . . 162	40 sq.	. . . 272
31 sq.	. . . 257	13	. . . 231	41	. . . 163
33 sqq.	. . . 265	20	. . . 159	42	. . . 273
38 sqq.	. . . 250	ix. 13	. . . 59	43	. . . 273
44 sq.	. 69, 179	14 sqq.	. . . 264	44	. . . 158
45	. . . 188	16 sq.	. . . 49	45	. . . 261
vi. 1 sqq.	194, 224,	22	. . . 231	45 sq.	. . . 159
	236, 253	29	. . . 231	49	. . . 272
5 sq.	. . . 30	35	. . . 124	52	. . . 48
6	. . . 240	x. 7	. 124, 162	xiv. 23	. . . 240
6 sqq.	. . 195	23	. . . 163	xv. 1 sqq.	63, 214
7 sq.	. . . 240	26	. . . 230	10 sqq.	. 32
14 sq.	198, 252	28 sqq.	. . . 194	28	. . . 231
16 sqq.	. . 264	29	. . . 260	xvi. 5 sqq.	. 50
17 sq.	. . . 30	32 sq.	160, 278	6 sqq.	. 236
19 sqq.	. . 268	37 sqq.	. . 224	14	. . . 142
22 sqq.	. . 229	xi. 11	. . . 142	18	. . . 16
24	. . . 190	12	. . . 141	24 sqq.	. 224
25 sqq.	188, 230	14	. . . 54	27 sq.	. . 163
26	. . . 260	16 sqq.	. . 158	xvii. 11 sqq.	. . 54
28 sqq.	. . 260	18 sq.	. . . 263	17	. . . 231
33	. . . 135	25	. 181, 240	20	. . . 231
42	. . . 254	25 sq.	. . . 192	xviii. 1 sqq.	. . 137
vii. 1 sqq.	. 252	xii. 1 sqq.	. . 58	3	. 161, 218
2	. . . 198	9 sqq.	. . 60	4	. . 237
7	. . . 240	11 sq.	. . 260	6 sq.	. 252
7 sqq.	. 187	24 sqq.	. . 262	8 sq.	224, 273
12	. . 56, 69,	28	. . . 134	12 sqq.	. . 187
	227, 250	33 sqq.	. . 213	13	. . 198
13 sq.	. . . 223	50	. . 7, 150	15 sqq.	. 252

II. PASSAGES OF THE BIBLE REFERRED TO.

MATTHEW.		MATTHEW.		MARK.	
xviii. 17 . .	16	xxiv. . . .	132	26 sqq. . .	165
21 sqq. .	252	30 . .	163	31 sq. . .	165
35 . .	198	37 sqq. .	163	36 sqq. . .	230
xix. 3 sqq.	61, 257	42 sqq. .	234	v. 34	231
13 sqq. .	138	45 . .	234	vi. 46	240
16 sqq.	57, 157, 223	48 sqq. .	277	vii. 1 sqq.	63, 214
		xxv. 1 sqq.	147, 234	15 . . .	32
18 . . .	251	13 .	162, 163	19 . . .	32
23 sq.	138, 268	14 sqq.	147, 200, 234, 277	21 sqq. .	216
26 . . .	193			29 . . .	231
28 . . .	163	30 . . .	273	viii. 14 sqq. .	50
xx. 1 sqq.	147, 196	31 . . .	163	15 sq. .	236
20 sqq. .	163	31 sqq.	152, 277	28 . . .	142
25 sqq. .	237	32 sq. .	272	34 sqq. .	224
28 . . .	224	34 sqq. .	250	38 .	160, 163
29 sqq. .	231	46 . . .	272	ix. 11 sqq. . .	54
xxi. 13 . . .	61	xxvi. 24 . .	52	23 . . .	231
15 sq. .	51	29 . .	163	33 sqq. . .	137
21 sq. .	231	31 . .	52	35 . . .	237
31 . . .	158	39 . .	192	42 . . .	252
33 sqq. .	200	54 . .	53	43 sqq.	224, 273
42 . . .	51	55 sq. .	52	50 . . .	252
43 . . .	144	64 . .	163	x. 2 sqq. .	61, 257
xxii. 2 sqq. .	147			13 sqq. . .	138
31 sq. .	61	MARK.		17 sqq. .	57, 157, 223
35 sqq.	56, 227	i. 14 sq. . .	162		
43 . .	48	15	124	19 . . .	251
xxiii. . . .	214	35	240	23 sqq.	138, 268
1-3 .	49	44	50	27 . . .	193
8 sqq. .	28	ii. 18 sqq. . .	264	35 sqq. . .	163
11 . .	237	21 sq. . .	49	42 sqq. . .	237
12 . .	237	23 sqq. . .	58	45 . . .	224
13	140, 240	iii. 1 sqq. .	60	52 . . .	231
16 . .	50	22 sqq.	134, 262	xi. 17 . . .	61
23 sq. .	55	35 . . .	150	22 sqq. . .	231
25 sqq. .	218	iv. 16 sq. . .	222	xii. 1 sqq. .	200
29 sqq. .	262	24 . . .	198	10 sq. . .	51

II. PASSAGES OF THE BIBLE REFERRED TO.

Mark.		Luke.		Luke.	
xii. 26 sq.	61	vii. 33 sq.	263	xii. 4 sqq.	194
28 sqq.	56, 144 sq., 190, 227	40 sqq.	197	6	260
		50	231	8	163
36	48	viii. 1	124	8 sq.	160, 278
40	240	13	222	10 sqq.	60
41 sqq.	215	21	150	13 sqq.	268
xiii.	132	23 sqq.	230	22 sqq.	188, 230
26	163	48	231	24	260
35	234	ix. 18	240	27 sq.	260
xiv. 21	52	19	142	31	135
25	163	23 sqq.	224	32	230
27	52	26	160, 163	33	253
49	52	28	240	33 sq.	268
62	163	41	231	36 sqq.	234
		46 sqq.	137	40	162, 163
Luke.		48	237	42	234
iii. 21	240	58	159	45 sq.	277
21 sq.	181	62	160, 233	47 sq.	276
iv. 8	229	x. 9	124, 162	54 sqq.	261
v. 14	50	11	124, 162	xiii. 19	165
16	240	18	141	21	165
33 sqq.	264	21	181, 240	24	223
36 sqq.	49	25 sqq.	56, 227	25 sqq.	149, 222
vi. 1 sqq.	58	30 sqq.	154, 250	28 sq.	162
6 sqq.	60	37	251	xiv. 1 sqq.	60
12	240	xi. 5 sqq.	240	5	260
27 sqq.	250	9	240	7 sqq.	238
31	250	9 sqq.	187	11	237
35	179, 188	15 sqq.	262	16 sqq.	147
37	252	20	134	25 sqq.	160
38	198	27 sq.	152	26 sq.	224
43 sqq.	213	39 sqq.	214, 218	xv.	198
46	149	41	253	xvi. 10	234
46 sqq.	222	47 sq.	262	13	190, 229
vii. 9	231	52	140	16	141
28	142	xii. 1	50, 236	17	66
29 sqq.	158	4	230	18	257

II. PASSAGES OF THE BIBLE REFERRED TO.

LUKE.			LUKE.			ROMANS.		
xvi. 19 sqq.	.	267	xxii. 28	. .	163	i. 1 sqq.	. .	73
29	. . .	48	32	. .	240	3 sq.	. .	177
xvii. 1 sq.	.	252	37	. .	52	18 sqq.	. .	190
3 sq.	.	252	42	. .	99	20	. . .	180
6	. .	231	53	. .	52	ii. 2	. . . .	199
10	. .	237	69	. .	163	6	. . . .	199
19	. .	231	xxiii. 34	. .	240	iii. 29 sq.	. .	191
20 sq.	.	131	46	. .	99	31	. . .	67
22 sqq.	.	163				iv.	. . . .	73
33	. .	224	JOHN.			v. 5 sqq.	. .	196
xviii. 1 sqq.	.	240	i. 14	. . .	307	vi. 1 sqq.	. .	74
8	. .	163	iii. 3	. 113,	161,	13	. . .	262
14	. .	237			219	23	. 196,	271
15 sqq.	.	138	16	. . .	196	vii.	. . . .	72
18 sqq.	57,	157,	iv. 21	. . .	29	6	. . .	74
		223	21 sqq.	. .	195	viii.	. . . .	72
20	. .	251	24	. .	29, 99	2	. . 7,	225
24 sq.	138,	268	v. 17	. . .	60	4	. . .	67
27	. .	193	vi. 35	. . .	307	6	. . .	178
31	. .	52	ix. 16	. . .	57	9	. . .	7
42	. .	231	xi. 41 sq.	. .	240	9 sq.	. .	233
xix. 10	. .	254	xii. 27 sq.	. .	240	14	. . 7,	177
12 sqq.	147,	234	xiii. 1 sqq.	.	237	15	. . .	182
46	. . .	61	35	. . .	7	15 sq.	. .	172
xx. 9 sqq.	.	200	xiv. 27	. 100,	232	19	. . .	178
17 sq.	. .	51	xv. 5	. . .	113	28	. . .	100
37	. . .	61	xvii.	. . .	240	29	. . .	177
42	. . .	48	xviii. 37	. .	287	x.	. . . .	73
47	. . .	240				2	. . .	66
xxi. 1 sqq.	.	215	ACTS.			12	. 151,	195
5 sqq.	.	132	iv. 13	. . .	28	xi. 16 sqq.	. .	73
22	. . .	53	x. 34 sq.	. .	153	33 sqq.	. .	192
27 sqq.	.	163	xvii. 26	. .	191	xii. 1 sqq.	.	193
36	. . .	234	27 sq.	. .	194	2	. . .	230
xxii. 18	. .	163	xix. 9	. . .	308	14	. . .	250
22	. .	52	xx. 32	. . .	287	17 sqq.	.	250
25 sqq.	.	237				18	. . .	252

z

330 II. PASSAGES OF THE BIBLE REFERRED TO.

ROMANS.

xiii.	8	67
	8 sqq.	228
	9	67
	10	67, 251
xiv.	4	252
	10 sqq.	252
	19	252
xv.	8	287

1 CORINTHIANS.

i.	2	23
	11 sqq.	252
ii.		73
	10 sqq.	182
	11 sq.	103
	12	182
iii.	3 sqq.	252
	16	23
v.		262
vi.	13 sqq.	262
ix.	9 sq.	76, 259
x.	1 sqq.	76
	6	73
	11	73
	32	23
xi.	16	23
	22	23
xii.		23
	4 sqq.	191
xiii.	1	98
	2	247
	13	7
xiv.	33	252
xv.	9	23
	24	123

2 CORINTHIANS.

i.	1	23
iii.		73, 75
	3	119
	6	119
	18	7
iv.	6	184
xii.	9	99
xiii.	11	252
	13	177

GALATIANS.

i.	13	23
ii.	5	287
	14	287
iii.		72, 73
	1 sqq.	74
	26 sqq.	28
iv.		72
	6	172
	10	29
	21 sqq.	76
v.	6 sqq.	74
	14	67, 228
	15	252
	19 sqq.	199
	20	252
	25	221
vi.	1 sqq.	252
	7	98
	7 sq.	199, 271
	14 sqq.	74

EPHESIANS.

i.	22 sq.	24
iv.	3	252
	3 sqq.	191

EPHESIANS.

iv.	6	112, 191, 194
	15 sq.	24
	18	177, 216
	25 sqq.	251
	32	252
v.	1 sq.	177

PHILIPPIANS.

iv.	6 sq.	243

COLOSSIANS.

i.	18 sq.	24
ii.	16	29

1 THESSALONIANS.

ii.	14	23
v.	13	252

2 THESSALONIANS.

i.	4	23

1 TIMOTHY.

iii.	5	23
	15	23
iv.	13	44

2 TIMOTHY.

iii.	16	77

HEBREWS.

xii.	14	252

JAMES.

i.	5	196
	12	271

II. PASSAGES OF THE BIBLE REFERRED TO.

JAMES.		2 PETER.		1 JOHN.	
i. 17	171	i. 4	8, 177	iv. 10	196
18	288			13	8, 183
21	288	1 JOHN.		15 sq.	177
27	8, 250, 262	i. 2	178	16	8, 99
ii. 8 sqq.	228	7	178	19	196
iii. 14 sqq.	252	ii. 9	248	v. 4	232
17	196	11	112	13	178
17 sq.	252	15	230		
iv. 11 sq.	252	iii. 1	172, 178	REVELATION.	
v. 9	252	4	216	i. 6	28
12	265	9	178, 221	ii. 10	234
19 sq.	252	14	98, 183, 248	v. 10	28
		15	212	xi. 15	21
1 PETER.		17	250	xx. 6	28
i. 23	288	24	183	xxi. 3 sq.	21
ii. 5	19	iv. 7	178		
9	19	8	112		
iii. 9	250				

14, HENRIETTA STREET, COVENT GARDEN, LONDON;
20, SOUTH FREDERICK STREET, EDINBURGH.

CATALOGUE OF SOME WORKS

PUBLISHED BY

WILLIAMS & NORGATE.

Abbotsford Series of the Scottish Poets. Edited by GEORGE EYRE-TODD. I. Early Scottish Poetry; II. Mediæval Scottish Poetry; III. Scottish Poetry of the Sixteenth Century. Price of each part, 3s. 6d.; fine paper, 5s. nett. IV. Scottish Ballad Poetry. Price 5s.; fine paper, 7s. 6d. nett.

Ainsworth (Rev. W. M.) Memorial of. With Portrait. Crown 8vo, cloth. 6s.

Barrow (E. P., M.A.) Regni Evangelium. A Survey of the Teaching of Jesus Christ. Crown 8vo, cloth. 6s.

Baur (F. C.) Church History of the First Three Centuries. Translated from the Third German Edition. Edited by Rev. ALLAN MENZIES. 2 vols. 8vo, cloth. 21s.

Baur (F. C.) Paul, the Apostle of Jesus Christ, his Life and Work, his Epistles and Doctrine. A Contribution to a Critical History of Primitive Christianity. By Rev. A. MENZIES. Second Edition. 2 vols. 8vo, cloth. 21s.

Beard (Rev. Dr. C.) The Universal Christ, and other Sermons. Crown 8vo, cloth. 7s. 6d.

Beard (Rev. Dr. C.) Lectures on the Reformation of the Sixteenth Century in its Relation to Modern Thought and Knowledge (Hibbert Lectures, 1883.) 8vo, cloth. (Cheap Edition, 4s. 6d.) 10s. 6d.

Beard (Rev. Dr. C.) Port Royal, a Contribution to the History of Religion and Literature in France. Cheaper Edition. 2 vols. Crown 8vo, cloth. 12s.

Bleek (F.) Lectures on the Apocalypse. Translated. Edited by the Rev. Dr. S. DAVIDSON. 8vo, cloth. 10s. 6d.

Booth (C.) Life and Labour of the People. Vol. I. The East End of London. Third Edition. 8vo, cloth. 10s. 6d.
—— —— Vol. II. London (continued), &c. With Appendix of coloured Maps. In 2 vols. 8vo, cloth. 21s.

Castorius' Map of the World, generally known as Peutinger's Tabula. Printed in colours, after the original in the Imperial Library, Vienna. 5s.

Cleland, Mackay, Young (Professors) Memoirs and Memoranda of Anatomy. Vol. I. 16 Plates. 8vo, cloth. 7s. 6d.

Collins (F. H.) An Epitome of the Synthetic Philosophy. With a Preface by HERBERT SPENCER. 8vo, cloth. 15s.

Conway (Moncure D.) Centenary History of the South Place Ethical Society. With numerous Portraits, a Facsimile of the Original Autograph MS. of the well-known Hymn, "Nearer, my God, to Thee," and Appendix containing an Original Poem by Mrs. ADAMS (1836), and an Address by WILLIAM JOHNSON FOX (1842). Crown 8vo, half vellum, paper sides. 5s.

Davids (T. W. Rhys) Lectures on some Points in the History of Indian Buddhism. (Hibbert Lectures, 1881.) Second Edition. 8vo, cloth. 10s. 6d.

Delitzsch (Professor F.) Assyrian Grammar, with Paradigms, Exercises, Glossary, and Bibliography, Translated by the Ven. Archdeacon R. S. KENNEDY. Crown 8vo, cloth. 15s.

Delitzsch (Professor F.) The Hebrew Language viewed in the light of Assyrian Research. Crown 8vo, cloth. 4s.

Drummond (Dr.) Philo Judæus ; or, the Jewish Alexandrian Philosophy in its Development and Completion. By JAMES DRUMMOND, LL.D., Principal of Manchester College, Oxford. 2 vols. 8vo, cloth. 21s.

Enoch, The Book of, the Prophet. Translated from an Ethiopic MS. in the Bodleian Library, by the late RICHARD LAURENCE, LL.D., Archbishop of Cashel. The Text corrected from his latest Notes by CHARLES GILL. Re-issue, 8vo, cloth. 5s.

Erman's Egyptian Grammar, Translated under Professor Erman's supervision, by J. H. BREASTED, Professor of Egyptology in the University of Chicago. Crown 8vo, cloth. 18s.

Ewald's (Dr. H.) Commentary on the Prophets of the Old Testament. Translated by the Rev. J. F. SMITH. 5 vols. 8vo, cloth.
Each 10s. 6d.

Ewald's (Dr. H.) Commentary on the Psalms. Translated by the Rev. E. JOHNSON, M.A. 2 vols. 8vo, cloth. Each 10s. 6d.

Ewald's (Dr. H.) Commentary on the Book of Job, with Translation. Translated from the German by the Rev. J. FREDERICK SMITH. 8vo, cloth. 10s. 6d.

Published by Williams and Norgate. 3

Frankfurter (Dr. O.) Handbook of Pali ; being an Elementary
Grammar, a Chrestomathy, and a Glossary. 8vo, cloth. 16s.

Gould (Rev. S. Baring) Lost and Hostile Gospels. An Account
of the Toledoth Jesher, two Hebrew Gospels circulating in the Middle
Ages, and Extant Fragments of the Gospels of the first Three Centuries
of Petrine and Pauline Origin. Crown 8vo, cloth. 7s. 6d.

Harnack (Axel) Introduction to the Elements of the Differential
and Integral Calculus. From the German. Royal 8vo, cloth. 10s. 6d.

Hatch (Rev. Dr.) Lectures on the Influence of Greek Ideas and
Usages upon the Christian Church. Edited by Dr.FAIRBAIRN. (Hibbert
Lectures), 1888.) 8vo, cloth. 10s· 6d.

Hausrath (Prof. A.) History of the New Testament Times. The
Time of Jesus. Translated by the Revs. C. T. POYNTING and P. QUENZER.
2 vols. 8vo, cloth. 21s.

Hausrath (Prof. A.) History of the New Testament Times. The
Time of the Apostles. Translated by LEONARD HUXLEY. 2 vols. 8vo,
cloth. 21s.

Hemans (Chas. I.) Historic and Monumental Rome. A Handbook for the Students of Classical and Christian Antiquities in the Italian
Capital. Crown 8vo, cloth. 10s. 6d.

Hemans (Chas. I.) History of Mediæval Christianity and Sacred
Art in Italy (A.D. 900—1600). 2 vols. Crown 8vo, cloth. 18s.

Hiller (H. Croft) Against Dogma and Freewill, and for Weismannism. Second and greatly enlarged edition. Containing, *inter alia*,
beyond the Original Text, a Concise Statement of Weismann's Theory, a
Controversy on its Application to Sociology, and an Examination of the
Recent Criticism of Professor Romanes. Demy 8vo, cloth. 7s. 6d.

Keim's History of Jesus of Nazara. Considered in its connection
with the National Life of Israel, and related in detail. Translated from
the German by ARTHUR RANSOM. Complete in 6 vols. demy 8vo.
Each 10s. 6d. (or 6 vols. for 42s nett.)

Kennedy (Rev. Jas.) Introduction to Biblical Hebrew. 8vo, cloth.
12s.

Kiepert's New Atlas Antiquus. Twelve Maps of the Ancient
World, for Schools and Colleges. Eleventh Edition, with a complete Geographical Index. Folio, boards. 6s.

King (John H.) The Supernatural: its Origin, Nature and Evolution. 2 vols. demy 8vo, cloth. 15s.

King (John H.) Man an Organic Community; being an Exposition of the Law that the Human Personality in all its Phases in Evolution,
both Co-ordinate and Discordinate, is the Multiple of many Sub-personalities. 2 vols. demy 8vo, cloth. 15s.

4   Catalogue of some Works

The King and the Kingdom: a Study of the Four Gospels.
Three Series, each complete in itself; with copious Indexes. Medium
8vo.   Each 3s. 6d.

Kuenen (Dr. A.) The Religion of Israel to the Fall of the Jewish
State. Translated from the Dutch by A. H. MAY. 3 vols. 8vo, cloth. 31s. 6d.

Kuenen (Dr. A.) Lectures on National Religions and Universal
Religions. (The Hibbert Lectures, 1882.) 8vo, cloth.   10s. 6d.

Kuhne (Louis) The New Science of Healing, or the Doctrine of
the Oneness of all Diseases. Forming the basis of a Uniform Method of
Cure without Medicines and without Operations. Translated from the
third greatly augmented German edition by Dr. TH. BAKER.   8vo,
cloth.   7s.

Laurie (Professor Simon) Ethica: or the Ethics of Reason. By
Scotus Novanticus. 2nd Edition. 8vo, cloth.   6s.

Laurie (Professor Simon) Metaphysica Nova et Vetusta: a Return
to Dualism. 2nd Edition. Crown 8vo, cloth.   6s.

Lloyd (Walter) The Galilean: a Portrait of Jesus of Nazareth.
Crown 8vo, cloth.   2s. 6d.

Lubbock (Sir John, F.R.S.) Pre-historic Times, as illustrated by
Ancient Remains and the Manners and Customs of Modern Savages. With
Wood-cut Illustrations and Plates. 5th Edition. 8vo, cloth.   18s.

Lyall (C. J., M.A., C.I.E.) Ancient Arabian Poetry, chiefly
pre-Islamic; Translations, with an Introduction and Notes. Foolscap 4to,
cloth.   10s. 6d.

Macan (R. W.) The Resurrection of Jesus Christ. An essay in
three Chapters. 8vo, cloth.   5s.

Malan (Rev. Dr. S. C.) Original Notes on the Book of Proverbs.
Mostly from Eastern sources. Vol. I. chap. i. to x., Vol. II. chap. xi. to
xx., Vol. III. Chap. xxi. to xxxi.   Each vol. demy 8vo, cloth. 12s.

Mind, a Quarterly Review of Psychology and Philosophy. Nos.
1—64. 1876-90. 8vo, each 3s. Vols. II.—XVI. in cloth.   Each 13s.
—— New Series, Vols. I. and II.   Each 13s.
—— Annual Subscription, post free.   12s.

Montefiore (C. G.) Origin and Growth of Religion as illustrated
by the Religion of the Ancient Hebrews. (The Hibbert Lectures, 1892.)
2nd Edition. 8vo, cloth.   10s. 6d.

Müller (Professor Max) Lectures on the Origin and Growth of
Religion, as illustrated by the Religions of India. (The Hibbert Lectures,
1878.) 8vo, cloth.   10s. 6d.

Nestle. Syriac Grammar. Bibliography, Chrestomathy and
Glossary. Translated by the Ven. Archdeacon R. S. KENNEDY, Professor
of Oriental Languages in the University of Aberdeen. Crown 8vo,
cloth. 9s.

O'Curry (Eug.) Lectures on the Social Life, Manners and
Civilization of the People of Ancient Erinn. Edited, with an Introduction,
by Dr. W. K. SULLIVAN. Numerous Wood Engravings of Arms,
Ornaments, &c. 3 vols. 8vo, cloth. 30s.

O'Grady (Standish H.) Silva Gadelica (I.—XXXI). A Collection
of Tales in Irish, with Extracts illustrating Persons and Places. Edited
from MSS. and translated. 2 vols. Royal 8vo, cloth. 42s.
—— Or separately, Vol. I., Irish Text; and Vol. II., Translation and Notes.
Each vol. 21s.

Oldenberg (Prof. H.) Buddha: his Life, his Doctrine, his Order.
By Dr. HERMANN OLDENBERG, Professor at the University of Berlin.
Translated by W. HOEY, M.A. 8vo, cloth gilt. 18s.

Pfleiderer (O.) Paulinism : a Contribution to the History of
Primitive Christian Theology. Translated by E. PETERS. Second
Edition. 2 vols. 8vo, cloth. 21s.

Pfleiderer (O.) Philosophy of Religion on the Basis of its History.
Vols. I. II. History of the Philosophy of Religion from Spinoza to the
Present Day ; Vols. III. IV. Genetic-Speculative Philosophy of Religion.)
Translated by Professor ALAN MENZIES and the Rev. ALEX. STEWART.
Complete in 4 vols. 8vo, cloth. Each 10s. 6d.

Pfleiderer (O.) Lectures on the Influence of the Apostle Paul on
the Development of Christianity. Translated by the Rev. J. FREDERICK
SMITH. (Hibbert Lectures, 1885.) 8vo, cloth. 10s. 6d.

Poole (Reg. Lane) Illustrations of the History of Mediæval
Thought, in the Departments of Theology and Ecclesiastical Politics.
8vo, cloth. 10s. 6d.

Pratt (Dr. H.) Principia Nova Astronomica. With 37 full-page
plates. Crown 4to, cloth gilt. 10s. 6d.

Protestant Commentary on the New Testament; with general
and special Introductions. Edited by Professor P. W. SCHMIDT and F.
VON HOLZENDORFF. Translated from the third German Edition by the
Rev. F. H. JONES, B.A. 3 vols. 8vo, cloth. Each 10s. 6d.

Renan (E.) On the Influence of the Institutions, Thought and
Culture of Rome on Christianity and the Development of the Catholic
Church. Translated by the Rev. CHARLES BEARD. (Hibbert Lectures,
1880.) 8vo, cloth. (Cheap Edition, 2s. 6d.) 10s. 6d.

Renouf (P. le Page) On the Religion of Ancient Egypt. (Hibbert Lectures, 1879.) Second Edition. 8vo, cloth. 10s. 6d.

Reville (Dr. A.) Prolegomena of the History of Religions. With an Introduction by Professor F. MAX MÜLLER. 8vo, cloth. 10s. 6d.

Reville (Dr. A.) On the Native Religions of Mexico and Peru. Translated by the Rev. P. H. WICKSTEED. (Hibbert Lectures, 1884.) 8vo, cloth. 10s. 6d.

Rhys (Prof. J.) On the Origin and Growth of Religion as illustrated by Celtic Heathendom. (Hibbert Lectures, 1886.) 8vo, cloth. 10s. 6d.

Sayce (Prof. A. H.) On the Religion of Ancient Assyria and Babylonia. Third Edition. (Hibbert Lectures, 1887.) 8vo, cloth. 10s. 6d.

Schloss (D. F.) Methods of Industrial Remuneration. Second Edition. 8vo, cloth. 10s. 6d.

Schmidt (A.) Shakespeare Lexicon. A Complete Dictionary of all the English Words, Phrases, and Constructions in the Works of the Poet. Second Edition. 2 vols. Imperial 8vo, 28s.; cloth. 31s. 6d.

Schrader (Professor E.) The Cuneiform Inscriptions and the Old Testament. Translated from the second Enlarged Edition, with Additions by the Author, and an Introduction by the Rev. OWEN C. WHITEHOUSE, M.A. 2 vols. With a Map. 8vo, cloth. Each 10s. 6d.

Schurman (J. Gould) Kantian Ethics and the Ethics of Evolution. 1882. 8vo, cloth. 5s.

Schurman (J. Gould) The Ethical Import of Darwinism. Crown 8vo, cloth. 5s.

Sharpe (Samuel) The Bible, translated by SAMUEL SHARPE, being a Revision of the Authorized English Version. 6th Edition of the Old, 10th Edition of the New Testament. 8vo, roan. 5s.

Sharpe (Samuel) The New Testament. Translated from Griesbach's Text by S. SHARPE, Author of "The History of Egypt." 14th Thousand. Fcap. 8vo, cloth. 1s. 6d.

Socin (A.) Arabic Grammar. Paradigms, Literature, Chrestomathy, and Glossary. Crown 8vo, cloth. 7s. 6d.

Spencer (Herbert) Works. The Doctrine of Evolution. 8vo, cloth,
First Principles. 16s.
Principles of Biology. 2 vols. 34s.
Principles of Psychology. 2 vols. 36s.
Principles of Sociology. Vol. I. 21s.
—— Vol. II. 18s.
Ecclesiastical Institutions. 5s.

Spencer (Herbert) Works—*continued*.
Principles of Ethics. Vol. I.   15s.
——— Vol. II.   12s. 6d.
The Data of Ethics. (Separately.)   8s.
Justice. (Separately.)   8s.
The Study of Sociology.   10s. 6d.
Education.   6s.
——— Cheap Edition.   2s. 6d.
Essays. 3 vols.   30s. (or each vol. 10s.)
Social Statics and Man v. State.   10s.
Man v. State. (Separately, sewed.)   1s.

——— Collins (F. H.) An Epitome of the Synthetic Philosophy. By F. HOWARD COLLINS. With a Preface by HERBERT SPENCER. 8vo, cloth.   15s.

Spencer (W. G.) Inventional Geometry. With a Preface by HERBERT SPENCER. 8vo, cloth.   1s.

Spencer (W. G.) A System of Lucid Shorthand. Devised by WILLIAM GEORGE SPENCER. With a Prefatory Note by HERBERT SPENCER. 8vo, cloth.   1s.

Spinoza. Four Essays by Professors LAND, VAN VLOTEN, KUNO FISCHER, and by E. RENAN. Edited by Professor KNIGHT, of St. Andrews. Crown 8vo, cloth.   5s.

Stokes (G. J.) The Objectivity of Truth. 8vo, cloth.   5s.

Strack (H. L.) Hebrew Grammar. Paradigms, Literature, Chrestomathy, and Glossary. Crown 8vo, cloth.   4s. 6d.

Strauss (Dr. D. F.) Life of Jesus; for the People. The Authorized English Edition. 2 vols. 8vo, cloth.   10s. 6d.

Waldstein (C.) Excavations of the American School of Athens at the Heraion of Argos. To be completed in about 4 Parts. Part 1, 20 pp. and 7 Plates. 4to, sewed.   12s.

Weizsaecker (C.) The Apostolic Age. Translated by JAMES MILLAR, B.D. 2 vols. demy 8vo, cloth.   21s.

Wright (Rev. J.) Grounds and Principles of Religion. Crown 8vo, cloth.   3s.

Zeller (Dr. E.) The Contents and Origin of the Acts of the Apostles critically investigated. Preceded by Dr. Fr. Overbeck's Introduction to the Acts of the Apostles from De Wette's Handbook. Translated by JOSEPH DARE. 2 vols. 8vo, cloth.   21s.

Ziegler (Th.) Social Ethics. Outlines of a Doctrine of Morals. Translated from the German. Crown 8vo, cloth.   3s.

Theological Translation Fund. A Series of Translations by which the best results of recent Theological investigations on the Continent, conducted without reference to doctrinal considerations, and with the sole purpose of arriving at truth, are placed within reach of English Readers.

Demy 8vo, cloth. 10s 6d per vol.

*** A selection of six or more vols. at 7s. nett per vol., instead of 10s. 6d.

1. Baur. Church History of the First three Centuries. 2 vols.
2. Baur. Paul, the Apostle of Jesus Christ, his Life and Work. 2 vols.
3. Bleek. Lectures on the Apocalypse. 1 vol.
4. Ewald. Commentary on the Prophets of the Old Testament. 5 vols.
5. Ewald. Commentary on the Psalms. 2 vols.
6. Ewald. Commentary on the Book of Job, with Translation. 1 vol.
7. Hausrath. History of the New Testament Times. The Time of Jesus. 2 vols.
8. Keim. History of Jesus of Nazara. 6 vols.
9. Kuenen. The Religion of Israel to the Fall of the Jewish State. 3 vols.
10. Pfleiderer. The Philosophy of Religion on the Basis of its History. 4 vols.
11. Pfleiderer. Paulinism. 2 vols.
12. Protestant Commentary on the New Testament. 3 vols.
13. Reville. Prolegomena of the History of Religion. 1 vol.
14. Schrader. The Cuneiform Inscriptions and the Old Testament. 2 vols.
15. Zeller (E.) The Acts of the Apostles Critically Examined. 2 vols.

Theological Translation Library. New Series. Edited by the Rev. T. K. CHEYNE, M.A., D.D., Oriel Professor of Interpretation in the University of Oxford, and Canon of Rochester; and the Rev. A. B. BRUCE, D.D., Professor of Apologetics, Free Church College, Glasgow.

Weizsaecker (C.) The Apostolic Age. Translated by the Rev. JAMES MILLAR, B.D. 2 vols. demy 8vo. cloth. 21s.

Harnack (A.) Dogmengeschichte. New Edition. Translated by the Rev. NEILL BUCHANAN. [In preparation.]

Kittel (R.) Geschichte der Hebräer. Translated by the Rev. J. TAYLOR, D.D. [In preparation.]

WILLIAMS AND NORGATE,
14, HENRIETTA STREET, COVENT GARDEN, LONDON; AND
20, SOUTH FREDERICK STREET, EDINBURGH.

www.ingramcontent.com/pod-product-compliance
Lightning Source LLC
Chambersburg PA
CBHW020240240426
43672CB00006B/586